Corbyn

Corbyn

The Strange Rebirth of Radical Politics

Second Edition

Richard Seymour

VERSO
London • New York

This updated edition published by Verso 2017
First published by Verso 2016
© Richard Seymour 2016, 2017

The moral rights of the author have been asserted

1 3 5 7 9 10 8 6 4 2

Verso
UK: 6 Meard Street, London W1F 0EG
US: 20 Jay Street, Suite 1010, Brooklyn, NY 11201
versobooks.com

Verso is the imprint of New Left Books

ISBN-13: 978-1-78663-299-9
ISBN-13: 978-1-78478-532-1 (UK EBK)
ISBN-13: 978-1-78478-533-8 (US EBK)

British Library Cataloguing in Publication Data
A catalogue record for this book is available from the British Library

The Library of Congress Has Cataloged the First Edition as Follows:

Names: Seymour, Richard, 1977– author.
Title: Corbyn : the crisis of British politics / Richard Seymour.
Description: London ; Brooklyn, NY : Verso, 2016.
Identifiers: LCCN 2016019162| ISBN 9781784785314 (paperback) | ISBN
9781784785321 (ebook : U.K.) | ISBN 9781784785338 (ebook : U.S.)
Subjects: LCSH: Corbyn, Jeremy. | Labour Party (Great Britain) – Biography. |
Politicians – Great Britain – Biography. | Legislators – Great
Britain – Biography. | Great Britain. Parliament. House of
Commons – Biography. | Labour Party (Great Britain) – History. |
Radicalism – Great Britain – History. | Democracy – Great Britain – History. |
Great Britain – Politics and government – 1997–2007. | Great
Britain – Politics and government – 2007– | BISAC: POLITICAL SCIENCE /
Political Process / General. | HISTORY / Europe / Great Britain.
Classification: LCC JN1129.L32 S443 2016 | DDC 328.41092 [B] – dc23
LC record available at https://lccn.loc.gov/2016019162

Typeset in Fournier by MJ & N Gavan, Truro, Cornwall
Printed and bound by CPI Group (UK) Ltd, Croydon, CR0 4YY

Contents

Acknowledgements

This book was proposed, researched and written in a flush of enthusiasm after Jeremy Corbyn won the leadership of the Labour Party – a most unexpected occasion for a book. It couldn't have been completed to my satisfaction without the input, encouragement and several friends, colleagues and many Labour members.

Marsha-Jane Thompson, Ben Sellers, Liam Young, Margaret Corvid, Phil Burton-Cartledge and Simon Hewitt were among those who gave up their free time and thoughts, often on numerous occasions, and I gained a lot from their experience and knowledge. I also am very grateful to Matt Zarb-Cousins for his insight and help. Tom Mills spent a long time giving me extremely thoughtful and incisive background on the BBC. Robin Archer at the London School of Economics gave me the benefit of his considerable expertise and thoughtful analyses. Jeremy Gilbert of Compass was also, as always, incredibly insightful.

In addition, there were many individuals, Labour activists, and others who, though too modest to be named, were happy to help fill in the blanks, and explained Labour politics in a way that the mainstream press generally can't. They did this despite knowing they may not agree with my analysis. Huge thanks to them.

My editor, Rosie Warren, has been amazingly efficient, tolerant and helpful throughout, and I'm immensely appreciative of everything she has done.

Finally, thanks to my agent, Susie Nicklin, for her advice, support, insight and hard work in helping this book to come about.

Preface to the Second Edition:
The Absolute Boy

Work as if you live in the early days of a better nation.

— Alasdair Gray

I

Rupert Murdoch, face heavy with thunder, got up and walked out of the election night party. Theresa May was reduced to tears. A Tory staff member was physically sick. Jeremy Corbyn, as his jubilant supporters crowned him the "Absolute Boy," quietly celebrated with a halloumi kebab and apple juice.

The Conservatives had won the most votes and the most seats of any party in the election. And yet for them, and especially for their leader, Theresa May, the result was comprehensively a disaster: the blues had bombed. It was not just that they'd failed to win the parliamentary super-majority which polls early in the campaign had said they were likely to get. It was not just that for once most polls had severely underestimated Labour's support. It was not just that Theresa May lost a parliamentary majority which she had called the election to fortify. The outcome was far more significant than that.

The exit poll had shown Labour gaining 40 per cent of the vote, and forcing a hung parliament. But worse than that, all over the country, it was making gains of the sort that it would only normally make if it was winning the election. Bellwether constituencies like Enfield Southgate, Warwick and Leamington, Reading East, Ipswich and Peterborough, went Labour. Mountainous SNP majorities fell. Supposed London marginals such as Ealing Central, Tooting, and Hampstead and Kilburn became safe seats. Canterbury, having been Conservative since the Great War, was won by Labour. Kensington, including the richest residents in the country, was swallowed in a vengeful blood-red wave across London as its forgotten working-class constituents took revenge on an atrocious Tory MP. The Labour candidate, an anti-gentrification activist, would later demonstrate why she was elected with her angry, passionate response to the horrific Grenfell fire, which consumed dozens of working-class residents. Portsmouth, a Tory–Liberal marginal, went Labour, as the party showed surprising strength across the South and South West. Labour had its biggest surge in vote share since 1945, with Corbyn racking up just short of 13 million votes, after coming from twenty points behind.

This was not supposed to happen. Jeremy Corbyn was the traduced laughing-stock leader of a broken and divided opposition, scolded by the liberal press, hounded by the right-wing press, condescended to by the broadcasters. Brexit had transformed the political terrain, and great swathes of the country were about to turn Tory. In traditional Labour heartlands, from the West Midlands to Wales to the rustbelts of the North, early polling suggested that the rush of former UKIP voters back into the Tory fold was likely to turn a number of Labour seats into Tory strongholds. Scotland was forever lost to Labour after a disastrous independence referendum campaign, in which the party, led by figures from the Blairite Right such as Jim Murphy, failed to distinguish itself from the Conservatives. Labour was twenty points behind in national opinion polls, seemingly adrift since Brexit, its leader scoring high negatives. May herself was glorified at the beginning of the campaign by Tory pundits such as A. N. Wilson and Matthew D'Ancona who claimed that her great secret was her matriarchal 'sex appeal'. Tory activists called her 'mummy'. The *Daily Mail*, a traditionalist Tory newspaper, salivated that May would 'Crush the Saboteurs'.

And yet as the campaign went on, May's weakness was exposed. Her wariness of debates, and unscripted interactions with the public, far from conferring on her the queen-like inaccessibility that she apparently sought, began to erode her aura of autocratic power. Her rare public appearances varied between competently boring and cringe-inducing. In fairness, most politicians would struggle with, for example, a question about the naughtiest thing they did as a child. May's answer, that she used to run through fields of wheat, upsetting local farmers, might in other circumstances have come across as a charming evocation of bucolic childhood innocence. But having made the election into a ranking of personalities, inviting the electorate to choose between a 'tough' Theresa May leadership and a 'weak' Jeremy Corbyn leadership, May had set herself up for critical scrutiny of her personality, her presentation, and her competence. And she failed her own test.

The Conservative Party's slowness in launching a manifesto was all the more damning when the actual document was produced. It included deeply unpopular attacks on core Tory supporters, above all pensioners. These included the promise to make social care users pay for it with the value of their homes. The Tories would also scrap the 'triple lock' guaranteeing increases in the value of pensions at either the rate of inflation, average earnings, or a minimum of 2.5 per cent (whichever was higher). And they would means-test winter fuel payments for the elderly. On top of that, the party proudly announced policies designed only to preach to the converted and annoy everyone else, such as the pledge to legalise fox hunting.

Meanwhile, Labour's campaign was far better than anyone had expected, and Corbyn in particular proved a star turn in debates and public appearances. Labour's manifesto – above all its core commitments to renationalising rail, mail, energy, and water; expanded public investment; abolishing tuition fees; building council houses; raising the minimum wage; and rolling out a new menu of workers' rights – was extremely popular. It was a promise of modernisation, a social upgrade, which addressed the needs of the working class in an age of austerity and stagnant capitalism. Corbyn's appearance at a Libertines concert and his interview with Grime star JME might for any other politician have come over as a patronising, baffled effort at panhandling for votes. For Corbyn, it was politics as usual: campaigning to mobilise the alienated and excluded was what he had built his leadership on. He took his audience seriously, as a political agency with aspirations, and so they took him seriously. One extraordinary result of this was that his name became a meme, a slogan, a sort of joyous battle cry chanted by the young at music concerts and football stadiums and outside pubs – to the tune of 'Seven Nation Army' by the White Stripes.

What Diane Abbott referred to in her election-night speech, celebrating a stupendous majority of 35,000, as 'the politics of personal destruction' – a politics designed to demoralise – had been dealt a lethal blow. The smear machine run by Tory PR men like Lynton Crosby, and their faithful tabloid amanuenses, had broken down. Weeks and weeks of acres and acres of febrile nonsense about Corbyn, his supposed 'links' to the IRA taking pre-eminence in an election campaign punctuated by two shocking terrorist attacks, had failed. Not that it had failed to convince Tory voters, and a layer of rightward-moving Labour voters, that Corbyn was a menace to Britain. There was at least anec-dotal evidence of older, white Labour voters defecting. Rather, it failed to sap the extraordinary energy, confidence, and aggression from Labour's campaign, or the buoyant pugnacity of its supporters. If anything, the attacks added to the sense that the political establishment was ganging up on an honest, principled outsider. The editors and press barons, the pundits and establishment politicians, still have their power. But increasingly they look like yesterday's men.

The result was a sharp increase in turnout in certain demographics, especially among the young and poor, who went heavily for Labour. The party won among the working-age population, only losing badly among retirees who went heavily for the Conservatives. Labour's increased turnout of its support more or less drowned the expected 'UKIP effect', which in part would have been a result of a long-term decline in the Labour turnout in core seats. A fifth of UKIP voters – made an offer addressing their immediate interests rather than pandering on immigration – defected to Labour. The party even held onto West Midlands marginals like Birmingham Edgbaston, and expected northern converts like Bury North, with dramatically increased majorities. Adding dozens of seats in an election in which it had been expected to lose dozens, Labour had what journalist Stephen Bush termed a 'glorious defeat'. Enough Tory seats were turned into potential swing constituencies, with tiny majorities – including Home Secretary Amber Rudd's constituency – that it would in principle only require a small further swing to Labour for Corbyn to be prime minister.

On election night, former chancellor George Osborne, whom May had sacked from the government, quipped that running through fields of wheat was no longer the worst thing she'd ever done. For now she had exposed the Tories to a brutal separation of wheat and chaff.

II

> Good evening. I know nothing. We, the media, the pundits, the
> experts, know nothing. We simply didn't spot it.
>
> Jon Snow, *Channel 4 News*, 9 June 2017

Here was a credibility crunch of gigantic proportions. Media corporations, think tanks, academics, and pundits had been acting like the ratings agencies, conferring credibility on politicians for years, determining who was electable and who wasn't. Corbyn, by common consent, simply wasn't electable. He was a good man, pundits might patronisingly concede, an honest man: but a disaster. He was toxic stock. Though hardly the first Labour leader to suffer from toxic stock syndrome, he was considered the worst by near-unanimous consent among commentators. And yet in recent years, media-conferred credibility had been losing its prestige. They had endorsed as blue-chippers those who turned out to be toxic stock, and vice versa. It was not simply that they hadn't seen Corbyn coming, either in the leadership election or the general election. They hadn't foreseen Brexit or Trump's victory either.

One could be charitable to the media, the pundits, and the experts, and argue that very few did 'spot it'. And why should they? Any knowledge economy is governed by scarcity; there are never enough facts around. The short-fall always has to be made up with a combination of theory, guesswork, ideology, and experience. Psephologists, communications specialists, and political strategists have to make working assumptions about how electoral systems operate, and their assumptions – however ideological, however much they are doctrine mistaken for fact – are usually grounded in some degree of experience. To spot the Corbyn surge, arguably, required breaking with truisms which had held for years.

But had they? When there is a shock to the system, when the old ways of knowing break down, it is only reasonable to ask whether the old assumptions ever really explained what they seemed to. What holds in the physical sciences must surely hold here. The experiments from the late nineteenth and early twentieth century using microscopes, which disproved Newtonian mechanics, wouldn't have been much use if people had excused the old laws of motion by saying, 'Well, no one could have predicted black body radiation.' It required years of painful rethinking and a fundamentally new view of the universe, replacing deterministic laws with probabilistic laws of motion, to account for the new data. Likewise, recent crises call for a paradigm shift, a fundamental rethinking of how politics works.

This should really have been initiated after the credit crunch. Not only did economists fail to predict the cataclysmic event, the worst crisis for capitalism since the 1930s; also, their theories denied it could happen. Elaborate mathematical models, based on the assumption of efficient, self-regulating markets, were developed to guide academic theory and policy. They ignored obvious, common sense facts, such as that house prices could not indefinitely rise above the value of incomes without producing a crash. Instead of recognising the full severity of this outstanding failure of orthodoxy, economists tended to blame either exogenous shocks or herd irrationality for the crisis. This was convenient for financial corporations who wanted to avoid any political backlash from the crash, and the same orthodoxy was invoked to justify austerity policies transferring the costs of the crisis to public service users, welfare recipients, and employees.

The credibility crunch, while long in the works, in part owes itself to the effects of austerity. In the first edition of *Corbyn*, I argued that Corbyn's leadership was made possible by a deep crisis in politics and representation. The secession of large parts of the electorate from the political system was evident in plummeting party membership and identification, and voter turnout. On the other side, politicians increasingly withdrew into the state, becoming less and less interested in the electorate except as a diminishing pool of participants to manipulate with good messaging. These were long-term processes, but the polarising effects of economic crisis and its austerian remedy accelerated them and produced a degree of hitherto unseen political instability.

Within the Labour Party, this produced an electoral crisis, the loss of Scotland – long a bastion of the Labour Right – and compounded an ideological crisis for the conservative old guard. It was in this context that Corbyn, addressing this profound political alienation, built his leadership campaign on an anti-austerity, anti-establishment prospectus. He was able, as a 200–1 rank outsider, to mobilise a radicalised minority in British society, a coalition that included politically polyamorous young people, trade unionists, and left-wing supporters of 'Old Labour'. With his opponents struggling to offer coherent answers to the party's crisis, and to the problems of austerity, he defied the pundits and experts and swept to the leadership with a landslide.

The question was always whether he could repeat the same feat within the country, and if so how long it would take to achieve this. His critics, who insisted he could not win the Labour leadership, now insisted that he could not change the country: only a moderate leadership could win an election and have any chance of stopping the Tories. Now that Corbyn has, by depriving the Conservatives of their majority and setting Labour up for a future win, proved the critics wrong, what needs to be rethought?

III

The world, for a start. In the past few decades, it has been taken for granted among the majority of journalists and politicians that something miraculous was taking place: globalisation.

The world was converging, under the relatively benign tutelage of Washington, toward a liberal world order. With the vast global expansion of trade availed by the global roll-back of capital controls and tariffs, a series of institutions of global governance sprang up, as well as a patchwork of regional trading alliances rolling out property rights, and rolling back barriers to trade such as public ownership, and environmental or labour protections. It was, to coin a phrase, capitalism *en marche*: investor rights *sans frontières*. A post-democratic world system in which the US trade representative would potentially have more power than any national monarch or president.

This situation was taken for granted. It was the way of the world. There was no alternative. The liberal journalist George Packer argued that 'rejecting globalisation was like rejecting the sunrise'.[1] And besides, it was benevolent: a rising tide would lift all boats, while judicious exertions of military force would iron out any wrinkles in an increasingly flat earth. But there are growing signs since the global financial crash that we have reached, as one of John McDonnell's advisors, economist James Meadway, put it, 'peak globalisation'. World trade is still growing, but far less rapidly than before the credit crunch, and more slowly than global GDP. According to the World Trade Organization, the ratio of trade growth to GDP growth fell to 0.6:1 in 2016. Financial internationalism, wherein banks extend their reach increasingly globally, is slowing down. Protectionism is on the rise across the G20, and various governments – notably the Chinese – have imposed capital controls.[2]

This is a crisis of globalisation, and, with that, a crisis of all the taken-for-granted wisdom about globalisation. Economists have been changing their minds, and so have voters. The crisis has exposed layers of people who never particularly cared for 'globalisation', but who were submerged in the rising tide. In the backwash, the economy is being politicised once more. Many of the most prominent expressions of this are on the Right. President Trump's repudiation of the Trans Pacific Partnership has cost hundreds of billions of dollars in revenue for US corporations. His threat to renegotiate NAFTA could have been even more costly if seen through. At the G20 summit in Hamburg, US negotiators actively opposed global liberalism on trade and climate change, to the dismay of Angela Merkel, recently dubbed the new 'leader of the free world' by an impressively broad array of journalists and columnists.

These moves were based on extraordinary political fantasies: that, for example, world trade had enriched a rising Asian middle class at the expense of white American workers, that America was being cheated by Mexicans at every turn, and that global warming was an expensive Chinese-perpetrated swindle. And all of this, of course, the Trump campaign blamed on cosmopolitan elites, 'globalists' who may have been born American, but lack national belonging. These fantasies are a kind of racist dreamwork, part of the same outlook which says that African Americans caused the global crisis and a Kenyan stole the presidency. But they have found fertile ground beyond their usual redoubts because they give coded expression to elements of experience. They work on the relative decline and economic isolation of those parts of America which did not benefit from the expansion of finance and communications technologies, where major corporations, lobbies, and parties did not have headquarters, and where the 'old economy' was still 'the economy'.

In Europe, an energised far Right has found a similar set of fantasies, wherein out-of-touch metropolitan elites are accused of collaborating with a Brussels despotism to ship national law-making powers to an incipient European superstate – a new Soviet empire, an 'EUSSR', with its own rouble. They charge the European Union with having allowed Eastern Europeans to cheat and undercut the work-forces of North West Europe and usurp national public resources, and with preparing a fresh influx of Turks to really kill off living standards. They charge that these politically correct, out-of-touch elites have made a nefarious alliance with the enemy, jihadists. In the United Kingdom, the Brexit campaign was suffused with this sort of racist paranoia.

But it wasn't just the Right that began to politicise the economy. The Left has also had its say, from Syriza to Podemos to La France Insoumise. The victory for Jeremy Corbyn in the Labour leadership, and even the tentative gains for the Left in the leaderships of the French and Spanish Socialists are part of the same process. This points to a crucial mistake which pundits and psephologists made about Brexit. They had assumed that, in Britain at least, the politicisation of the economy would only effectively benefit the hard, nationalist Right. They assumed that the only strategy open to the Left was a defensive, centre-seeking strategy. That the Left's only option was to depoliticise the economy, accept the verities of 'globalisation' and of the post-Thatcherite settlement, and uncritically defend the European institutions.

The Left has long had criticisms of the European Union, from the Commission to the central bank, the single market, the customs union, and the Eurozone. But, so the logic ran, it had to suppress these for the sake of unity in a Remain campaign pivoted on a technocratic defence of 'the economy' – as if anyone still believed that the economy was socially neutral. The kernel of truth in this was that, though Corbyn's leadership signalled a revival of the Left's fortunes, it was still relatively fragile and unprepared for the European referendum campaign. A Left exit campaign would surely have little social resonance in a terrain dominated for so long by the hard Right. For that reason, Corbyn had campaigned for leader on the basis not of his traditional Euroscepticism, but as a critical Remainer – he argued that the EU needed to be reformed, but that leaving would be worse than staying in.

Nonetheless, Corbyn's mild criticisms of the EU from within the Remain campaign, and his refusal to campaign alongside David Cameron, were regarded by journalists as weakening the campaign, and by Labour centrists as sabotage. This became the basis for a failed coup attempt against his leadership within Labour. And in the aftermath, Brexit having won, the logic became that Labour's urgent task was to give up its insurgent leftism and cleave to the nationalist Right by taking a hard line on immigration. The long-gathering commentariat chorus, especially from its liberals, had suggested that Labour's electoral problems were crucially about its failure to connect to the nationalism of ordinary voters, and speak in an unembarrassed way about patriotism. This found a fitting apotheosis in the absurd persecution of Emily Thornberry for implicitly 'disrespecting' the flag-toting white van man. Unsurprisingly, then, when the liberal knee jerked after Brexit, it jerked right in the direction of immigrants. Typical of this was Polly Toynbee, who faulted Corbyn for defending 'free migration on the eve of a poll where Labour was haemorrhaging support for precisely those metropolitan views', before adding, 'if Labour wants to get its voters back, it can't block its ears as Corbyn, the party's leader, does.' Likewise, Andy Burnham insisted that the Brexit vote was 'against free movement' and that Labour must now find a new 'balance'. He added the gloss, shared by UKIP, of blaming free movement for 'a race to the bottom' in living standards.[3]

The Left indeed looked weaker and more isolated as a result of the Brexit vote; Labour seemed aimless and adrift, and having recovered some of its lost core vote in the year before the decision, it began losing more seats than it won. The loss of the by-election in Copeland and the just-about-victory in Stoke, precipitated by two right-wing Labour MPs resigning, appeared to have seriously weakened the leadership. As with the independence referendum in Scotland, the Brexit referendum looked to have remoulded politics in England and Wales along nationalist lines. And immigration was the number-one issue. The Tories took a huge lead in national opinion polls, and it was predicted that with UKIP votes filtering back into the Conservative fold, many Labour majorities in traditional heartlands of the North, the West Midlands, and Wales would succumb to a blue tide.

With a few notable exceptions, that did not take place. Labour politicised the economy from the Left, promising nationalisations, redistribution, an offensive against the wealth-hoarding rich, an end to the public sector pay freeze, workers' rights, a higher minimum wage, housing, and an expanded social wage especially in terms of free education. The Labour manifesto completely changed the terrain, so that class was as important as nation to the final outcome.

On Brexit, Labour insisted that it would not oppose the referendum verdict, and adopted a position of productive ambiguity as regards any final settlement, although Corbyn let it be known that he would prefer tariff-free trade outside the single market. On free movement, Corbyn stated that Labour was 'not wedded' to it, but also refused to offer any target for reducing migration, and refuted right-wing arguments blaming immigrants for low wages and austerity. Many media outlets interpreted the election result as a surge of young middle-class people furious about Brexit – the 'revenge of the Remainers', as Robert Ford claimed, despite his predictions about the impact of Brexit having been falsified. According to studies by Loughborough University, the course of the election campaign saw a definite shift away from Brexit as the number-one issue.[4]

It would be glib to reduce Labour's appeal entirely to a class-populist one, not least because class is so critically tied to other social distinctions, such as race, gender, and generation. The effects of precarious employment and low wages, of welfare cuts and the marketisation of the university system, are all borne disproportionately by the young. The lethal effects of poor housing and gentrification, as Grenfell tragically showed, are disproportionately borne by ethnic minorities and migrant populations. And Corbyn was swimming with the generational tide on a whole range of issues, from trans rights to Trident. The younger generations are, to put it crudely, less impressed by flags, authorities, and men with guns. This generational polarisation was painfully apparent during a special BBC *Question Time* edition in which both Corbyn and May, separately, faced questioning from the assembled audience. Corbyn was grilled intensively on his opposition to nuclear weapons, his meetings with Hamas representatives, and his supposed 'IRA links' by a number of older white men in the crowd. In particular, the fact that he refused to commit to pushing the button infuriated these audience members, leading a young woman to comment, 'I don't understand why everyone in this room seems so keen on killing millions of people.'

However, what this showed, and what the punditry largely did not understand, was that the working class was changing. The assumption for a long time had been that the melancholic, older, 'white working class' was the authentic voice of working-class Britain. Corbyn's campaign demonstrated that this was yet another point on which received wisdom was wrong.

IV

What did the punditry misunderstand about class? In part, the melancholic ideology of the 'white working class' was corroborated by polling practices. The majority of polling organisations called the result badly wrong. Only YouGov and Survation consistently showed results close to the outcome, and YouGov made some final adjustments on its standard polling to reduce Labour's share to 36 per cent. Why did this happen? In some ways, for perfectly good reasons. In 2015, polling companies had significantly over-stated the level of Labour's support, suggesting that there might be a hung parliament, when the Tories won the election with a comfortable lead. Their own inquiries suggested that they had overrepresented the young and the unemployed, groups with a tendency to show a low turnout. On the basis of this, the polling companies made weighting adjustments to account for likelihood to vote based on past turnout.

In 2017, for YouGov's and Survation's estimates to be correct, one had to believe that these voters, especially the young, would buck the trend and turn out in much bigger numbers. This, of course, is exactly what they did. Turnout among eighteen- to twenty-four-year-olds rose by 16 per cent in 2017, according to Ipsos Mori figures.[5] However, while this shocked most pollsters and pundits, it did not surprise those involved in the Labour campaign. When I interviewed one of Corbyn's aides, Marsha-Jane Thompson, for the first edition of this book, she argued that the polls might have been underestimating Labour's support because they were assuming that the electorate would be the same as in 2015. Indeed, part of Corbyn's strategy was precisely to reach out to previous non-voters with a programme of radical social democracy.

On what basis did psephologists and commentators assume this couldn't be done? Simply, a senior Labour advisor told me, because it was a truism: non-voters never turn out. The empiricist model of polling didn't bother to ask *why* non-voters were non-voters in the first place; it simply noted habitual non-voting and weighted the results accordingly. Insofar as anyone did attempt an explanation for non-voting within the commentariat, it was often insulting. A *Times* column published before the election summarises the main idea nicely. Taxing Corbyn for a 'cynical' approach to young people, promising them all kinds of goodies to get their votes, it added,

> As everyone knows, come election time under-25s are the worst group at showing up to vote. This isn't for any profound reason: some young people are, as Catherine Tate would put it, simply not 'bovvered' about politics and may not even know who Theresa May is, let alone be able to make educated choices about her or her rivals. The left, which can only win by exploiting their ignorance, therefore sets about trying to buy them with gimmicks, whether it's Snapchat videos or promises of student funding which don't stack up.[6]

To reiterate, this piece was arguing that it was Corbyn who was cynical about the young. The unspoken fear of such pieces, that the young would actually turn out for a party that offered them something to vote for, was echoed in the cynicism of Rod Liddle in the *Sun*, who advised readers that 'the civic thing to do is to stop them voting'. 'Let them lie in,' he suggested, 'introduce them to LSD' or 'tell them the election is tomorrow'.[7] Notwithstanding this contempt for the young as a vacuous horde of un-bovvered, lazy, ignorant social media addicts, as Chapter 1 shows there is ample evidence that non-voting has been linked to protest against the choices on offer, and that those least likely to turn out are not just young, but more likely to be poor and unemployed.

The gerontocratic fear of the young was in part also a fear of the disobedient working class. Nonetheless, most polling firms insisted that they wouldn't turn out, and most pundits agreed.

The problems with polling go deeper than its tendency to reproduce received wisdom. Polling measures individual opinions as though they were roughly equivalent units, and the resulting 'public opinion' is the aggregate of these units. Methodologically, it makes the assumption that those answering the questions each have the same force of conviction and the same range of competences, before applying post hoc 'weighting' to surveys of voting intention based on past turnout. But opinions don't work that way. People are often conflicted in their views, an ambivalence that becomes obvious when the same question worded slightly differently produces sharply different results. Posed a question that they don't care about or feel competent to answer, respondents often feel pressured to give an answer that may not reflect how they will in fact act. Often, moreover, people form opinions in group contexts, organised by class, religion, race, occupation, or gender, in ways that aren't individualised. Therefore, an opinion asked for in an individual context, on a subject on which the respondent may not yet have reflected, may be more a reflection of media buzz than of conviction. The overstatement of Nick Clegg's support in 2010 – the lamentable 'Cleggasm' – might be a case in point.

The final way in which polling is giving us a fundamentally misleading impression of what is happening in the country is directly related to class. To figure out what is going on with class, most polling companies use a poor measurement called 'social grades'. This is a system devised by the National Readership Survey approximately half a century ago, which helps market researchers split respondents up into consumer blocs: A, B, C1, C2, D, and E. The standard way in which pollsters and media interpret these grades is to say that ABC1 grades are 'middle class' while C2DE grades are 'working class'.[8] On the basis of this, some pundits using YouGov's post-election polls have claimed that the 2017 election showed a complete class dealignment, since the Tories and Labour were evenly split in the two blocs.[9]

A couple of obvious questions arise here. First, what is the 'middle class' in the middle of? Where is the upper class? Where is the class of employers and owners? If there is no upper in this schema, then what we're calling the 'middle' is the upper – which is absurd. Second, what does it mean to be in the 'middle'? According to this standard reading of the scheme of 'social grades', the middle includes everyone in 'white-collar' work, from clerical workers to professionals, supervisors, and senior managers. This, surely, is an illusory levelling, as if to say that everyone who works in a call centre, from the receptionist to the chief executive, is 'middle class'.

But the world evoked in this conception of class isn't really the modern world, where there even are such things as call centres. It is a world in which workers use their hands and leave the brain-work to their social betters. Therefore, as long as you don't use your hands, or if you have a degree, you can be patronisingly called 'middle class' even when you're working precarious shifts for minimum wage. The nation tacitly evoked here isn't even the Britain of fifty years ago; it is an imaginary past, an *Upstairs Downstairs* ideology of class relations. Weirdly, the same ideology which tells us that the middle class is a majority, and that class voting is a thing of the past, on another level communicates that nothing fundamental has really changed.

This practice will likely persist due to the business model of polling organisations. Part of the value of their output derives from the fact that their results can be compared across the decades. A new, more relevant definition of social class would create a break in the results, undermining comparison. However, these figures are ultimately only as powerful as the way in which they are interpreted and used. Had there not been, since the Thatcher era, a determined drive in the political class to declare an end to the class war, and to insist that 'we are all middle class now', journalists and academics would be more careful about invoking such trite readings based on social grades.

Likewise, this melancholic ideology of class, which tends to invoke the working class as an ethnic rump – a tea-towel memory of better days, a nostalgic, left-behind hangover – is the product of ideology, not polls. Since the middle of the New Labour era, there has been a conspicuous effort to identify and console an ageing, patriotic 'white working class'. They were the excluded remainder of an otherwise benign liberal order. The allegation was that these workers were excluded above all by multiculturalism and mass immigration, a claim floated by New Labour intellectuals like David Goodhart, but taken up with gusto and gratitude by UKIP and the far Right. Absent that vital groundwork, no one today would see fit to classify young, urban, disproportionately poor, multiracial Labour voters, as the 'liberal metropolitan elite'. And yet, even today, as the election shows the absolute futility of dividing electorates in this way, the *Telegraph* still felt comfortable characterising the election result as the 'revenge of the liberal metropolitan elite', angry about Brexit.[10]

Labour's success in 2017, in destroying the aura of invincibility around the Conservatives, also laid waste to the seeming unilateral command that the nationalist Right hoped to exert on Britain's future by means of the 'white working class'. It demonstrated that not everyone who worked for a wage was hypnotised by the abstraction we call 'nation'. The fizz of angry exuberance after the election celebrated an abrupt widening of the horizons of the thinkable, precisely in part because millions of working-class people refused to reduce their class experiences and aspirations to the demands of angry white men for immigration controls and nuclear megadeath.

V

Perhaps the biggest blind spot of the media, however, concerned their own role, and the sudden, sharp diminution of their power. It wasn't just that they didn't see it coming; for most of the media, it was a matter of they couldn't stop it coming. Chapter 6 covers this in more detail, but here it can be said that the British media terrain could not have been more favourable to the Conservatives. The press were divided between newspapers that were institutionally and ideologically loyal to the Tories, and those from the liberal centre whose anti-Corbyn animus was only marginally lesser. The broadcasters tended to cluster around what they perceived the centre to be, but also took their cue about what was newsworthy to a large extent from the newspapers, thus ensuring that the Lynton Crosby spin machine would reach them both directly and indirectly.

The raw facts of anti-Corbyn bias, vehemently denied by journalists, could hardly be news. A 2016 study by the London School of Economics noted that 'most newspapers' had been 'systematically vilifying the leader of the biggest opposition party, assassinating his character, ridiculing his personality and delegitimising his ideas and politics'. A review of the BBC's coverage of the 2016 coup by the Media Reform Coalition noted that twice as much airtime had been given to Corbyn's critics as to his supporters, while the tone of reports about Corbyn was strongly pejorative.

In a notorious incident which was to play a role in the snap election, the BBC's political editor Laura Kuenssberg had been found by the BBC Trust to have seriously misrepresented Corbyn's opposition to shoot-to-kill policies, depicting it as an answer to whether he would be happy for police to 'pull the trigger in the event of a Paris-style attack'. The BBC News director James Harding simply shrugged off the finding, and the misleading report was left online, becoming one of the most viewed BBC video segments during the election – an attitude bespeaking a sense of regal impunity. This is not because television news is pro-Conservative. The bias of broadcasters, particularly the

BBC, tends to be toward a notional 'consensus', which tends to boil down to news chiefs' estimate of where the political centre is. But as ample evidence has shown, they also tend to be 'press-ganged' by the newspapers into framing the issues in a way that favours the Tories. Studies by Cardiff University and Loughborough University showed that the same patterns persisted throughout the 2017 election – even during the worst moments for the Conservatives, such as the catastrophic third week of campaigning.[11]

And yet all these big guns turned out to be so many misfiring blunderbusses once Labour's campaign got under way. Why? The annual World Press Trends report shows the big picture. Between 2012 and 2016, advertising revenues for the world's press shrank from almost $90 billion to $68 billion. A mild increase in audience revenues caused by increasing the cover surcharge or introducing Internet paywalls is nowhere near making up for the loss.[12] In Britain, the Pew Research Centre findings are even more stark: only half of those aged sixty-five and over read a daily paper. Under the age of forty-five, less than a quarter read the papers. Under the age of thirty-five, it's less than a fifth. Only 16 per cent of eighteen- to twenty-four-year-olds read a paper.

Year after year, sales are collapsing. In 2014–15, national newspaper sales fell by half a million, or 7.6 per cent. The losses were as grave among the 'popular' press as in the broadsheets, with the *Sun* readership declining by 10 per cent, and the *Guardian* falling by 9.5 per cent. In 2016–17, losses continued more slowly for the broadsheets but just as rapidly for the tabloids, with the *Mirror* losing 11.7 per cent, the *Sun* down by 10.5 per cent and the *Guardian* and *Telegraph* losing approximately 3 per cent each.

As the *Guardian*'s media columnist Roy Greenslade points out, this is reproducing on a national scale something that has already happened to the regional newspapers. 'The newspaper industry's business model is wrecked,' Greenslade writes. 'The inevitable result will be cost-cutting on an even greater scale than has been apparent for the past decade.' As audiences move online, advertisers are increasingly switching to digital rather than print publications. The newspaper magnates know they're losing out to a new attention economy led by platforms like Facebook and Google, which together claimed 89 per cent of new advertising spending and 64 per cent of total audiences in the platform economy. Last year, the moguls met to agree the terms of a likely ill-fated bid to form a cartel around advertising sales. The broadcasters are also losing out, in some cases faster than the newspapers. The average age of a BBC News viewer rose from fifty-two in 2009 to fifty-nine in 2014. The number of hours of television news watched in a year by sixteen- to twenty-four-year-olds is twenty-five compared to 108 for all adults, and has declined every year since 2010.[13]

This is not, however, purely an economic crisis, and it would be a gross mistake to reduce it to that. Insofar as the newspapers have been part of the political establishment, a fourth estate wielding significant influence not just in shaping opinion but also in the making of policy, this crisis is a political and ideological crisis. As World Press Trends points out, the drop in sales is congruent with a crash in trust in the newspapers. Currently, more people globally trust search engines (64 per cent) than traditional media (57 per cent). Online-only media still have the kind of bad reputation that attaches to clickbait or conspiracy websites, but still 51 per cent trust them, which is not much lower than trust in traditional press and broadcasters.

In the UK, moreover, these trends are more advanced than elsewhere. The number of people who said they trusted the press in Britain has fallen precipitously, year on year. In 2012, trust in red-top journalists was already rock-bottom, at 10 per cent. Comparatively, BBC and ITV news journalists were comparatively well trusted (44 per cent and 41 per cent respectively), as were broadsheet journalists (38 per cent). But this already reflected a sharp drop for all groups – 37 per cent for BBC journalists, 41 per cent for ITV journalists, and 27 per cent for broadsheet journalists. In 2016, trust in the entire media stood at 36 per cent, and within a year it had fallen to 24 per cent.[14]

It is worth pausing to comment specifically on the role of the BBC, which draws a lot of complaint from Corbyn supporters on social media. The BBC, as a globally powerful and respected media organisation, also produces the most widely watched and listened to news programmes in Britain, and is the dominant content provider in the online news market. Its global legitimacy derives from the fact it is a public service broadcaster, nominally independent from the government and advertisers. So, one could argue that Corbynistas are just expecting more of the BBC than other broadcasters, who don't have the same public legitimacy. But one would be overlooking the evidence. I asked Tom

Mills, author of one of the few critical histories of the BBC, about this.[15]

'All the evidence', Mills argues, 'supports the underlying assumption of the Corbyn movement about BBC bias. That doesn't mean that every single example is right. But the thrust and underlying assumptions of the critique are factually correct. In terms of evidence, I know of no study which has said the BBC tends to reflect marginal or critical perspectives or ignores powerful interests. There is no evidence on that side. The problem is that bias gets discussed as if it reflected a hidden personal political agenda.'

So what, if not a hidden agenda, would explain systematic bias? Partly, Mills argues, it is a matter of the circulation of powerful milieus between media organisations, consultancies, political parties, and the state. Partly it is a matter of the BBC's dependency on the government not just to ensure continued funding, uphold its charter and appoint its board members, but also for a great deal of its news content. And partly it is a matter of journalists who have built their expertise and political networks through Oxford PPE degree programmes. But to really understand the current situation, one would need to take into account what happened to the BBC in recent decades.

'The BBC became more integrated into markets. John Birt, hired by Thatcher's appointees on the Board of Governers, was a neoliberal in a narrow sense. This wasn't understood at the time. People thought he was just a managerial maniac, some even called him a Leninist. They didn't understand what was happening, because they thought neoliberalism was about privatisation. It was a more ambitious project to remodel state and society, and this was taking place under the first wave of New Public Management [a neoliberal doctrine that would have the public sector organised on market principles]. The BBC was obliged to commission from the private sector, it was divided into buying and selling units, old correspondents were fired, and new personnel brought in people from the private sector sympathetic to Birt's managerial ethos.

'There were also changes in the reporting structure. In the seventies, the BBC had correspondents who covered both business and trade union news. The social democratic settlement, reflecting the power of both capital and labour, was built into its reporting structure. After the Miners' Strike and the Wapping dispute, trade union correspondents became redundant. Editors decided that what unions said didn't matter any more. Birt brought in Peter Jay, the financial journalist who famously wrote Callaghan's speech declaring a monetarist policy, and Evan Davis. Their journalistic beat was dry economics reporting. This treated the economy as something which a narrow subset of experts deal with. Then they had more populist business programmes on the Thatcherite model, promoting the idea of a nation of shareholders.

'By the time of the credit crunch and the austerity projects, there was a consensus around neoliberalism. Particular centres of expertise were valued – for example, Jeff Randall had been brought in from the *Telegraph* to be the first business editor. So that when the crisis hit, the sources they had on television were people from the City, neoliberal think tanks and, of course, politicians who had been won over to neoliberalism. The media academic Mike Berry looked at the *Today* programme's coverage of the crisis, and even the Keynesian liberals didn't get much of a look in. So you end up with an institution which has a very close relationship to official sources from the state and business elites, who have been won over to neoliberalism. This is the BBC that confronted Corbyn in 2015. Corbyn's political positions are not only alien but, also, he is not of that world. It wasn't just a matter of hostility. Arguably, the BBC didn't know what to make of him, because they didn't think this was how politics worked, and had no sources in that world of left-wing activism.'

The gulf that has opened up between Corbyn supporters and the BBC, then, is not the result of a single biased agenda. The BBC's biases emerge from an overlapping and cumulative series of structural pressures and historical changes which had the effect of creating a consensus at the top of British politics and media around neoliberalism. The radicalisation of a new generation has called into question the precepts of that consensus, and this is particularly a problem for the BBC, because – whatever its actual record – it is expected to be impartial and represent a range of views. This raises questions as to whether the BBC will now feel under pressure to broaden its perspectives and reporting.

At the centre of this collapse is, however, not the state broadcaster but the traditional print empire, driven by the grand ideological designs of a sole proprietor like Rupert Murdoch, or, in Germany, Axel Springer. The idea that such a capitalist success story could be constructed around a hard-right ideological project was forged in the high point of Cold War-era industrial print capitalism, when prohibitively high costs of production favoured monopolies and one-way ideological traffic. This situation also favoured the 'newspaper of record' linked to a major governing party, like *El Pais*, so long the dominant newspaper of post-Franco Spain and fierce guardian of the political centre. Six hundred years of print culture is, if not over, being abruptly displaced by the Internet. Coupled with a crisis of confidence in the political class, this has forced media empires to diversify ideologically. In Germany, the Axel Springer media empire, publisher of the hard-right tabloid *Bild*, and long the backbone of right-wing populism in the country, has been responding to the crisis by shifting to online investments in single-issue and progressive publications like *Mic* and *Ozy*. *El Pais*, by contrast, has been unable to make this adaptation, is too deeply imbricated with a crisis-ridden Socialist establishment, and finds itself forced to consider liquidating its print edition in a country where 80 per cent of newspaper revenues still come from print.

This is a giant shift in the edifice of capitalist civilisation with, in all likelihood, much farther-reaching and deeper shifts entailed than has yet been apprehended. But some of the immediate political consequences are becoming increasingly clear. The crisis of representation finds its echo in a crisis of the representation of representation. The same distrust for the political establishment extends to distrust for the media establishment which reflects on their doings. But distrust is only a part of it. If Internet neutrality, the advent of social media, and relatively low online production costs had not come along contemporaneously, there would not be the range of easily accessible alternatives, and the one-way ideological traffic of the old media would still obtain.

It is difficult to see Corbyn having won the Labour leadership contest, in the absence of a well-organised Left, had he been forced to rely on the coverage given him by the press and broadcasters. Likewise, the general election would have followed a very different course had Corbyn's campaign team not been able to reach out to social media users with a range of easily digestible and shareable content, bypassing and sometimes challenging the messages of the old media. As it is, pro-Corbyn websites like the *Canary* were able to beat the BBC, the *Mirror* and the *Telegraph* in terms of shares on Facebook, while *Another Angry Voice*, run by a dedicated individual blogger, beat the *Daily Mail* and the *Express*. The most widely shared stories on this platform were pro-Corbyn and anti-Tory, accentuating Corbyn's celebrity support and polling improvements, thus undermining the demonisation taking place in the traditional print and broadcast media. Labour understood this advantage and invested more energy in posting and sharing social media content than all of its rivals.[16]

Some journalists and centre-right politicians have responded to this change with unavailing moral panic about 'online abuse' and 'fake news'. As with all moral panics, they express real tendencies, but in a way that distorts, exaggerates, and scapegoats. Certainly, the emerging attention economy has allowed sensationalist websites and sources of infotainment to exert influence and claim advertising revenue, but neither sensationalism nor infotainment are original products of online media. Clearly, the dark side of the Internet is populated by trolls, doxxers, bullies, and witch-hunters, but the newspapers involved in Hackgate can hardly have clean consciences about bullying and doxxing. The media which have indulged in what Diane Abbott, herself one of the major targets of online abuse, called the 'politics of personal destruction' are in no position to lecture. And all too often, politicians have muddied the waters by qualifying any mildly intemperate political criticism as 'abuse', invariably with the wry rider: 'so much for the new kinder, gentler politics.'

The moral panic is a substitute for appropriate journalistic curiosity about complex new developments. Particularly striking is the complete lack of interest in learning anything about Jeremy Corbyn and his supporters, who have instead been demonised, condescended to as silly and dangerous fanatics uninterested in wielding real power, and subject to gossip and red-baiting. And, with newspapers once again returning to form with rumours of Corbynite purges and hard-Left 'bullying', there is no sign of that changing any time soon.

VI

When Corbyn first took the Labour leadership, his critics surmised that it was a return to the discredited, squalid, and angry past: the 1980s. To them, this meant that Corbynism was a project for a permanent opposition, an eternally subaltern protest party rather than a realistic attempt at political and social change. And they began preparing their lines of attack as if this were true. They were wrong. Corbyn's

Labour has demonstrated its ability not just to critique existing failures, not just to protest the limitations of the old governing centre, but to catch the forward motion of technological, cultural, and social change. It has proven to be a *modernising* project, giving a collective and radical expression to popular ambitions.

When the Right and centre can no longer seriously claim to offer 'opportunity' to underemployed and precarious workers, Labour offered workers' rights, a cradle-to-grave free education service, and investment to create jobs. When 'aspiration' is no longer plausibly championed by the Tories; when home ownership is increasingly out of the question even for professionals like teachers, nurses, and junior doctors; when landlords drive up rents for ever dingier properties with impunity and oligarchs drive gentrification, Labour offered to build council homes, control rents, bring back housing benefits for the young, and impose new minimum habitation standards. In this, Labour was addressing the problems of twenty-first-century Britain, something that was already clear in Corbyn's 2015 leadership bid, but was largely ignored by his oblocutors.

In the 1980s, modernising meant moving to the right, accepting 'free markets', marginalising the left-wing 'dinosaurs' (such as Corbyn), and imposing an obsessive, managerial, focus-grouped control in messaging in order to win support across classes. Today, modernisation is a left-wing goal, the Blairites are the dinosaurs, and obsessive message control has been abandoned, with the result of rebuilding Labour's support faster than anyone expected. The boisterous celebrations among Corbyn's social media prize-fighters are entirely justified. They woke up on 9 June in a country they didn't know existed: that, arguably, wouldn't have existed had it not been for Labour's breakthrough campaign. So, to an extent, are the outbursts of angry triumphalism from those who have been belittled, patronised, and vilified for so long. Many an erring pundit has been christened a 'melt' and invited to 'eat your tweet' or, better still, 'delete your account'. At some point, however, this has to give way to a more sober appraisal of the dilemmas facing Labour.

The problem is not just that Labour must now find a way to turn its advantage into electoral victory, which raises a question about where to find the necessary voters in a first-past-the-post system, and how. Even if a fresh election is called soon and Labour does win, it will be in the position of having to try to implement a radical programme in an economy where there is very little investment. It will have to persuade corporations to invest, in spite of the higher taxes, regulations, and workers' rights they will face. It will have to convince the City and businesses that paying toward an upgraded infrastructure is better for them than hoarding capital in the form of low-risk securities or in offshore tax havens.

Most difficult of all, it will now have to manage the giant task of Brexit, an economic and political minefield. The issue of whether to leave the European Union was settled by the referendum, but the issues of single-market membership and free movement were not. And while pundits may have overestimated just how much people care about Europe per se, the issue of migration cuts to the heart of a cultural and generational divide in Britain today. Not only that, but if the EU isn't forthcoming with a viable deal, if it decides to punish the UK for Brexit, then Labour would need to immediately win support for an emergency economic programme, far more radical than anything that is currently being contemplated.

Moreover, the divisions within the Labour Party are far from over. The Labour Right is divided, defanged, and demoralised, but there are fresh lines of attack opening up already. Nor is its power completely gone. Most Labour MPs are still well to the right of the leadership and the membership, as indeed are most trade union leaders. Their influence is demonstrated in Labour's manifesto commitments on NATO, Trident, and policing, as well as, arguably, Labour's ambiguous position on migration. Nor are the strategic and organisational problems for the Left resolved. Labour has had a rocky two years under Corbyn, in no small part thanks to open sabotage, and the Left has had to think on its feet. If the overall effect of this turbulence has been to weaken and discredit the Labour Right even further, it has also exposed weaknesses on the Left. Momentum, the left-wing Labour activist group, has experienced crises. More broadly, there is evidence that most of Corbyn's membership base, while it will rally to defend the leadership, abstains from local party activism. This raises the question whether they're abstaining because there are other forms of activism they would prefer to be engaged in, because they just haven't been approached properly, or because they're waiting for the leader to act on their behalf.

Above all, this raises a fundamental strategic question.

What is the ultimate goal? In the traditional Labourist view, the goal is a Labour government, plain and simple. It is to elect 'our' government and defend it as it, hopefully, achieves some incremental gains. There was never any reason to reflect too much on the structural limitations imposed on any government's ability to act as long as Labour wasn't trying to do anything too radical. But Labour's leadership is, perhaps for the first time, systematically trying to pull British politics to the left, something it will no doubt also try to do in office. And it will be that much harder if it confronts a situation in which the balance of power in British society still overwhelmingly favours the owners of the country, and in which workers and communities are so poorly organised. Corbyn's own experience and perspective foreground the necessity of extra-parliamentary, grass-roots organisation: 'people-powered politics', as his campaign put it. Corbyn won the leadership in part because the idea that change simply, or adequately, follows from winning elections is no longer persuasive. It is no use being in office without power, as Tony Benn once put it. But Corbyn can't build movements by decree, even if it was in his style to lead in that way, so finding the right way to organise is a crucial problem for his supporters.

These are difficult enough problems, but they happen to be the problems of success. And it would be a fool who would bet the farm on failure at this point. Corbyn began, we can hardly forget, as a 200–1 outsider to win the Labour leadership. At the outset of the snap general election, he cheerfully reminded critics of this fact before confounding their expectations yet again. Everything Corbyn, his allies, and his supporters have achieved has been against the odds – against *all* odds.

August 2017

Introduction:
Against All Odds

There's Something about Jeremy

Early 2016, and Tony Blair is 'baffled'. What with Jeremy Corbyn in Britain, and Bernie Sanders in the United States, he sighs: 'I'm not sure I fully understand politics right now.'[1]

His confusion is to be expected. He had warned Labour, to no avail: 'if your heart is with Jeremy, get a transplant'. His former confederate Peter Mandelson joined in, telling that bastion of Labour values the *Financial Times* that: 'The Labour Party is in mortal danger.' And his old ally and sparring partner Gordon Brown exhorted Labour not to become a 'party of permanent protest'.[2] What more could they have done?

But since Blair left office, the world has been changing, one regime at a time, and he is no longer at ease. Sarkozy has gone, Bush has gone, Aznar has gone, Mubarak has gone, Qadhafi has gone. Soon, his last ally in office will be the Kazakhstani dictator, Nursultan Nazarbayev, for whom he provided invaluable service in managing his image after a notorious regime massacre.[3]

As abroad, so it is at home. Where once the Blairites seemed unshakeable in their power, their ruthless sodality has finally bitten the dust in Labour's leadership elections of 2015, when they received 4.5 per cent of the vote. Officially, the burial was executed by an unassuming anti-war socialist named Jeremy Corbyn, who won with a landslide 59.5 per cent of the vote in the first round.

It would be underselling this to call it the most unlikely political comeback in history. It is true that there was a time when socialists operated openly in the Labour Party, unashamed and relatively vocal. Yet rumours of their former power have always been exaggerated. And this is the first time in Labour's history that it has a radical social-ist for a leader.

It does the novelty of the situation no justice at all to compare Corbyn to Michael Foot, as some commenta-tors prematurely did. Foot was of the soft Left, and his political roots belonged in a form of radicalised liberalism. Despite a certain amnesia on this point, moreover, he was far more dependent upon the party's right-wing than its hard Left – it was the former which ran the ill-fated 1983 election campaign. His long record of peace campaigning didn't prevent him from supporting Mrs Thatcher in the Falklands, in a way that it is difficult to conceive of Corbyn doing. A closer historical comparison might possibly be made with George Lansbury, a left-wing pacifist with an activist past, who was elected Labour leader in 1931 after Ramsay MacDonald's defection to join a Conservative-led National Government. That one has to look back this far for comparison is a register of precisely how unprecedented the current position of the Labour Party is, and even here it only goes so far: Lansbury had been a popular local mayor and a cabinet member by the time he was elected, whereas Corbyn has held no executive office. That this rebounded to his advantage in this campaign tells something of how unpopular the governing strata has become.

Jeremy Corbyn is one of the last standing Bennites in the Labour Party. Those whose memory of Tony Benn is chiefly of a gentle elder radical in the anti-war movement and incomparable diarist, rather than as a threat to the British establishment hounded by spooks and monstered on the front pages, may not immediately grasp the significance of this. For Benn had been an upper-class rebel, a noble by birth who rejected his title, and a former cabinet minister who had seen inside the vaults of power and concluded that it called for something rather more wide-reaching than mere tinkering. He could, by all accounts, have led Labour himself had he not veered so hard to the left having experienced office. But the experience of 'office without power', as he described it, radicalised him.[4] Labour's problem, he argued, had been that it attempted to manage capitalism rather than do anything to undermine the serious inequities of wealth and power that existed at the time. As a result, it was presiding over a system that was losing legitimacy, generating major discontent, and as a result was in danger of being reversed by the Right.

To remedy this perceived failure, Benn had called for Labour to implement a round of sweeping reforms, akin in its depth and ambition to the achievements of the 1945 Labour Government. This meant redistributing wealth, reforming unelected state apparatuses, and nationalising key industries in order to place them under workers' control. One of his major criticisms of the post-war settlement had been that nationalised industries were still not democratic, but run on the same top-down basis as private industry – often by the same people. Within the framework of democratic socialism, he argued, it should be possible for parliament to pass laws giving workers the right to manage and to elect their managers.[5] The very idea that Labour should ever aspire to such drastic reforms was precisely what New Labour existed to destroy.

Corbyn, from a more humble background in rural Shropshire, where he worked on local farms, has never been considered a likely Labour leader. As he put it,

> The difference between Tony and me was that whereas he was one of those very unusual politicians who was actually very successful in a conventional career pattern, I have been monumentally unsuccessful in the conventional career pattern.[6]

Yet in another way, his political background was more favourable to a course as a socialist agitator than Benn's. The son of middle-class political activists who met while campaigning for the republican side in the Spanish Civil War, he grew up in a family steeped in radical ideas. And the evidence is that he genuinely obsessed about politics and little else. As a grammar school student, he foreswore study the better to spend time with his politics. As a Voluntary Service Overseas worker in Jamaica, he was radicalised by the 'imperialist attitudes, social division, and economic exploitation' he found there. As a trade union organiser, first in the National Union of Tailors and Garment Workers, and then in the National Union of Public Employees, he tirelessly attended meetings, protests and picket lines. He seems to have found no time at all either for money or drink or for the hedonistic pleasures of counterculture, prefer-ring instead to practise the teetotal strain of socialism for which Benn was famous. On the plus side, this meant that he was, as his former partner Jane Chapman recalled, 'very principled, very honest ... a genuinely nice guy'.[7]

These characteristics are consistently evident through-out Corbyn's career as constituency MP for Islington North, which he has represented since 1983. Even his most sceptical biographer, the *Telegraph* journalist Rosa Prince, acknowledges that he 'is known as a "good con-stituency MP", meaning he takes great pains over helping those who need him, and he is universally considered to do an exemplary job'.[8] As a member of the Socialist Campaign Group, representing the Bennite wing of Labour, he has consistently opposed the government whichever party was in office. Ever the activist, never an operator, he was more likely to be found working for the Anti-Apartheid Movement or the Palestine Solidarity Campaign than wheeling and dealing for favour and influ-ence. He was found, during the expenses scandal that befell British parliamentarians in 2009, to have claimed the smallest sum of expenses of any MP – £8.95 for a printer cartridge.[9]

His activism is not just a moral calling, but also a matter of a conscious political strategy. 'People are saying the job of the PLP is to go for the middle-class suburban vote,' he explained during the Kinnock era,

> but the Campaign Group must be on the picket lines and at the workplace level. In inner-city areas where there are no major employers except local government and some public services, there just isn't trade union experience, and school-leavers know nothing about the trade union or labour movement.[10]

For Corbyn, the relative weakening of the Left and the labour movement was not a reason to move to the right, but to patiently rebuild. This is far more fundamental to his perspective for reviving the Labour Party than the necessary compromises and reassurances offered to parliamentary backbenchers. As he explained in one of his campaign speeches, the Conservatives were able to win because people were not mobilised and thus didn't vote:

> Their parliamentary majority is based on a low turnout, it's based on the support of 24% of the electorate as a whole … There is a fairly small political party membership in Britain, really. The Labour Party membership is 240,000. I've no idea what the Conservative Party membership figure is … Liberal Democrat membership I have no idea; I suspect it's not very big. And so there isn't a vast number of people in political parties in Britain, but that's not to say we're living in a totally depoliticised society. Look at the 250,000

that came on the anti-austerity march last weekend; look at the vast number of people who were on the Pride march in London yesterday, and the demonstration. People are involved in politics in a different way ... I think we need to build a social movement.[11]

This is not to claim that Corbyn's campaign *was* the social movement, but it used the techniques of movement building in a way that conveyed what Corbyn wanted for the Labour Party. This way of doing politics, greatly underestimated by the media and political classes, was critical to Corbyn's success. The exhausting sequence of packed public meetings in towns and cities across the country, for example, were a typical part of Corbyn's calendar. As he explained, 'I did over a hundred events during the leadership campaign and by the end of the year I will probably have done 400 to 500 public meetings.'[12] This political style had been largely forgotten in the era of focus groups, marketised politics and the obsessive shaping of news cycles. Corbyn, far from evincing embarrassment at his militant record, plentiful images of which circulated on social media sites during his campaign, embraced it as a virtue. He was elected as a man of the movements, not of the markets.

And through such means, he has assembled a surprising breadth of support. The ideas that he champions haven't had a powerful mainstream voice for years, and the last time anyone remotely this left-wing got close to the Labour leadership was during Tony Benn's run for deputy leader in 1981, which Corbyn played a leading role in organising. As Phil Burton-Cartledge, a Labour Party member in Stoke, astutely observed, Corbyn seems to have personified something that people of various political hues feel is missing from politics. 'Whether you're a Green, self-described Old Labour, a recovering Trotskyist, or some other permutation', there is 'something attractive about Jeremy's politics'.[13]

This is what has taken the party establishment and its sympathisers in the media most by surprise. The ideas with which Corbyn won are ones that have largely been ignored, suppressed, or regarded with amused condescension since the Blairites took control. It was not just that Corbyn was prepared to oppose the government's austerity programmes and support higher public spending, nationalisation and redistribution. This was all bread and butter for the social-democratic Left. And on these issues, there is some evidence that the British electorate is more left-wing than is conventionally assumed.[14] Corbyn also defied what is supposed to be the common sense view on immigration, refusing to give an inch to the resentful UKIP-style nationalism that had permeated both of the dominant parties. This suggests that Corbyn is prepared to challenge more than the establishment; he aims to run against popular prejudice, and win. His first gesture as leader, utterly characteristic of him, was to attend a pro-refugees rally in central London, where he received what the *Mirror* called a 'hero's welcome'.[15]

The agenda on which Corbyn was elected is not, however, the stuff of which revolutions are made. He has pledged to end austerity, and in its stead implement a People's Quantitative Easing programme with money invested in infrastructural development, job-creation and high-technology industries. Canadian Prime Minister Justin

Trudeau won office on an agenda like this. Even the OECD is anti-austerity these days.[16] He promises to address the housing crisis through extensive home-building, to fully nationalise the railways, and to bring all academies back under local democratic control. These objectives are to be funded, not so much by squeezing the rich like a sponge to water the gardens of the poor, as by closing tax loopholes, stimulating growth, and spending less on controversial programmes such as Trident.

This is in most ways a classic social-democratic remedy, which could easily have come with some Wilsonian vocables about 'the white heat of technological revolution'. The problem for the establishment is not necessarily Corbyn's agenda. It may be too radical for today's Labour Party, today's media and today's parliamentary spectrum, but business could live with it, and the consensus would shift if Corbyn gained popular support. The problem is the type of politician that he is. The political tendency represented by Corbyn was supposed to be finished, the very idea of an alternative to capitalism interred since 1989 and all that. Now, it is not terribly shocking to read of surveys that show British people to be slightly 'keener on socialism than on capitalism'.[17] It is not the case that the Left is suddenly vibrant and full of beans and power. It is the case that, in circumstances which defy analogy, there is a chance for radical politics to make an utterly unexpected rebirth.

How did he do it? In this book, I argue that Corbyn intelligently exploited an opening which has come about from the decay of the old parties. This isn't just Labour's problem, despite the obvious complacency and enervation of the party's traditional elites. As of writing, the Tories are undergoing the latest spasm of a chronic crisis pivoted on Europe, but affecting a far wider range of issues. Corbyn, despite the weakness of his position and the extraordinary belligerence of his back benchers, has succeeded in exploiting these divisions to force policy retreats on a series of issues, from tax credits, to the Saudi prisons contract, to disability benefits cuts. But his own party is in no better shape. The logic working itself out in all the major parliamentary parties tends toward splits and realignment. This malaise goes deeper than policy and leadership.

The story of Corbyn's victory is one in which parliamentary democracy, and the traditionally dominant parties, have been slowly sliding into a crisis of legitimacy for some time – and that crisis suddenly became acute with the onset of economic stagnation and austerity. The representative link, between the people and the government, has been breaking down for decades. Now it is throwing up new forms of political volatility. The SNP's surge in Scotland, and UKIP's surge in England, are recent manifestations of this breakdown and realignment of political loyalties. If Corbyn's surge was far more rapid and less anticipated, he and his team were just the latest group of radical Leftists to punch well above their weight because they saw where the establishment was failing and articulated the right ideas. Whether it is Syriza in Greece, or Podemos in Spain, or even Sanders in the United States, the sudden surges in support for individuals and groups who were previously marginalised arises from the same type of crisis.

These examples, of course, also contain certain warnings to Corbyn and his supporters. Podemos, despite having led in the polls, was ultimately unable to secure an election victory. Syriza, having won, was unable to change policy despite forming a government. Sanders may yet win, but is already warning his supporters that even as president the scale of resistance he would face from 'the billionaire class' could make it all but impossible for him to implement his goals. Corbyn, of course, is some way from being in a position to tangle with 'the billionaire class'. He has first to face down the bile of his own parliamentary colleagues such as David Blunkett, Tristram Hunt, Simon Danczuk, Sadiq Khan, Caroline Flint, John Mann, Michael Dugher and Ben Bradshaw. He also has to keep a shadow cabinet together against a steady drumbeat of more subtly undermining behaviour on the part of Hilary Benn, Maria Eagle and deputy leader Tom Watson. And he has to weather the attacks from the Conservatives and the media, whose criticisms invariably seem to resonate with those of Corbyn's Labour critics.

In the coming chapters, I will explain how Corbyn faced down 'Project Fear' and won, before delving into the broader context and history of British politics and Labour's role in it. In asking whether Corbyn has any chance of success as a Labour leader, let alone as a prime minister, the answers I give won't leave anyone entirely comfortable. Those awaiting a return to 'politics as usual' will find a lot to be worried about. The Blairites and Labour's 'moderates' will find the analysis hugely disagreeable. Corbynistas, meanwhile, won't find a tone of cheerleading optimism here. Above all, although this book is written in sympathy with Corbyn, it is not written with any loyalty to the Labour Party, of which I am not a member. That fact allows me to put my finger on what might be the raw nerve of any Labour loyalist, left or right: that the party may simply be untenable in its current form. Because the most difficult challenges that Corbyn faces have to do with the question he was elected to answer: whither Labour? Labour's decline is what Corbyn was elected to address. Labour's decline is what gave him the space to lead. And Labour's decline will now constitute the major obstacle to his success.

1

How 'Project Fear' Failed

Let us remind ourselves of the extraordinary facts of this leadership election. When the race began, Corbyn was considered a no-hope candidate. As an anti-austerity, anti-war campaigner, he was far too remote from the conventional idea of a successful politician to win. Channel 4 journalist Michael Crick summed up this logic when he wrote to his Twitter followers: 'Under my law of leadership elections – that the freshest and/or youngest contender usually wins – you should bet on Liz Kendall.'[1] Corbyn was initially estimated by bookkeepers to be a rank outsider, with 100–1 odds of winning, behind the favourite Andy Burnham, and the runners-up Liz Kendall and Yvette Cooper.[2]

However, under the seemingly calm political surface, something was already stirring. There had been, in the wake of the Conservative victory, an angry reaction by Labour supporters, and a large anti-austerity march through central London attended by Corbyn. The Labour establishment from which Burnham, Kendall and Cooper were drawn had responded to the defeat by blaming Miliband for being too left-wing. The 'Blue Labour' guru Jon Cruddas fed mangled and misleading research to the *Guardian* newspaper claiming to support this idea.[3] Such claims were rejected by the British Election Study, which pointed out that the major factor dogging Labour was the 2008 economic crash, Labour's version of the 1992 ERM crisis.[4] But more importantly, they were rejected by a growing number of Labour supporters. Labour's defeats in the 1980s might have been blamed on the Left, but this one was blamed firmly on the Right. As a result, Corbyn's 'dark horse' challenge had a certain momentum from the beginning. Corbyn's early meetings were extremely well attended, even if this fact was largely ignored by the media.

As the media belatedly began to pick up on 'Jeremy Corbyn mania', with some bewilderment and alarm, high-profile Labour figures including Tony Blair began to make public statements, using their presumed moral authority to warn against a gamble on Corbyn. The unease among senior Labour figures was exacerbated by the decision of major unions, such as Unite and Unison, to support Corbyn – chiefly on the grounds that he was the only candidate to offer more than lukewarm opposition to the Tories' planned anti-union legislation. The release of the first poll for the leadership showing Corbyn with a serious lead over all rivals prompted a slew of panicky and counterproductive interventions from Gordon Brown, Jack Straw, Alistair Campbell and others.

What Blair, Brown, Straw, Campbell and the rest could

not understand was that for Corbyn's supporters, they were the very epitome of the problem, the right-wing establishment that they were rebelling against. Labour-supporting celebrities who rallied behind the mainstream candidates – for example, Steve Coogan's boasting about Andy Burnham's 'radical leftwing plan' for Britain[5] – also had little impact. Yet another poll was released, this one giving Corbyn a lead in the first round, with at least twenty points over his nearest rival. The panic from the Labour machine, as it sought to purge potential pro-Corbyn 'infiltrators', was matched by a public fear campaign from the likes of Labour MPs John Mann and Simon Danczuk, who demanded that the election be stopped, or that Corbyn be overthrown during his first days in office. Once again, this was counterproductive, since those who were likely to vote Corbyn were already convinced that the old leadership was undemocratic and didn't take members seriously.

With little support from any of the traditional media, Corbyn's campaign team turned to social media. Just as the UK Independence Party (UKIP) had exploited Twitter and Facebook to their advantage during the general election, even showing up the mainstream media to their supporters, Corbyn and his team were able to do the same. Through these means he built his mass meetings without recourse to the old media that were denying him due publicity, while the other candidates' meetings struggled to attract a dozen or so stragglers despite ample coverage. In the end, despite (and in part because of) the purges and fearmongering, Corbyn's victory was a first-round landslide, as he emerged with just under 60 per cent of the vote.

From Out of Nowhere

The story of Corbyn's challenge begins shortly after the 2015 general election. While the dominant narrative coming out of Labour's right-wing was that Labour had lurched to the unelectable left, a core of activists on the Left were drawing very different conclusions. Few, when Corbyn first stood as a Labour leadership candidate, expected him to get on the ballot, much less stand a chance of winning. This was as much true of his close supporters and advisers as it was of his rivals. But there was a need to counter the Blairite narrative and create a space for an alternative point of view. The campaign's social media organiser and London regional organiser Marsha-Jane Thompson explains:

> We didn't think he had a chance of getting on the ballot paper. We had a strategy of holding regional meetings with figures like Owen Jones and Jon Trickett MP, publicising an alternative manifesto, explaining what we would say if Jeremy Corbyn did get on the ballot ... It was part of a wider anti-austerity initiative. There had been some good stuff in Ed Miliband's election manifesto which was downplayed by the right-wing, so our idea was to highlight the aspects of it that called for social justice and to highlight that there was a shift to the left there. We also wanted to challenge the Blairite narrative, which was that Labour lost because we had moved too far to the left. In fact, we lost because we didn't present a coherent alternative.[6]

Nevertheless, there was a sense quite early on that the situation was very different from that five years before, when the most left-wing candidate, John McDonnell MP, didn't even get on the ballot paper. Ben Sellers, a long-standing Labour activist and founder of *Red Labour*, recalls that while there was no guarantee that Corbyn would get on the ballot, there was a palpable current of discontent among party members:

The grass roots was not particularly left-wing, but at the same time they were not happy with the cards they had been dealt by New Labour, or the exclusion of members from the decision-making process. They felt they were just there to do door-knocking, leaf-leting and so on. And even then, there was a controversy when the party started collecting data from door-knocking and gave people scripts, as if they couldn't cope with having conversations with people on the door-step. So there was a kickback against the lack of trust in the party membership. Then there were a hell of a lot of people keeping quiet, who you would see at People's Assembly events, but would never say they were in Labour, and for that reason weren't seen as the voice of the party. People thought the party was just full of Blairites, but the truth is, the Blairites were always a small minority in the party – they just happened to be the ones in positions of power in constituencies, or regional officials, or councillors. So, the left was silenced: they kept their paper member-ship, but they stopped going to meetings.[7]

For this discontent to be channelled into a leadership elec-tion process, however, there were some hoops to jump through. For all the talk of one-member-one-vote, the par-liamentary party still has a veto on who gets to stand for leader. Prior to 2014, a candidate had to have the support of at least 12.5 per cent of Labour MPs. After the implementation of reforms recommended in the Collins Review, the required level of support was increased to 15 per cent. This meant that Corbyn needed at least thirty-five nominations to even stand. Given that the dominant explanation in the party for its electoral defeat seemed to be that Ed Miliband was a recalcitrant socialist who dragged the party to the left, it was not obvious that MPs would give Corbyn the nominations he needed.

However, it was also glaringly apparent that without Corbyn the debate would be deathly dull and narrower than ever before. And there was a core group of activists with a degree of social media savvy, who were able to leverage the existing discontent in the party to put pressure on MPs to at least allow the debate to happen. Using Twitter, Facebook and email campaigns, they were able to build a momentum behind Corbyn's campaign that would not otherwise have existed. As Thompson put it:

> We sensed that this time it was different and they wouldn't be able to ignore us and sideline us as they historically had. The parliamentary party were under a lot of pressure from people who supported Jeremy's candidacy on social media … One MP explained that she'd had a hundred constituents email her in one day demanding that Jeremy be admitted to the ballot.[8]

Newcastle MP Chi Onwurah explained on her website that she was nominating Corbyn not because she agreed with his policies but because 'I asked members and supporters in my constituency who I should nominate and the overwhelming feedback ... was that Jeremy Corbyn should be on the ballot.'[9] Some of those who welcomed Corbyn's candidacy did so the better to see his ideas clearly defeated. Labour activist Luke Akehurst explained, 'I want their ideas taken on democratically and defeated in an open contest of ideas.'[10] There was, in short, no expectation among his nominees or seasoned activists that Corbyn could win. But the mere fact that they were talking about him, in a way that they hadn't talked about previous campaigns mounted by John McDonnell, already suggested that something novel was happening. Corbyn squeezed past the nominations barrier at the last minute with just thirty-six nominees.

Some of the energies that would appear in the campaign began to make themselves visible in a significant public protest that summer. In June 2015, for the first time in several years, an anti-austerity protest drew tens of thousands of people to the streets. This would not have been the largest such protest if it had happened in 2011, the year of the Arab Uprisings, the Occupy movement and a series of mass demonstrations, public sector strikes and even riots in the UK. But on this occasion, it followed years of demoralisation and defeat, in which every crisis seemed to favour the Right. Labour's long retreat from its brief experiment with anti-austerity politics, its welfare-bashing and its feeble attempt to triangulate UKIP on immigration, had resulted in yet another election defeat. Labour's biggest problem, it had turned out, was motivating the younger electorate, who largely either did not turn out, or gave their votes to the Greens. Many of them now took to the streets and, as a major speaker at the concluding rally, Jeremy Corbyn set the direct and morally straightforward tone that would characterise his whole campaign. It was not a polished, rehearsed performance, and the candidate was not naturally charismatic. And far from sticking to the relatively easy critique of austerity, he made a point of defending the immigrants and 'welfare scroungers'[11] reviled both by Tories and previous Labour governments. From anyone else, a call for a 'kinder politics' would come across as a greasy, hypocritical shibboleth. In Corbyn's case, it was the core of his politics reduced to its simplest expression. He appealed for a new type of society where, 'we each care for all, everybody caring for everybody else: I think it's called socialism'.

This was only one crowd and far from the last of a series of large public events that Corbyn addressed. Soon, his meetings, held in cities across the country from Exeter to Newcastle, were as packed as those of his rivals were threadbare. But this one crowd in mid-June alone would have suggested that, if Corbyn could channel the discontent of Labour activists, he had the basis for a serious leadership challenge. As Stephen Bush wrote in the *New Statesman*, the size of the crowd in London – however exaggerated by organisers – pointed to the existence of a large enough activist base to win the Labour leadership:

> Let's say that just 10,000 of them can be convinced that the Labour Party, even one led by Corbyn, is worth the candle. Then they each need to recruit five friends. If just *one* of those five friends recruits another friend, Corbyn could be Labour's next leader.[12]

So it turned out. On one Saturday in August, Corbyn addressed 1,800 people in Manchester; 1,000 people in Derby; 1,700 in Sheffield's Crucible and a further 800 outside.[13] The patterns were repeated in Coventry, Plymouth, Liverpool, Birmingham and in London, where the Camden Centre was filled to bursting point with 2,000 people inside, and a crowd of several hundred outside. By the end of that month, it was announced that a total of 13,000 people had signed up to volunteer for his campaign. The daily growing list of celebrities supporting Corbyn in writing or in public events seemed to extend well beyond the list of 'usual suspects' who might be spotted at People's Assemblies – a motley cohort ranging from Emma Thompson and Daniel Radcliffe to Mary Beard and Lord Skidelsky. Labour membership soared wherever Corbyn touched down. In Colchester, following a meeting of over a thousand people, the biggest local political meeting for decades, the Labour Party membership quadrupled. The spectacle of thousands upon thousands of enthusiastic participants signing up to have anything to do with the Labour Party would have been unthinkable a few months before. The fact that there was a 'registered supporters' category also helped the Corbyn campaign team, since it gave them a chance to make a unique and compelling offer to those Leftists who were wary, on account of bitter experience, of joining Labour. As a senior advisor put it, 'the offer was, pay three quid and help smash Blairism for good. Many people would pay a lot more than that for such a privilege'. But while 100,000 people did sign up as registered supporters, almost twice that number, 183,658, signed up as full members. The number of new members alone was more than twice the membership of the Conservative Party.[14]

The campaign's ability to summon enthusiastic participation was matched by its online reach, and indeed the two aspects of the campaign were mutually supporting. Marsha-Jane Thompson recalls:

> There is a lot of exaggeration about social media, but we went from nothing to reaching 2.5 million people within four weeks of our Facebook page being launched. At the moment, our page reaches 11 million people every day ... In Colchester, this meant that when we put the announcement out about our meeting on Facebook, all thousand tickets were gone within forty-five minutes. This was before the polls showed Corbyn leading the other candidates.[15]

In addition to organising meetings, the social media campaign was able to play off against negative media coverage, rebutting the scare stories, and also make a virtue of those aspects of Corbyn's ideology and career that the media would try to vilify. As Sellers explains,

> There were three strands to the social media campaign. There were the official [social media] accounts which consisted mainly of standard fare, official statements and so on. They grew huge, naturally. But there were also a number of semi-official accounts which we ran, where we had contact with press officers and people working on the ground in the offices in London, with whom we could discuss rebuttal strategies informally. We also had a slight distance from them. The campaign office didn't want to get involved in rebuttals, but we felt there were some things that needed to be taken on. So

we began to plug away at what Corbyn stood for, the fact that he had a consistent ideology, had remained principled since the 1980s, and we turned this into a positive. We simplified his messages and put them out in easily digestible formats, memes and stuff. Then there was a huge volume of people doing smaller projects that were nothing to do with us or even necessarily the Labour Party – pages like 'Kittens 4 Corbyn', and so on. We had some tangential contact with these pages, and we could discuss things with them now and again, but they actually did a lot of the rebuttal work off their own back.[16]

This is not a dynamic that is peculiar to the Left. It is part and parcel of a political scene in which the ideological monopoly of the traditional media is breaking down. With the rise of alternative sources of information – and according to YouGov, some 57 per cent of Corbyn's supporters received most of their information about the campaign from social media[17] – there is far less deference to the dominant television and press outlets than there had been before. Meanwhile, the antagonism of the news media to Corbyn tended to compound a sense among supporters of both the authenticity of the candidate, and the general untrustworthiness of the traditional media.

One of Corbyn's most important assets in the campaign was his ability to say exactly what he thought, and to express it in a straightforward idiom that anyone could grasp without insulting anyone's intelligence. This rapidly distinguished him from his rivals, who waffled and looked unconvincing when not delivering prepared remarks. There was, indeed, something unreal about their detachment, their lack of direction, and their confusion in the face of Corbyn's rising star. It didn't help their cause that there were three candidates from the party's broad right-wing. The Labour Right, and its media supporters, couldn't agree on which of these to support. The *Mirror* backed Andy Burnham, The *Guardian* supported Yvette Cooper and the Tory press tended to favour Liz Kendall. The differences between the three candidates were miniscule, but the fact that they all competed for the same shrinking ideological space meant that there was no cohesive opposition from the Labour Right to Corbyn's brand of socialism.

It also didn't help that the candidates looked and sounded like special advisors rather than political big-hitters. Jeremy Gilbert, an associate at the soft-left group Compass, recounts that at the inception of the New Labour project, there was a clear divide between special advisors and the loyal MPs parachuted in to safe seats,

> and the architects like Mandelson and Gould, who are more robust intellectually. But they could never persuade serious intellectuals or serious composite political organisers of their case, so they had to recruit banal and unthinking figures – and we saw the outcome of this in the leadership election.[18]

So, after years in government, ideologically and intellectually exhausted, divided into three candidates, the Right faced Corbyn in a curiously hesitant mood. Sellers recalls that 'they didn't talk a lot about policy, and they didn't challenge the policy stuff that we put out – in a way, we weren't facing a serious opponent, which was odd. This wasn't the strong, efficient machine we were familiar with.'[19]

In a clip from LBC radio, which rapidly became viral, the four Labour candidates were asked by a member of the public to say whether Ed Miliband would feature in the shadow cabinet if they were elected. Corbyn gave a straight answer, in contrast to the waffling of the other candidates, prompting the host to remark: 'This is exactly why Jeremy Corbyn is shown in this *Times* poll this morning as way ahead of the rest of you, because he's given me a straight answer to a straight question, and the three of you can't do that.'[20] Participants at a typically packed meeting in Plymouth's Guildhall emphasised precisely that he spoke convincingly *as a Labour candidate*, in a way that none of his rivals did:

> 'He's saying things in a way that people can understand,' said Jo, a former secondary-school teacher. 'He says things that aren't patronising, that are talking to working people, and that feel like what the grassroots of this party is all about,' she said. 'Change is the word,' said Kate Taylor, a feminist and Labour councillor who was elected at age eighteen, three years ago. 'I'm a bit sick of having to constantly put aside my own opinions and beliefs for the Labour Party. I would like to get the Labour Party back to what it was made to be, for working people,' she said.[21]

So it was that, as branch and union nominations began to come in, Corbyn was far ahead of his leadership rivals. Constituency Labour Parties had not been bulwarks of Leftism for some time, but here they gave Corbyn a clear advantage, with 152 constituency branches backing him. By contrast, 109 voted to support Yvette Cooper, 111 backed Andy Burnham and a humiliating 18 backed Liz Kendall. This should not be exaggerated: less than half of the branch nominations went to Corbyn, and he gained fractionally under half of the votes of full members in the final result. Yet no one expected a Left this vibrant in the Labour Party. The results suggested that a long dormant Left, the survivors of old and almost forgotten battles, had reanimated and fused with a younger generation radicalised through participation in social movements and single-issue campaigns.

Far more shockingly to the Labour establishment, Corbyn also gained the support of the largest trade unions, UNISON and Unite, as well as the endorsements of the postal workers union, the CWU, the transport workers' union, ASLEF, and the other transport workers' union, TSSA. Andy Burnham and Yvette Cooper divvied up the endorsements of the Musicians' Union, the depleted husk of the miners' union, the NUM, the builders' union, UCATT and the shop workers' union, USDAW. Liz Kendall gained no union endorsements. The advantage of having union support was that it meant there was a well-funded electoral machine working for Corbyn, which there simply hadn't been for previous left-wing leadership campaigns.

Why did the leaderships of the larger trade unions, which were not helmed by radical Leftists and had no history of supporting left-wing Labour leadership candidates, back Jeremy Corbyn in this instance? With few exceptions, such as the union backing for Tony Benn's deputy leadership campaign, the traditional stance of the trade unions in Labour's internal politics has been to support moderate leadership factions and equally moderate policies. It is true that since the election of a number of left-wing leaders dubbed 'the awkward squad', the general trend in trade union support has been to the left, but this has never before led to such a rift with the Labour Party establishment. It is also true that, of the range of alternative leadership candidates available to them, none would fight for union-backed policies in parliament in the way that Corbyn would. But the union leaders are accustomed to bargaining for minor concessions within the existing framework of the Labour Party, rather than, as they have done by supporting Corbyn, trying to fundamentally alter it.

In the case of UNISON's support, one could discern a pragmatic consideration. The threat of a looming election for general secretary Dave Prentis might have inclined him to think carefully about whether he could justify supporting any of the other candidates, none of whom supported union policy in the way that Corbyn did. And while that disciplinary pressure did not apply to any of the other unions, those involved in the Corbyn campaign could see other pressures at work. 'Union leaders are more connected to the grass roots than we give them credit for sometimes,' Thompson argues,

and they could see which way their membership was going. They could see that members in their unions were signing up to support Jeremy. The data on their websites, where people could register to vote and back a candidate, showed that they were overwhelmingly backing Jeremy.[22]

Perhaps the most important consideration was hinted at in the CWU's official rationale for supporting Corbyn. They argued that Corbyn's victory would help break the 'grip of the Blairites ... once and for all'.[23] Throughout the whole period of Blairite dominance, the unions had been slowly sinking into an existential crisis. Their social depth has declined, the legislative climate has remained abysmal, industrial action has sunk to all-time lows, levels of manufacturing have continued to decline and the private sector is overwhelmingly non-unionised. Furthermore, the ability of the unions to do anything to reverse these trends has been seriously undermined by a series of reforms which have hacked away at their political clout within the Labour Party. The most recent of these was a package of measures recommended in the Collins Review, which in one manoeuvre disenfranchised millions of trade unionists. The spark for the reforms had been the Falkirk controversy, in which Unite was baselessly accused of rigging Labour's selection procedures. That Miliband instrumentalised this fake scandal in order to further weaken the union link ought to have put the unions on their guard. But, not wishing to embarrass Ed Miliband in the year before an election, and having been promised that the process would be continuously reviewed, they backed the reforms. This strategic blunder only compounded their crisis and it is likely that the victory of any other candidate would have led to their further marginalisation.

Corbyn's momentum, however much it enlivened the Labour Party, was met with a growing chorus of fury among Labour Rightists. As soon as it became clear that he was the favourite to win, with polls beginning to give him a clear lead as early as mid-July, panicked battle cries began to fly.

'Project Fear'

During the campaigns for and against Scottish independence, the leadership of the Unionist 'Better Together' campaign comprising both Labour and Conservative parties embarked on an offensive privately dubbed 'Project Fear' by the organisers.[24] The idea was, rather than selling the benefits of the Union, to terrify Scottish voters with visions of political and economic chaos should they vote to leave the UK. At its peak, Project Fear brought together leading figures in the state, business and media operators. The *Financial Times* reported[25] that the government twisted the arms of business leaders – 85 per cent of whom supported the Union – to go public with a series of warnings about economic disaster in the event of independence. Meanwhile, the civil service abandoned its customary pretence of neutrality, as the head of the Treasury Sir Nicholas Macpherson argued that there was no need for neutrality when 'the very existence of the British state was at stake'. Sir Jeremy Heywood, the cabinet secretary, drafted the Queen's intervention in the debate, while the Treasury published unusually partisan advice. Research showed that the main broadcast media, above all the BBC, were on board with the fear campaign, overwhelmingly publicising negative claims about independence.[26]

A remarkably similar pattern was to emerge in the case

of the Left's capture of the Labour leadership. During the leadership election, three Labour MPs from the party's right-wing – John Mann, Barry Sheerman and Graham Stringer – called for the process to be halted, claiming to be worried about infiltration by the far Left and Tory trolls.[27] They argued that the new rules under which the election was being conducted made it impossible to vet participants. As Stringer put it, with the influx of registered supporters, 'We do not know and could never know whether these people support other political parties.' Sheerman likewise contended that among infiltrators, only a few of the 'usual suspects' could possibly be detected by vetting measures. Mann suggested that 'long-standing members' might be 'trumped by people who have opposed the Labour Party', invoking the danger of a return of the old Trotskyist faction, Militant.

The *Sunday Times* joined in, leading the charge with a front-page story amplifying calls for Harriet Harman to cancel the leadership vote: 'Hard left plot to infiltrate Labour race.'[28] The only solid evidence of such a plot was a call by a groupuscule called the Communist Party of Great Britain for members to join Labour and support Corbyn. This was a group whose membership didn't exceed two dozen, and whose major claim to fame was its weekly news-sheet, recognised among the cognoscenti as the *Heat* magazine of the far Left. Otherwise it rested entirely on over-heated claims by right-wing Labour MPs and anonymous officials. Nonetheless, the piece succeeded in framing Corbyn's supporters as a deviant demographic, a trope that persists in the punditry of the traditional media. Dan

Hodges, a Blairite pundit and former spin doctor who had complained about Corbyn even making it onto the ballot, evoked a distorted image of Labour Party constituency meetings swarming with 'dozens of proto-Trotskyists … demanding a people's revolution, and shouting down anyone who disagrees with taunts of "Red Tory"'.[29] Andy McSmith, a journalist sympathetic to the Labour Right, was less excited about infiltration plots, yet he too rather sneeringly characterised Labour's registered supporters as '£3 day trippers whose idea of political involvement is to log on, vote Corbyn, and tell your mates via Facebook'.[30]

In fact, the rules that these people now complained about were exactly the same rules as had been approved overwhelmingly by conference, with 86 per cent of the vote and with opposition largely coming from the Left, in the year before the leadership election.[31] They were part of the wider series of transformations recommended in the Collins Review, which weakened the union link and were welcomed at the time as a radicalisation and deepening of previous Blairite reforms.[32] The logic of such reforms was to achieve a transformation that even Blair could not. Labour, at its inception, federated the institutions of the labour movement into a broad political party, with trade unionists making up the organised core. The New Labour project had been, in part, to replace this federal structure with one in which the organised core was the professional strata that ran the party, while the base consisted exclusively of individualised supporters and members. By weakening the union link, and replacing the levy-paying trade unionists with a mass of largely passive supporters paying a small fee, the party would be anchored firmly in the political centre.

What Labour's party managers had sought, ironically, was precisely the political day tripper – a cash cow, and voting fodder, but otherwise not likely to make life difficult for the party professionals. If no one at the time worried about the possibility of Trotskyist infiltration, this was because it would make precious little difference to anything even if it did happen. That analysis still holds. Almost 300,000 people signed up as members and registered supporters of the Labour Party during the election campaign. The total weight of the far Left in the UK is, based on the acknowledged (and often exaggerated) memberships of its organisations, less than 5 per cent of that total. What is more, most of its members wouldn't be seen dead in Labour – indeed, many of them have spent years eagerly working to replace it with a British equivalent of the Continent's radical Left parties.

Yet, rather than clearsightedly dismissing most of these largely confected complaints of infiltration, the Labour Party management decided to act on them, and began a process of purges. In doing so, they took a fairly broad interpretation of their remit, purging for example the general secretary of the civil servants' union, the PCS, Mark Serwotka. It is not clear how many were excluded in total. Some alarmist reports, apparently encouraged by acting leader Harriet Harman, who talked up the number of supposed 'infiltrators', gave the impression that up to 100,000 people might be purged. The total number of people expelled by the end of the process was reportedly closer to 3,000. Many of those who were banned were targeted for having previously been members or supporters of other centre-Left parties such as the Greens. The perfect idiocy of this defies measurement. For most young political activists, in an era when party identifications are weaker than they have ever been, and when the electoral system is showing signs of unusual volatility, a degree of political polyamory should be expected. It would be remarkable, and something Labour should regret, if it were unable to win back those who might have dallied in the past with the Liberals, the Greens or the Scottish National Party (SNP) – and odd for a party that used to proudly brag about former Tory MPs it had lured into the Blairite fold. To react to success on this front as evidence of 'infiltration', when the party managers know perfectly well that there is no evidence of organised entryism, bespeaks some form of political derangement. Worse, many of those who were expelled were not driven out for anything as substantive as an impure political past. The party simply had 'reason to believe' that they did 'not support the aims and values of the Labour Party'. These and similar expulsions appear to have been based on vexatious complaints emailed from local constituency chairs eager to ward off the Corbynite offensive.[33]

While the Labour Party machinery experimented with excluding party members and supporters on the basis of near-Jesuitical distinctions, the media dutifully advised the public of the coming danger. The near-unanimity of the media's offensive, supported by the Conservative Party, a section of the Labour Right and actors within the state, was hard to miss. The Media Reform Coalition, set up in the wake of 'Hackgate' – the infamous scandal exposing *News of the World* phone-hacking and the shady relationship of the Murdoch press to top politicians and police chiefs – studied the press response to Corbyn's victory and found that the papers 'systematically undermined' Corbyn from the first day of his leadership. A survey of 494 articles across the press found that 60 per cent of the coverage was negative, with only 13 per cent positive.[34]

The right-wing newspapers predictably augured 'chaos'. The *Telegraph* predicted that union leaders would try to use 'coordinated strikes and demonstrations' to 'topple the Government', while another columnist warned of Corbyn's supporters 'seizing the means of production and distribution directly through strikes and organised demands'.[35] The *Daily Mail* published a delirious fantasy about Jeremy Corbyn taking office and the first days of his administration, which began: 'The night sky over London was thick with choking black smoke…'.[36] Invoking an indebted basket-case economy torn apart by rioters, demonstrators and revolutionaries, it was practically salivating over the apocalyptic scenario it conjured up. One can't help but see in such eristic a degree of projection and nostalgic wish-fulfilment: the right-wing yearning for the old fighting days of the Cold War, when they could crush the Left in the name of the Free World. Even the seemingly sober *Financial Times* was at it, complaining of an 'air of menace' stalking Corbyn's campaign: 'National socialism, it was once called. One side waves the flag, the other demands a bigger state. Both rail against outsiders – the right against immigrants, the left against international capitalism.'[37] Here, the exuberant followers of a bearded, anti-war socialist were found to be analogous to the Third Reich. The *Financial Times* not only reached the threshold of Godwin's Law, in three sentences, it also compared powerful multinational capital to the desperate refugees being left to drown in the Mediterranean and subject to racist persecution across Europe.

One of the most insidious attacks from the Right was organised by the *Jewish Chronicle*, edited since 2008 by the Tony Blair–worshipping neoconservative pundit Stephen Pollard. In an article published a month before the outcome, the *Chronicle* posed a series of 'key questions Jeremy Corbyn must answer'.[38] Most of these were insinuation, guilt-by-association tactics. So, for example, it queried his links to Carlos Latuff, whom it characterised as 'the notorious anti-Semitic cartoonist'. Latuff is notoriously pro-Palestinian, but support for Palestine is a far cry from anti-Semitism. Even the Jewish daily *Forward* considers it a 'stretch' to call his cartoons 'antisemitic'.[39] Far more insidious was the attack on Corbyn for supporting Raed Salah, whom the *Chronicle* depicted as 'a man convicted of the blood libel'. This was particularly obnoxious, because Salah had been the subject of a deportation struggle, in which these claims of anti-Semitism were used by the government to support his expulsion from the UK. What the *Chronicle* failed to mention was that Salah won that court case precisely because these claims were shown to be false and based on mistranslations.[40] The fact that Salah was being slandered by the government is the reason why Corbyn, quite ethically, stood by him. Nonetheless, the *Chronicle*'s article provided material for reams and reams of similarly insinuating media attacks, such as Dan Hodges's claim that Corbyn's victory would be 'cheered by terrorists and racists'; and it served as ammunition for Labour's mayoral candidate Sadiq Khan to attack Corbyn in the *Daily Mail* for 'encouraging' terrorism.[41]

The centre-Left press had its own lines of attack. The *Guardian*, a long-standing ally of the Labour Right, played a particularly shoddy role, both in its journalism and its comment pages. Its comment pages were filled with condescension toward Corbyn and his supporters from comment editor Jonathan Freedland, leader writer Anne Perkins, columnist Suzanne Moore (a former eurocommunist pugilist from the pages of *Marxism Today*) and veteran columnist Martin Kettle (another former *Marxism Today* writer) – all essentially repeating the habitual refrain of Corbyn's Labour critics that he and his supporters were obsessed with their narrow concerns and oblivious to his unelectability.[42] Its sister paper, the *Observer*, was little different, with senior journalist Andrew Rawnsley deriding Corbyn's 'promised land', belittling its 'fantasy' politics and invoking Labour's 'near-destruction at the hands of the Bennites'.[43] The paper's editorial repudiating Corbyn finally induced an exasperated response from the *Observer*'s senior journalist Ed Vulliamy, who wondered why the paper had joined in the chorus of attacks, leaving 'a lot of good, loyal and decent people who read our newspaper feeling betrayed'.[44] Symptomatically, the flood of disobliging column inches about Jeremy Corbyn in these newspapers was marked by constant harking back to the 1980s. As if nothing fundamental had changed that might bear think-ing about. As if the same battles could be restaged – and indeed, the *Guardian* gave space to one of Labour's wealthi-est donors to suggest that a Corbyn victory could be met by an SDP-style split.[45] As if those rallying to Corbyn might not be responding to the problems of twenty-first-century Britain. As if part of the problem might not be the palpable inadequacy of the candidates whom liberal commentators seemed to think had a right to win, regardless of the paucity of their campaigns. One is entitled to wonder who it is here who was really stuck in the past, and really mired in self-serving fantasy.

One of the main methods of obloquy from the centre-Left papers – aside from the claim that Corbyn's supporters were either spaniel-eyed naïfs, gently prancing around in cloud cuckoo land, or dangerous ideological zealots – was to bait Corbyn's supporters as sexist. The *Guardian* had backed Yvette Cooper for the leadership, partially on the grounds that she would be the first female leader, bringing 'down-to-earth feminism' to the role, and challenging aus-terity policies that hurt women. Its leading columnist and former Social Democratic Party (SDP) star Polly Toynbee seconded the endorsement, announcing: 'Labour needs a woman leader.'[46] This prompted a reply by the seasoned feminists Selma James and Nina Lopez, who pointed out that Cooper not only supported 'sexist austerity' but had also implemented it in government, abolishing income support and extending work-capability assessments for the sick and disabled.[47] Nonetheless, having supported Cooper as a 'feminist', it didn't require much imagination to notice

that Corbyn was not female and thus to indict his supporters 'brocialists'. Suzanne Moore complained that as Corbyn
was 'anointed leader' – that is to say, elected leader – 'not
one female voice was heard'.[48] The remarkable thing about
this complaint was that Corbyn won among women by a
landslide. The polls showed that 61 per cent of women eli-
gible to vote in the election supported Corbyn, while the
two female candidates, Liz Kendall and Yvette Cooper,
gained 4 per cent and 19 per cent respectively. The polling
company YouGov pointed out that 'women who are eli-
gible to vote are dramatically more likely to vote Corbyn
than men'.[49] What Moore meant was that she hadn't listened to the women who supported Corbyn, an important
distinction.

This campaign spread to the *Independent*, which published a surreal piece headlined, 'If it's truly progressive,
Labour will have voted in a female leader – regardless of
her policies'.[50] It was also mirrored in the *Telegraph*, which
gleefully wondered if Corbyn had a 'women problem'.[51]
Cathy Newman, a *Channel 4 News* reporter who had
recently made headlines by falsely reporting an example
of sexist exclusion at a mosque, authored a piece for the
Telegraph which sneered: 'Welcome to Jeremy Corbyn's
blokey Britain – where "brocialism" rules'.[52] Newman's
complaint did not concern policy, on which Corbyn was
difficult to attack, but representation. She alleged that none
of the 'top jobs' went to women. Corbyn's shadow cabinet,
it must be said, was notable for being the first to have
more than 50 per cent of its posts occupied by women[53] –
as opposed to the pathetic 22 per cent representation that

women have in wider public life. The shadow ministries of Defence, Business, Health, and Education were all run by women. The shadow cabinet was, in other words, more gender-egalitarian on this front than any previous Labour shadow cabinet. It is perfectly fair comment to lament that important posts such as shadow chancellor have never been held by a woman, but the force of the point is blunted if it is simply used in an opportunistic way to belabour Corbyn. Likewise, the *New Statesman*'s effort to pour cold water on Corbyn's victory, with the headline 'Labour chooses white man as leader', would have been far more convincing if the publication had not generously supported every previous white man elected as Labour leader.[54]

Another major theme of the ongoing campaign was Corbyn's supposed unelectability. A typical example of this was the *Independent*'s misleading story, originally accompanied by a false headline that read: 'Jeremy Corbyn "loses a fifth of Labour voters"'.[55] The substance of the story, carefully obscured within prevaricating formulations, showed something completely different. Sixty-three per cent of Labour voters said they were more likely to vote Labour in the next election with Corbyn as leader, as opposed to 20 per cent who said they were more likely to vote Conservative. Over a third of SNP voters, approximately a third of Liberal Democrats, about one-fifth of UKIP voters and 8 per cent of Tories were more likely to vote Labour with Corbyn as Labour leader. And four-fifths of Tory voters were more determined to vote for their own party, just under a fifth of SNP voters would be more likely to vote Tory, while a third of Liberals and 40 per cent of UKIPers would be more likely to vote Conservative. Corbyn had not lost voters: he had polarised them in a new way.

The class valence of Corbyn's supposed unelectability varied, depending on whom one was listening to. According to an opinion piece in the *Telegraph*, Corbyn's 'sub-Marxist drivel' showed that he had 'no understanding of the British people',[56] whose great middle class had no need of the types of Leftist reforms he proposed. A similarly splenetic piece in the *Guardian* held that Corbyn's Labour was so 'poncified' that working-class voters had turned off in droves.[57] These claims reached a comical zenith during an otherwise unremarkable by-election. The *Times* had insisted that Labour was 'counting the cost' of Corbyn's peacenik antics in Oldham, where a UKIP challenge was ready to reduce Labour's majority to a margin of error.[58] John Harris, in a video report from Oldham for the *Guardian*, held that 'Corbynmania' was about to collide with 'reality'.[59] Corbyn's leadership was 'looking increasingly fragile', Harris averred, and cited an encounter with an anti-Corbyn Labour voter to suggest that perhaps the only remaining Labour voters would be the hardened tribalists who put the party first. There being no polling in this by-election, journalists relied on a combination of anecdotes, vox pops and their own prejudices. In the end, Labour held the seat not only with a sizeable majority of over ten thousand, but increased its share of the vote with a 7.5 per cent swing in its favour. The anticlimax was palpable, and the *Telegraph* wondered whether 'Muslims worried about war' might not be to blame for the victory.[60]

Other hit pieces strained for effect. For example, a story in the *Telegraph* – a paper that, more than any other, has been out for Corbyn's blood – referred to claims that Corbyn had a consensual relationship with Diane Abbot in the late 1970s as 'damaging'.[61] Janet Daley of the *Telegraph* recounted a horror story from Haringey in the seventies in which Jeremy Corbyn, as a local councillor, may or may not have been indifferent to the squatters residing in a house next to hers.[62] Anne Perkins of the *Guardian*, with a tone so stiff as to be almost beyond satire, complained that Corbyn had not sang the national anthem at a commemoration service: 'it is his job to sing it'.[63] The *Sun* published a false story alleging that Jeremy Corbyn was a 'hypocrite' since, as a republican, he was willing to bend his knee and kiss the Queen's hand in order to secure state funds for Labour.[64] This was complemented by another *Sun* 'scoop', claiming, again falsely, that Corbyn 'refused to bow' to the Queen, in an apparently trivial defiance of protocol.[65] Such contradictory characterisations suggested something of an internal conflict in the smear department: was Corbyn an inflexibly, excessively principled left-winger, or a conniving opportunist? This dreary sequence of contrived stories reached peak absurdity with the media's extraordinary attention to Corbyn's precise comportment in the laying of a wreath at the Cenotaph, with piece after piece suggesting that his solemn nod of the head was not quite solemn enough.[66]

As the government prepared for war in Syria, and Corbyn tried to rally his MPs to oppose it, pro-war Labour MPs continued to generate tittle-tattle for the press. For example, as the parliamentary vote neared, these seasoned warriors – closets groaning with skeletons, minds keenly attuned to the location of buried bodies – suddenly discovered an extraordinarily delicate temper when faced with criticism, online or offline. News reports listed examples of 'bullying' and 'intimidation' of pro-war MPs, such as protesters gathering outside the constituency office of Peter Kyle MP; an email sent to Labour MPs by someone claiming to be a Labour Party member to the effect that, if they voted for war, they would face votes of no confidence in their constituencies; a Labour councillor suggesting that MPs who voted for war should face re-selection ballots; a tweet sent to Stella Creasy pointing out that 'in the digital age there is a lot more accountability to voters'; Labour MPs being called mean things such as 'warmonger', and 'red Tory'; and finally, in December 2015, a news story emerged, based on social media rumours, that anti-war protesters had marched past Stella Creasy MP's home. As it transpired, the story was wholly untrue, but it provoked a series of denunciations of 'bullying', and calls from Deputy Leader Tom Watson to expel any Labour members who were found to have participated.[67] A perverse logic thus unfolded, in which Labour MPs, claiming to be victimised, bullied and threatened with excommunication, demanded that activists with whose politics they disagreed be victimised, bullied and purged. Without evidence to support their case, MPs launched a campaign to force Corbyn to disband the nascent Labour left group Momentum. They were not able to inculpate the group in any bullying, but feebly suggested that some of its members probably were involved – and thus the leader of the Labour Party should act with monarchical haste to crush the insurgents.[68]

These frivolities were interwoven with another, ongoing line of attack. The Tories had responded to Corbyn's victory with a series of messages and social media memes designed to identify Corbyn as a threat to 'national security' – or, less euphemistically, as an anti-British weirdo who doesn't know how to bow properly at the Cenotaph, won't sing the national anthem, will not (or, nefariously, will) kiss the Queen's hand, and has a romantic affiliation to the nation's enemies. Characteristic of this obnoxious campaign was a *Telegraph* piece by Tory MP and former soldier Tom Tugenhat, who expostulated that Corbyn was a terrorist ally who 'wants to see Britain defeated'.[69] But far more alarming were the interventions by the military leadership in this debate. The first came via the *Sunday Times*, which published without comment or criticism the statements of an unnamed senior army general who claimed that a Corbyn government, if it abandoned Trident and cut military spending, could be subject to an armed forces mutiny.[70] The fact that this was not widely regarded in media or Westminster circles as an outrageous attack on democracy, suggested that at least some of the British media was prepared to take a positively Venezuelan turn, allowing itself to become a mouthpiece for the most belligerent elements of the anti-Corbyn chorus. Later, as the campaign over Trident heated up, the chief of staff of the British armed forces used an appearance on the BBC to state that he would be worried if Corbyn's views were 'translated into power'. This was an explicit and probably planned breach of neutrality, but more notably it was then defended by Corbyn's own shadow defence secretary, whose differences with Corbyn on Trident had been made clear. No discipline was applied to the chief of staff.[71]

Here, then, were all the classic ingredients of a 'Project Fear' campaign: a toxic combination of falsehoods, insinuation, trivialisation, scaremongering, and pointed political interventions by the supposedly neutral apparatuses of the state. By and large, it did not work. This is not to say that it went without benefit for those undertaking it. Corbyn would have to struggle under any circumstances to define a radical agenda that would work in modern Britain, win the media battles to gain a voice for his objectives and assemble a viable electoral coalition behind it. In the context of 'Project Fear', he and his allies have had to navigate an almost daily sequence of contrived outrages, neutralise hundreds of petty but toxic talking points, and continually negotiate a truce with his own back benchers. Yet Corbyn won by a mile and remains in the leadership with the overwhelming support of the party membership. Despite dire predictions, there has not been a crash in the Labour vote, although it has not markedly improved either. The fact that Corbyn's opponents have been unsuccessful thus far suggests that there's something they're missing.

The Rage of the Labour Right

Adam Phillips suggests that our rages disclose what it is we think we are entitled to. We become infuriated when the world doesn't live up to our largely unconscious assumptions about how it should be for us. What might the fury of Labour's right-wingers, as well as their media allies, tell us about their entitlement? Their denial about the depths of Corbyn's support within Labour, their seeming belief that they have a right to be safeguarded against the critical and sometimes harsh words of activists, not to mention against the mere suggestion that they may at some point be answerable to members for their actions, all suggests an almost proprietorial attitude to the party.

They, of course, prefer to see their efforts as an attempt to spare the party electoral oblivion. Labour had lost the 2015 election, as a prominent former advisor to Tony Blair claimed, because it was led by an incompetent left-winger.[72] There was always something about this that smacked of wishful thinking: as if the problems facing the Labour Party were reducible to an easily rectifiable political deviation. In fact, as the right-wing commentator Tim Stanley acknowledged,

> we live in a post-Cold War world where both Left and Right have already triangulated towards a narrow middle. The Left has swerved far, far to the Right. Labour has dumped nationalisation, industrial democracy, pacifism and socialist internationalism. Given this fact, I fail to buy the argument that only by moving dramatically Rightward can the party become competitive.[73]

Nonetheless, the logic is clear. If Labour had swung too far to the left, how could electing the most left-wing leader in the party's history possibly be the solution? In fact, it is evident that for many of Corbyn's opponents in the Labour

Party, even if he *was* the solution, they would rather not resuscitate the party in that way. As Tony Blair put it with refreshing candour, 'I wouldn't want to win on an old-fashioned leftist platform. Even if I thought it was the route to victory, I wouldn't take it.'[74]

Blair's case is exactly as it has always been. In the name of modernity and its outward manifestations – globalisation, technological innovation, 'change' – Labour must abandon the shibboleths of 'the past', and learn to govern a twenty-first-century society. It must accept markets and harness them, rather than attempting to control them. A party which tries to govern on any other basis is destined for the charnel house. Given this, it is not just a matter of thinking that Corbyn can't win for Labour, but also of hoping that he never does.

And indeed, as one of Blair's ideological comrades, Dan Hodges, wrote in the Tory-supporting *Telegraph*, Labour 'moderates' were confessing that they wanted the party to lose under Corbyn:

> 'It's crazy,' one Labour MP confides to me. 'The decent people of my constituency and I have to act out this charade. We keep talking to each other about fighting hard for [Labour mayoral candidate Sadiq Khan], and secretly we're all thinking, "But I hope he loses."'[75]

This chronicles the evolution of the positions of Labour's right-wing zealots. First, the Left can't win. Second, it shouldn't win. And third, it would be better to crash Labour than to let it win under a left-wing leadership. It is one small step from this reasoning to outright defection. Here, the

Blairites are a little more cautious. While some are more or less open in calling for a split,[76] there appears to be a general recognition for now that this can't work. Polly Toynbee, a veteran SDP splitter, warns that it would fail: 'Unlike Foot, Corbyn has compromised on Europe and Nato, so there is no single break point.'[77] John Rentoul, Blair's biographer and a vitriolic opponent of the Left, argues,

> The conditions for a new centre-left party are less favourable than they were when the Social Democratic Party was launched in 1981 – then, the Conservatives had moved to the right while the London liberal middle class and the media were all for a new party.[78]

The fact that the historical spectre of the SDP is even raised in this context is indicative of the scale of alarm on the Labour Right. One does not, in the context of the Labour Party, so nakedly dispense with the 'broad church' rhetoric and openly dally with the idea of desertion, unless one is scared out of one's wits. The party's right-wing has usually found the 'broad church' trope a convenient one, dignifying its grip on power and its marginalisation of the Left. And it has long benefited immensely from the matchless tribalism of party culture.

After all, 'everyone knows' – and not wholly without reason – that the SDP split confirmed Thatcher in power for the rest of the 1980s. Breaking up the traditional Labourist electoral coalition into two jagged fractions – middle-class liberals on one side, and the working-class Left on the other – they handed the Tories an indestructible parliamentary majority with which to annihilate one quarter of Leftist potency after another. This is engrained into Labour's folk memory.

The Blairites have to be panicking to talk like this – and panic they might. They can handle their party losing electoral appeal. Labour shed some 5 million votes, largely from the working-class heartlands, between 1997 and 2010. They can handle being unpopular on major policy issues. Blair was happy to campaign in 2001 on the flagship policy of Private Finance Initiatives, though they were opposed by some 80 per cent of the public, and later staked his leadership on the invasion of Iraq. They can even stand to be out of power in their own party for some time. Ed Miliband's leadership was not the one the Blairites had sought, yet they did not panic.

What they are now panicking about is that, whereas Miliband at least shared the Blairites' axioms for judging success or failure, Corbyn does not. As the BBC's Mark Mardell put it,

> Journalists and politicians based at Westminster ... measure daily success and failure through a set of unwritten rules reached by instinct rather than reflection ... It is often about a tug of war between positive and negative headlines, trials of strength over internal and external opponents, with all the fragility of narrative within a bubble. One of the reasons Mr Corbyn attracts so much opprobrium from those whose orbit circles planet Westminster is he will not accept their measure of his worth.[79]

Meanwhile, their fetishes are being turned against them. New Labour once idolised modernity, its slick, Britpop-friendly electoral mercenaries extolling the virtues of novelty and change, however vapidly, at every opportunity. Now they appear every bit as dated as Britpop; or as the Oasis front-man Noel Gallagher, whose valiant defence of Blairism raised a universal shrug.[80] The 'modernisation' demanded by Labour's millennials and its post-credit crunch support-ers has little to do with focus groups and courting Rupert Murdoch.

One can hardly blame Labour's 'moderates' for feeling aggrieved. By their own standards, they achieved an out-standing success. The litany, usually delivered in staccato sentences, is by now well-worn. A national minimum wage. Investment in public services. A raft of new mecha-nisms to deliver 'social inclusion'. Ambitious measures to combat rough-sleeping and child poverty. A more toler-ant society, with gay rights widely accepted. Again and again, New Labour intellectuals insist, Blair and Brown shaped an agenda that their opponents were forced to accept. They built a ruthless, powerful electoral machine that secured 'hegemony' and changed Britain for the better. The Tories were excluded from office for three terms until they finally abandoned an unavailing neo-Thatcherite path, and chose a liberal leadership. Though the New Labour intelligentsia would never put it like this, Cameron was as much Blair's legacy as Blair was Thatcher's achievement.

Meanwhile, they assert, the current Labour leadership will overreach and achieve nothing. However legitimate the indictment of austerity politics and inequality, they insist, Corbyn simply can't win power. Blair's strategist,

Peter Hyman, argues that a left-wing party of the sort that Corbyn would like to lead

> could gain the support of 15 per cent to 20 per cent of the public and possibly, with the infrastructure, money and backing of the big trade unions, up to 25 per cent to 28 per cent of the vote. Let's not forget Michael Foot's Labour Party got 27.6 per cent of the vote in 1983. But this is a party that will never be in power.[81]

At most, the Blairites claim, a Labour Party led from the left can expect to win some arguments, but it can't win elections; it will never dominate the conversation, or lead, because its social basis is too narrow. Is there anything to this argument? There could be, if the Corbyn leadership only sought to represent its own core support. Jeremy Gilbert of Compass points out,

> Corbyn rallied the metropolitan left vote: not just in London, but in the other big cities. This represents consistently about 25 per cent of the electorate, and they now demand representation. The assumption that the hard-Left represents only a negligible minority is wrong; they didn't disappear. A quarter of the public, if you look at the British Social Attitudes Surveys, are socialists, whereas about 8 to 15 per cent are fascists. It's interesting to think about why that is invisible and what it implies about the hegemony of liberalism in the media.[82]

Corbyn, then, has a base, but just not enough to win an election by itself. The 'moderate' case, then, is that Labour has to choose between being a left-wing organisation, and being an electorally successful organisation. And, as Peter Mandelson reminded the Blairite faithful in a 'leaked' memo written after Corbyn's success, 'electability remains the party's founding purpose from when the trade unions first created the Labour Representation Committee. If we cannot represent people in parliament and government what is the point of the party?'[83] There is something to all of this. Labour is an electoralist organisation first and foremost, and always has been. And winning elections does mean building coalitions, since the core vote is never enough. The problem for the 'moderates' is this: they aren't actually anywhere near as good at winning elections as they like to think.

Even in their reputed 'golden age', beginning in the bright summer of 1997, New Labour was the beneficiary of timing and fortune far more than of the strategic genius of Mandelson and company. The Tories had already decisively lost the support of a stratum of 'secular' voters who tend to vote with their wallets. Any general election held after the 1992 ERM crisis would have been Labour's to lose.[84] (Admittedly, that is no surety that they would not have lost it; Mandelson's savvy did not prevent the loss of the 1992 election.) New Labour's first term in office, between 1997 and 2001, saw their electoral coalition shrink by 3 million voters, largely from the poorest parts of the country. Were it not for the ongoing crisis wracking the Conservative Party, and the oddities of Britain's electoral system – two factors over which electoral gurus and spinners had little control – such a haemorrhaging of support could have been fatal, leaving Blair another one-term Labour Prime Minister.

Blair's third general election victory in 2005 was obtained with just over a third of the popular vote, and a total number of votes (9.5 million) similar to that achieved by Ed Miliband (9.35 million) in the disastrous 2015 election, in which Labour finally lost the entirety of Scotland. What was the big difference between a record third election victory and a crushing defeat? The revival of the Conservative vote. The Tories had undergone a detox operation, with a youthful, glabrous-cheeked leader doing his best Blair imitation. The deranged Right had largely decamped to UKIP. A period in coalition government with the Liberals had persuaded middle-ground voters that the Tories were no longer dominated by rancorous flag-wavers and pound-savers. (One might add, since it has become a psephological commonplace, that the credit crunch was 'Labour's ERM crisis', but this is only partially true: Labour decisively lost this argument in retrospect, and it was by no means inevitable that they should have done so.)

What about today? Whatever they think of Corbyn's electoral chances, the Blairites own electoral prospects are not necessarily better. Polls taken of the prospective Labour candidates before the leadership election found that, of all the candidates, Corbyn was the favourite.[85] The 'moderates', lacking an appealing message, were also about as charismatic as lavatory soap dispensers. Labour's poll ratings under Corbyn are poor, but hardly worse than before despite the ongoing media feeding frenzy. There is no reason to believe that any of his lacklustre rivals would be doing any better than Corbyn presently is.

Why might this be, and why have the pundits been so

easily impressed by the claims of Labour's right-wing? Thinking through the electoral arithmetic on the Blairites' own terms, it was never obvious that the electoral bloc comprising people who think the same way as they do is even close to 25 per cent. The reason this hasn't been a problem in the past is that elections in Britain's first-past-the-post system are usually decided by a few hundred thousand 'median' voters based in marginal constituencies. As long as Labour could take the votes of the Left for granted, they could focus on serenading the 'aspirational' voters of Nuneaton. Even the erosion of 'heartland' votes didn't register, so long as this erosion was happening to mountainous, seemingly unassailable majorities.

What happens, however, when left-leaning electors defect in sufficient numbers and sufficient geographic concentration to pose serious questions about Labour's medium-term survival? What happens when it is no longer just the odd Labour seat going to George Galloway or Caroline Lucas in sudden unpredictable surges, but the whole of Scotland being lost in a single bloodbath? What happens when votes for left-of-centre rivals surge (the SNP vote trebling, the Green vote quadrupling), millions of potential voters still stay at home, and all of this takes place while the Conservatives reconstitute themselves as a viable centre-Right governing party? This is one of the reasons why Corbynism has emerged in the first place: in that circumstance, Blairite triangulation turns out to be as useful as a paper umbrella, only any good until it starts raining.

This Is Not 1981

In the last analysis, Corbyn's victory was decisively enabled not by organisational changes or by 'infiltration'. Nor was it a result of the dynamism of the Left. In a way, the Left punched well above its real weight to secure this victory. Corbyn won because the Labour Party was weak, and the traditionally dominant party ideologies, and the normally effective modes of political control, had broken down. At the core of this was the degeneration of the union link, which had been hacked away at over years, with the result that the traditionally cautious union bureaucracies seized on a drastic opportunity to reverse their losses. The intellectual and ideological enervation both of the New Labour project and of those who had governed as New Labour ministers meant that Corbyn was able to answer the existential questions posed about Labour's future far more convincingly than any of his rivals.

It is the denial of this state of affairs that lies behind the fantasy of Labour's Right that the party's problems will only be solved by re-enacting the battles of the 1980s. Faced with the Corbyn ascendancy, some seasoned Labour Rightists have reacted with familiar relish. Roy Hattersley, who had spent years ineffectually bemoaning the Blairites, suddenly seems to have recovered his élan. Recounting his travails in right-wing Labour politics in the early eighties, he exhorts Labour 'moderates' to take the battle to Corbyn in the spirit of Denis Healey. The battle must be fought 'all over again', he declaims. 'The sooner the fightback begins the better.'[86] But anyone looking for Cold War reheats in this manner is wasting their time.

There are a number of reasons that Hattersley, Healey and other hammers of the Left were able to defeat the Left in the early-to-mid-eighties which simply don't obtain today. One is that the wider climate of opinion was moving sharply to the right at the time, while the Left – whether of Militant or Bennite variety – was far weaker than its national profile allowed it to believe. There is no such pronounced and generalised shift to the right today, and all the movement in the Labour grass roots is to the left. Another is that the soft Left was inordinately belligerent toward the hard Left, and was happy to work with activists and politicians from the right in order to take control of the Labour Party. This profound realignment of forces, culminating in the victory of New Labour, was seen as a necessary modernising project, junking the unyielding dogmas of the past. Today, the soft Left, having experienced the traumatic years of Blairism, is more likely to achieve some of its objectives with a left-wing leadership, and currently appears to be happy to live with such a leadership. And today's modernisers are in the Corbyn camp: 'socialism with an iPad', as John McDonnell put it.[87]

And for those not wearing the Cold War blinders, it is patently obvious that 'left-wing' means something far more cautious than it used to. Corbyn has sought to steer a careful course, compromising with the right-wing over NATO membership and the European Union. He has called for Labour councils to set legal budgets with deep spending cuts rather than defying the government. His shadow chancellor John McDonnell has dropped early plans for the nationalisation of energy firms, despite how popular such measures would be. There is also the difference made by the breakdown of the traditional media's ideological monopoly. Whereas the popular press in the early eighties was overwhelmingly right-wing, if not downright Thatcherite, the tabloids exert no such dominance today. However culpable and complicitous national media outlets may be, social media has broken their grip on the national conversation. And there is the very different role of trade unions in today's Labour politics. Whereas once, powerful right-wing union leaders could be relied on to battle their left-wing counterparts and give ballast to the red-hunters, there is little sign of even relatively right-wing union leaders signing up for sabotage.[88] Moreover, this time around there is no SDP to act as a right-wing pressure on the party, and there is little space for such a vehicle. Those looking for centrist politics with no trade union strings attached already have it in the Cameron–Osborne leadership. Finally, in the absence of the USSR, there is simply no groundswell of anti-socialist feeling which could be harnessed to a red-hunting crusade. Unilateral nuclear disarmament was once a policy nostrum associated with 'fellow travellers'. Today, the majority of the public, and much of the military establishment, favour scrapping it.[89]

None of this is to say that Corbyn's position is assured until the next election. The next chapter will deal with the considerable obstacles he faces. One might say that, even if he were to survive until the 2020 general election, and even if he were to win it, that is where his real problems would begin. However, those attempting to fight yesterday's battles in the hope of yielding yesterday's results call to mind Anna Freud's famous saying that 'in our dreams, we can have our eggs cooked exactly how we want them, but we can't eat them'.

2
The Crisis of British Politics

Labour's Mess

In the BBC series, *The Thick of It*, hapless opposition leader Nicola Murray tries to win credit from a sceptical electorate by agreeing with a government policy. To appear tough, she decides to agree with a particularly mean-spirited austerity policy, cancelling funding for 'breakfast clubs' for primary school children. 'We are in concurrence with the government,' she intones, 'because we are in unity with the British people.' Just as she announces her support, however, the government backtracks. Her spin doctor, Malcolm Tucker, is furious: 'Nicola is about to adopt a policy that is so toxic that this stony-hearted government of fucking puppy killers is dropping it?'

Nothing else in popular culture captured so accurately the air of sheer pointless and self-defeating cravenness that has hung around Labour in recent years. Shadow Chancellor Ed Balls declaring, before a general election, that he would reverse none of the spending cuts that the government has introduced. Acting leader Harriet Harman, faced with a draconian welfare bill, whipping Labour MPs into the bold stance of abstaining. Unable to form a government, they couldn't form an opposition either. Labour had rarely looked this pitiful. And it is this Labour, ideologically vacuous, politically timid, unimaginative, that Jeremy Corbyn set out to change. In the event, this very weakness is what enabled Corbyn to win.

Corbyn's victory is evidence, then, not of the power of the Left but of the enervation of the Labour Party and of the traditional political centre. It would be a mistake for Corbyn's supporters to be too impressed by their own sudden feeling of vitality. It is equally a mistake for analysts to take too seriously the reports, red-faced and spittle-lathered, on the strength of Corbynism in the Labour Party. The new left-wing Labour group, Momentum, has attracted considerable support within the party, and recently won the Labour youth elections. Yet, that was on a turnout of 3.5 per cent.[1] The group, though talked up in the press the better to monster it, has as yet little clout in the real centres of power in the Labour Party. Constituency members are overwhelmingly supportive of Corbyn, but it would be too hasty to presume that they are all single-mindedly socialist.

On the same day that Corbyn won the Labour leadership, the old stalwart of the Labour Right Tom Watson won the deputy leadership. Diane Abbott was later defeated in the selection race for Labour's London mayoral candidate by the uninspiring Sadiq Khan, while the elections to the Conference Arrangements Committee that year were lost by the Left.[2] There are reasons why these candidates won apart from their politics. Watson is regarded as a decent politician who took on Murdoch and the child abuse scandals. Sadiq Khan is seen as having a certain personal charisma that Abbott lacks. But that is partly the point. Corbyn's supporters incline to the radical left, but they are by no means as experienced and programmatic in this as, say, the veterans of Eighties Leftism.

How, then, could a current so marginal within the Labour Party, so painfully at a loss for so many years, suddenly find itself swept to the leadership by a fusion of young, radicalised members and supporters with the existing networks of the hard Left? Some of the answers to this question are contingent, and have to do with organisational changes to the Labour Party and tactical mis-steps on the part of its managing elites. Some have to do with the austerity politics which, until Corbyn's election, enjoyed bipartisan support in the House of Commons. However, the most important factor is also the most intractable – a secular crisis of the labour movement and its grass roots. As Ed Miliband put it in an important piece for the Fabian Society shortly after winning the leadership election: 'Five million votes were lost by Labour between 1997 and 2010, but four out of the five million didn't go to the Conservatives,' he wrote. 'One-third went to the Liberal Democrats, and most of the rest simply stopped voting. It wasn't, in the main, the most affluent, professional voters that deserted Labour either,' he continued. 'You really don't need to be a Bennite to believe that this represents a crisis of working-class representation for Labour – and our electability.'[3]

In this analysis, Miliband was undoubtedly influenced by the arguments of his close advisor Jon Trickett from Labour's soft Left.[4] However, Miliband was not able to reverse the losses. Labour's vote had crashed to its lowest level since 1918 in the 2010 election, and barely shifted in 2015. Labour's internal focus-group reports suggest that it may never win these voters back, as they have shifted to the right and are 'a hair's breadth from becoming Conservatives'.[5] It is an open question how representative such focus groups can be, and neither the British Election Study nor the Beckett Report into the party's defeat found much evidence for the idea that Labour wasn't right-wing enough for the voters.[6] However, where most analyses converge, it was on the idea that Labour lost first and foremost on the economy. The 'credit crunch' had destroyed its reputation in much the same way as 'Black Wednesday' had destroyed the reputation of the Conservatives. As it approached the election, Labour seemed able neither to defend its record nor to admit fault.

The decline was also felt in terms of party membership, which had fallen from over 400,000 in 1997 to 156,000 by the end of 2009. The fall was partially reversed in the first months of Miliband's leadership, rising to 194,000 by December 2010, but only during the Corbyn surge did it increase to anything like previous levels.[7] The official labour movement has been in a similar freefall, though over a much longer period, with trade union density falling from over 50 per cent in 1979 to just over a quarter in 2012. The fall has been pronounced in the public sector in recent years as austerity measures and recession have eroded employment, but the worst coverage continues to be in the private sector, where over 85 per cent of workplaces have never seen a union rep – and it is part of a global decline, registered first in the United States but apparent in all the core industrial economies.[8] In a weakened condition, unions had put up little resistance to austerity measures, barring a brief flurry of strike action against pension reforms in 2011, after which the rate of strike action fell to the lowest levels on record.[9] The labour movement, having become more top-down, more politically timid and more constrained by hostile legislation, has been poorly placed to put up much of a fight – in a way, supporting Corbyn's candidacy, as the big unions did, was by far the most radical thing they have yet done to address their existential decline.

As its institutions have become more top-heavy, and its social base weakened, the Labour Party has become more right-wing, more managerial and more dominated by middle-class professionals, hostile to the traditional aims of the Left. And just as it adjusted to the post-Thatcher consensus, so in recent years it embraced the austerian agenda of its opponents, offering only to temper its excesses – which, as Miliband discovered, was not enough to attract progressive voters to the polling booths. Instead, Labour ran the risk of what party activist James Doran called 'Pasokification', following in the doomed footsteps of its centre-Left sister party in Greece as it administered austerity policies.[10]

Ironically, this very weakness, which left the Labour Party open to Corbyn's surge, is now one of the most significant impediments to his success. And Corbyn's success as yet has shown no tendency to reverse Labour's difficulties: it may even compound them in the short-term. It is true that throughout his campaign, hundreds of thousands of people signed up as members or registered supporters of the Labour Party. In the days following his success, further tens of thousands joined Labour. The evidence now is that these are sustained increases, and that the majority of the new members remain supportive of Corbyn's attempt to rebuild Labour from the Left. Yet the fragility of this project is visible in the abysmal poll ratings for Labour, which are not even remotely strong enough among constituencies that it needs to be winning over, particularly young people and ethnic minorities.[11] Meanwhile, the constant barrage of attacks on the Labour leader from a coterie of his own MPs, echoed and amplified by a rabid media, ensures that whatever Corbyn attempts to achieve is repeatedly undermined by a series of confected crises.

Democratic Decline

Labour is in trouble, then, but its problems are inseparable from a wider democratic deadlock. In 2000, just as the British electoral system was about to experience its lowest participation rate in history, the political scientist Colin Crouch coined the term 'post-democracy'.[12] From the standpoint of post–Cold War triumphalism, such an emphasis must perforce seem misplaced and unnecessarily gloomy. At what time in history has democracy ever been more globally institutionalised? In this strict and narrow constitutional sense, within the framework of what could be called capitalist democracy, the total number of people who could participate in elections to change their governments was probably greater at the turn of the millennium than it had ever been. So what was there to be gloomy about? The end of history had turned out alright, had it not?

Clearly, there is a great deal more to democracy than the formal existence of party-political competition and representative structures. Mass democracy has always depended upon popular engagement, and that engagement is undergoing a long decline. Parties and representative chambers are only as democratically robust as the power that is invested in them. If the locus of power shifts elsewhere, democratic capacity is lost. Further, for democratic institutions to be viable, they require a healthy degree of participation. Precisely what level of participation counts as healthy is a value judgement, but where there is a significant decline in voting turnout and party membership, there is a prima facie reason to begin asking questions. And this is exactly what we find. As Peter Mair puts it,

> Party democracy, which would normally offer a point of connection and site of engagement for citizens and their political leaders, is being enfeebled, with the result that elections and the electoral process become little more than 'dignified' parts of the modern democratic constitution. That is, elections have less and less practical effect, because the working, or 'efficient' part of the constitution is steadily being relocated elsewhere.[13]

In the period between 1950 and 1990, there was a steady state of trendless fluctuation in election turnouts across the industrial democracies. After 1990, the average turnout began to fall significantly, from 81.7 per cent in the previous period, to 77.6 per cent in the 1990s, and 75.8 per cent in the 2000s. The trend was most advanced in the UK, where the turnout in the 2001 general election was 'the lowest level of turnout since the advent of mass democracy'. Most of the record lows in turnout for other nations were recorded in these two decades.[14]

In the British general election of 2010, average turnout was 65.1 per cent, but the turnout varied across constituencies according to the social classes concentrated in those areas, with a range between 44 per cent and 77 per cent. Generally speaking, the more working-class a constituency, the higher its rate of unemployment, the lower its turnout.[15] Unsurprisingly given these trends, Labour has been the biggest loser from declining turnout. Party membership has also slumped across European democracies. In the 1960s, party membership as a proportion of the total population averaged 14 per cent. In the 1990s, the proportion averaged 5 per cent.[16]

But there is another feature of modern democracies that is relevant here, and that is the heightened electoral volatility of those who do still vote. If, as Mair argues, elections no longer count as much as they did, then the likelihood of strong party identifications declines, and choices become more likely to be based on factors other than tribal filiation. And, indeed, this is what one finds. Across European democracies, without exception, there has been a marked decline in strong party identification between the 1960s and the 1990s.[17]

What explains these trends? One way to approach this is to ask why it is that people are decreasingly inclined to participate in the system. Traditionally, abstention is viewed as a matter of 'apathy'. People decline to vote or join political parties, not from dissatisfaction, but from a sense of sufficient security and contentment in their consumer lifestyle that they have no motivation to vote. This was, in fact, the response of New Labour to a series of low electoral turnouts in 1998 – people stayed at home from contentment rather than disaffection. How well did this perspective explain the record low turnout in 2001? In part, the patterns of voting decline could be explained by the peculiarities of the electoral system. As Pippa Norris pointed out,

> Voting tumbled most sharply in safe Labour seats – places like Liverpool Wavertree, Stockport, Bootle – while falling far less in marginal Conservative seats such as Norfolk North and Hexham, where parties had greater motivation to mobilize support and voters had more incentive to feel that casting a ballot could make a difference to the outcome.[18]

But the broader picture was one of demoralisation and at most 'lukewarm support' for the government. One study found that for the first time the majority, some 62 per cent, of non-voters were deliberate abstainers – their non-vote counted as a rejection of the choice on offer. The same patterns are found repeatedly in subsequent elections with, one study suggests, all of non-voting in the 2005 general election accounted for by deliberate abstention.[19] The turnout never recovered to previous levels, and was never higher than 65 per cent. In both 2001 and 2005, non-voters constituted a larger share of the electorate than the vote for the winning party. A local study of non-voters by the University of York found that 80 per cent of those who didn't vote in 2005 cited a lack of difference between the major parties. As one respondent put it: 'Parties are all brands nowadays. Brands of the same product.'[20] In 2015, BBC News interviewed likely non-voters and found a pervasive sense of broken trust and cynicism: 'they're all the same', and 'it won't make any difference', just two of the more typical responses.[21]

The biggest non-voters are typically those who are most likely to vote Labour: younger voters, poorer voters, and those from ethnic minorities. In the 2010 general election, only half of men aged 18–24 voted, while 39 per cent of women from the same age range voted. Younger black and Asian voters in particular began to peel away from Labour in the 2005 general election, an election overshadowed by the war in Iraq. And it is likely that while many of those who did vote abandoned Labour for other parties such as the Liberal Democrats or, in a few localities, Respect, perhaps less than half of those voters actually turned out. By 2015, only 33 per cent of black and Asian voters considered themselves certain to vote, compared to 52 per cent of white voters.[22]

The evidence is overwhelming. There is a political withdrawal across the board, it is most pronounced among those who were already least enfranchised, and the biggest resultant losses in the UK have been sustained by the Labour Party. What accounts for this? If non-voters see themselves as being in protest against a system that seems unintelligible, distant and impervious to their concerns, what is the real basis for their alienation? To ask this is to ask something about what electoral participation is for. In the nineteenth century struggles over democracy, the concern of those who sought to prevent it was that it would lead to the erosion of the principle of private property. The reason that elites ultimately opted to extend the franchise to workers, however, was that they came to regard it as the easiest way of managing social disturbances. By committing, through a long and deliberately protracted process, to redistribute a proportion of wealth and power, they might avoid challenges to that power by other means. As Earl Grey, proposing the reforms, suggested: 'I am reforming to preserve, not to overthrow.'[23]

One way of characterising this state of affairs is to say that parliamentary democracy offers the possibility of some form of class compromise which ameliorates the conditions of those without property, while protecting the institution. In modern parlance, this is given a banal gloss in the form of Clinton's slogan on the key to electoral success: 'it's the economy, stupid'. Where there appears to be stable growth and employment, governments are popular, and political volatility is minimised. But this is to treat the economy as merely a technical factor in governing. In this view, the goal of efficient government would be to make investors as happy as possible, and watch the wealth and contentment pile up. But the economy is inherently political. It works, insofar as it does, through a tacit compromise between owners and wage-earners. Despite the hallelujahs and hosannahs for 'wealth creators' that politicians of centre-Right and centre-Left are inclined to engage in, businesses only bother to generate prosperity if the circumstances are acceptably profitable to them.[24] Employees, meanwhile, have to at least implicitly agree to the conditions that are necessary for profit-making. Stable governments are those which are able to secure a compromise between classes on the conditions of future growth.

In post-war Britain, it fell to a Labour government to begin the work of rebuilding a stable profit regime in which the state mediated between politically organised expressions of business and wage-earners. This class truce was accepted by the Conservative Party, which did little to undo it once in office. This was the high point of social democracy and, for approximately a quarter of a century, the peace held. Profits rose, but wages also rose in line with productivity, while a welfare state made up for the failures of the market with a social wage. For the duration of this period, electoral participation and party identifications remained strong, with turnout peaking in 1950 at 83.9 per cent, even if party membership showed a slight tendency to fall.

Following the deep-going crises of the seventies, the balance of the compromise was shifted such that organised labour was weakened, welfare was re-tooled as 'workfare' – a new disciplinary system to keep the unemployed on their toes – and the state took a growing interest in enhancing private sector profitability by reducing wage costs and removing regulations that businesses found obstructive, and opening up the public sector to commodification. These changes were legitimised by neoliberal ideology, and to some extent directed by those educated in it. Neoliberalism, broadly speaking, initially emerged as a break with classical liberal thought. Its pioneers were those like Ludwig von Mises and Friedrich von Hayek who, in the early twentieth century, regarded with horror the effects of mass democracy on the liberal order of private property. Regarding the emerging welfare state as a threat to property-based liberty, they initially looked to authoritarian Rightists to protect property, and then sought to reinvent the liberal state to protect it from democracy. According to their story, the essence of liberty was the ability to make choices with one's resources in a free market. Meanwhile, the essence of economic efficiency was unimpeded, quasi-Darwinian competition between rival producers, in which good ideas and practices would ineluctably out-compete the bad. Get the market out of the way and a pacific 'spontaneous order' would emerge which was far better for human welfare than government programmes. This, of course, was the soft sell. The slightly harder sell was General Pinochet. That is to say, this 'spontaneous order' had to be underwritten by a violently interventionist state, one whose repressive capacities were enlarged even as the democratic and welfare functions atrophied. Moreover, far from empowering 'markets', whatever this might mean, they tended to empower the largest, most economically powerful financial and industrial corporations on whose cooperation national governments depended.[25]

Perhaps one of the most sophisticated means of constraining democracy was the series of recommendations endorsed by the 'public choice' school developed by James Buchanan and William Niskanen.[26] Arguing that state bureaucracies were necessarily inefficient and self-serving, and that any 'public service' ethic was hypocrisy writ large, they favoured the subordination of most public functions to market-like mechanisms. Services should be privatised or, if not actually run by corporations, should emulate corporations where possible. Markets should be introduced between providers, and competitive mechanisms set in place. Services should be removed from direct political control where necessary: aside from full privatisation, the proliferation of quangos in British political life was one of the early alternatives to democratic control. This, of course, was anything but efficient. The companies brought in to run services inflated costs drastically. Internal markets notoriously inflated overhead costs in the NHS to scandalous levels.[27] But what it did achieve was a crony relationship between state actors and privileged businesses, involving the state more deeply in making life easier for business, while reducing its democratic capacities.

This internal reorganisation of the state was soon accompanied by its integration into a network of international institutions – the World Trade Organization, the European Union, and soon the Transatlantic Trade and Investment Partnership – which collectively constrain governments in an 'iron cage' of regulations demanding fiscal austerity, competition and privatisation in public services, and the rolling back of laws deemed uncompetitive. The scope for democratic participation grows narrower by the day. The net result is precisely what Crouch refers to as 'post-democracy':

> While elections still exist ... public electoral debate is a tightly controlled spectacle, managed by rival teams of professionals expert in the techniques of persuasion, and considering a small range of issues selected by those teams. The mass of citizens plays a passive, quiescent, even apathetic part, responding only to the signals given them. Behind this spectacle of the electoral game politics is really shaped in private by interaction between elected governments and elites which overwhelmingly represent business interests.[28]

In this view, it is not apathy that characterises a growing chunk of the electorate so much as their *exclusion* from effective political power. And matters are likely to get worse. One reason for this is that, since the credit crunch, the owners of capital are hoarding money rather than investing it.[29] This phenomenon is by no means restricted to Britain, yet in the UK alone, hundreds of billions of pounds are set aside rather than put to work to create jobs or growth. Profit rates being too low in the private sector, firms instead look to government to improve investment conditions by reducing the cost of labour and by creating new opportunities for them in the public sector: this is a far more important part of what the government calls 'austerity' than its spending cuts.[30] This exacerbates the peculiar and particularly corrupt form of relationship between the state and privileged sectors of business that is emblematic of the neoliberal era. But it also leaves Britain's economy weak, sluggish and ongoingly susceptible to crisis, and forces the state to be on hand, ever ready to lend new support and to extract more from a weary public. As the state becomes less and less democratic, and more geared toward crisis-management, the alienation and volatility of the electorate is likely to increase.

The other aspect of the popular withdrawal from parliamentary democracy that this brought about has been the withdrawal of governing elites 'into the institutions of the state'. As parties have lost their social roots, they have become more oriented toward 'office-seeking' in a way that is increasingly detached from their electoral success.[31] The extreme case of this is the technocratic coalition government wherein parties of whatever hue and social basis find themselves seeking to win a share of governing power in order to lead from the centre. Party leaderships are increasingly inclined to conceive of their power in terms of influence within the existing state apparatuses and non-elected institutions, assets which they can build up even as they lose electoral support.

A particularly crass example of this could be found in the run up to the 2015 general election, in which Nick Clegg (having won influence by securing the support of disaffected Labour voters anxious about the extent of planned austerity measures and increased tuition fees – subsequently to squander this support once in coalition) warned that a government without the Liberal Democrats would lack legitimacy.[32] Of course this proved to be untrue, but it suggested that Clegg's strategy for ongoing influence was not to win as many votes as possible – even then, the looming Liberal Democide was apparent to all – but to situate his party as parliamentary king-makers in exchange for some policy incentives and influence on select committees. But coalition governments of the centre are merely an extreme and unusually express example of what is generally taking place in a more granular, gradual and tacit way, visible in the growing profile of political professionals, special advisors, pollsters and focus groups whose existence increasingly appears to be about representing the government to the electorate, rather than the reverse. This partially explains why, given the choice between breaching an established governing consensus and cleaving to it while losing electoral support, party leaderships tend to choose the latter.

It is not that politicians are completely oblivious to their growing detachment and insulation from the public. Following the 2015 general election, Hansard described a 'deeply disillusioned citizenry that will be hard to motivate' to vote.[33] Later the same year, the House of Commons Liaison Committee began a series of hearings intended to address the decline of parliamentary institutions in British society.[34]

Its first report notes that, already in the late nineteenth and early twentieth centuries, the professionalisation of party machines, the strengthening grip of the executive of the state and the decline of parliament were already grounds for concern regarding the status of democracy in Britain. In its potted history, it also goes on to acknowledge the emergence of a stream of disengaged, 'antipolitical' sentiment rising in the Britain of the sixties, and the efforts made by some parliamentarians to reform an increasingly out-of-touch Westminster. Strange to relate, the closer its historical sketch gets to the present day, the wider the gap appears between the problem and the proposed solutions, which involved improving the functioning and powers of select committees. The political establishment knows that it is losing touch – it just doesn't have the smallest clue what to do about it.

'I read some Marx and I liked it': The Young Radicals Looking for a Political Home

It has been customary for some commentators, particularly those aligned to Labour, to bemoan the non-voting young as either huffy Kevin-the-Teenagers or Lauren Coopers, or as excessively discriminating to the point of self-indulgent. Polly Toynbee hits this particular sweet spot of commentariat arrogance with a regularity that can't be accidental. Speaking of those who refuse to vote in defence of political principle – the majority of non-voters – she scolds,

> Their vote is far too precious to bestow on any of the parties on offer. No one is good enough for them, as if they expect a personal bespoke party, regardless of the necessary compromises in assembling a majority, blind to how parties work as portmanteaus of ideals and interests willing to travel together. Did those over-fastidious ones ever roll up their sleeves in the past five years to start a new party or movement, or shift an existing one?

Yet in the same breath, Toynbee complains about those who have rolled up their sleeves for anything other than the palest pink social democracy, above all those inclined to 'vote Green'. 'A vote', she stiffly rebukes, 'is not a personal accessory to show the world who you are.' Naturally, these very same commentators are those who have been most likely to complain about the mobilisation of the young behind Corbyn for 'ignoring the electorate'.[35]

Another way of looking at it is to suppose that those disproportionately young people who mobilised to support Corbyn have a longer perspective than the next election. That the ways in which they are, in fact, rolling up their sleeves to shift an existing party is a recognition that political change takes place on registers other than the parliamentary. That by trying to change Labour, they have reference to something more than the few hundred thousand voters in swing constituencies who typically decide election outcomes. What is at stake here is a generational change that, though it has been seen in other countries first, is now intersecting with Britain's democratic decline to produce this challenge to the status quo.

From the first ruptures of the anti-capitalist movement to Occupy; from Ecuador, Bolivia and Venezuela to Spain, Portugal and Greece; Leftist success has been propelled in large part by new movements of the young. Even in the United States, hardly a typical case in other respects, Bernie Sanders's support is overwhelmingly concentrated among the under thirties.[36] Much is written, not wholly incorrectly, of how these activists are shaped by 'post-materialist' values – support for peace and gay rights, for example. But far more fundamentally, this generation is the one to suffer the most from the consolidation of neoliberalism, as they are paying more for access to higher education, have far less access to diminished public services and welfare, and suffer far higher rates of unemployment. Their housing situation is, particularly in large urban areas, abysmal, and they are far less likely to have a chance of affordable rent, let alone home ownership. They face a more financially uncertain future and later retirement than previous generations, as more of their old age income will be dependent on financial products. And they have inherited a political system that is less responsive and more insulated from public influence than at any point since the universal franchise was first achieved. But if all that explains their militancy, it does not explain why it should now take the form of a highly improbable mass entry into Labour. What else could these activists be doing if they were not trying to pull Labour to the left?

One of the major casualties of neoliberalism as it has been rolled out across Europe has been the classical social democratic party. Almost uniformly, albeit at different paces and to differing degrees, they found themselves overwhelmed by the transformations in the global economy and the resistance of business to their attempts to keep the old status quo going. As the priorities of national states switched from full employment, as a condition for the old class compromise, to counter-inflation and balanced budgets, as a condition for businesses to keep investing, social democracy abandoned the policy instruments that had made it distinctive. Only in Sweden and Austria was there a brief period in which counter-inflation existed successfully alongside extensive public sector investment and an institutional commitment to full employment, but this did not survive the turn of the nineties. In Britain, New Labour had consecrated neoliberal orthodoxy before its election in 1997, such that nothing else was expected. In France, a 'plural-Left' government led by the Socialist Party was elected just as the European Stability and Growth Pact was passed, committing all signatories to fiscal discipline. Although it was committed to a modest Keynesian programme, such as the thirty-five-hour week, it did not have to be coerced into respecting budgetary orthodoxy, keeping public investment under control and restraining wage demands. And in Germany, the Social Democratic Party was elected in 1998 with the Greens as coalition partners and with some idea of an interventionist state, but was already committed to fiscal orthodoxy and deep welfare cuts inspired by Clinton's move to 'end the welfare state as we know it'.[37]

In short, social democracy has lost its purpose in line with the loss of agency of parliamentary democracy to represent the electorate. In place of social democracy, a strange new hybrid form has emerged, sometimes called 'social-liberalism'. Although still functionally social democratic in the relationship to organised labour and the working-class electoral base, the leadership of such parties is undeniably neoliberal, and the direction of policy is aimed at gradually converting the base to a neoliberal common sense. This has proved costly in electoral terms, as this new breed of social-liberal parties have struggled to adequately distinguish themselves from their centre-Right rivals. One result of this is that since 1989, a series of radical Left parties have emerged across Europe, to challenge the rightward shift of social democracy.[38] Pinning their hopes on a 'vacuum thesis', according to which the evacuation of a traditional social-democratic political space should leave space for a new Left, parties including the Rifondazione Comunista in Italy, the Front de gauche in France, and Die Linke in Germany, were launched to occupy the vacant space. Emphasising a modern combination of left-wing themes, from class politics to 'post-materialist' and left-libertarian concerns, they have fused old elements with the new: the remnants of traditional Communist Parties fused with defecting left-wing components of social democracy, a range of revolutionary fragments and activists schooled in the social movements and public assemblies.

Socially, these parties are far less supported by industrial workers than their equivalent older formations, the communist parties, and far more by the lower end of the salariat. Their support base also tends to be far more concentrated among those under thirty-five years old. These parties have thrived above all when they have remained aloof from coalitions with centre-Left parties and maintained a policy of frontal criticism on markets, privatisation, redistribution and Europe, but their electoral success has been far in excess of their real social depth. These parties, it must be frankly admitted, have struggled to turn their electoral profile into real power. They have only in two cases, Spain and Greece, succeeded in fundamentally altering the dynamics of party competition. And in no case have they changed the neoliberal constitution of state power. Nevertheless, in terms of gaining some form of representation for a left-wing constituency that had been neglected, they have enjoyed some success.

So why did Britain not see an equivalent party form? It was not for want of trying: the ultimately abortive experiments in launching such ventures in the UK range from the Socialist Alliance, to Respect, to Left Unity. Only in the case of Respect were electorally significant results obtained, and even these were short-lived. These organisations proved to be far too narrow, based on ramshackle coalitions of the fragments of the far Left and the odd Labour refugee, to make a sustained bid for a national political presence. They gained minimal union backing and, in contrast to continental rivals, were not nourished by the addition of major splits from social democracy. Essentially, what prevented them from being more than protest parties was the demoralisation and defeat of the Labour Left.

The defeats that were inflicted on the British Left in the 1980s were, cumulatively, far more traumatic and disabling than anything comparable visited on their continental allies. From the miners to municipal socialism, every political and cultural organisation of the Left and the labour movement had defeats handed to them both by the Thatcher government and by a Labour leadership determined to free itself to adapt to the new order. By the time Blair had taken control of Labour, their expectations were set to somewhere below zero. The broad lines of policy which they were compelled to accept were such that, however disappointed people may have been, there was no great galvanising shock when a New Labour government began to implement policies previously associated with its electoral opponents, such as Private Finance Initiatives and market-based public sector reform. Only the prime minister's strange alliance with a right-wing US president in the prosecution of adventurist war produced a potentially life-threatening crisis for the Labour leadership, and even then only a single MP decamped – George Galloway, who was expelled rather than walking out of his own accord, much less leading any kind of split. Rather than split like other social-democratic parties, Labour simply haemhorraged members as well as voters.

Insofar as the young generation of radical activists have had a party orientation, therefore, it has taken the form of a weak identification with an alternative centre-Left party such as the SNP or the Greens. Otherwise, where they have been active it has tended to be in movements like Occupy and Radical Independence in Scotland, or single-issue campaigns such as Climate Camp. Corbyn emerged to articulate their discontents following several years of quiet demoralisation, as the UKIP Right held the initiative while the movements of 2010–11 went eerily quiet. As one Labour organiser put it, many activists had in the interim put down their copies of *The Coming Insurrection* and picked up the writings of Antonio Gramsci. They were thinking about how to build a movement as a 'system of alliances', as Gramsci had put it. One in which all who had lost out from the system, who were not represented in parliament, and whose voices were generally not heard in the media, would fuse into an effective political bloc.

Corbyn's advantage in this respect is his ability to

personify the things that Britain's diverse progressive currents have in common, and to federate them. No other
political format has as yet been up to the task. The Greens
have assembled broad electoral support and increased their
membership in recent years, largely by reducing the influence of its middle-class, right-leaning layers. However,
precisely because of the existence of those layers and
their record where it counts – for example, its management of Brighton council – it is distrusted by some on the
Left. The SNP has succeeded in galvanising most left-of-
centre voters in Scotland, but of course is limited by its
strict national scope. Plaid Cymru, though it currently has
a left-wing leadership, has thus far failed to make much
impact on the Left.

Corbyn's offer, in this context, was simple and unique.
In joining the Labour Party or registering as supporters,
they could bypass the need to patiently build an alternative party or start a new one. Instead, they could take the
leadership in an existing mass party with union backing,
money, and a record of electoral success far greater than
any of its rivals, and drive it to the left. This did not mean
turning Labour into a radical-Left party. It did not even
mean giving Labour a radical-Left agenda. Corbyn's prospectus for a Labour government may be one that only a
hard-Left leadership could secure today, but it is also one
that would once have been advocated by the party's mainstream. Barring foreign policy, there is nothing in principle
that Roy Hattersley couldn't support in Corbyn's agenda.
It did mean pushing back against neoliberalism on several
fronts, by rolling back privatisation, defending public

investment, supporting welfare and placing local services back under local authority control. It did mean reversing Labour's usual foreign policy nationalism, and breaking with the previous bipartisan consensus on Trident.

What Corbyn's leadership did mean, for his supporters, was putting the Right on the defensive for once. It did mean turning Labour into a party where the radical Left could organise with resources and significant networks of activists. It did mean having some influence over policy, and beginning the task of opposing the austerity narrative in its fundamentals rather than some of its specifics. It did mean a once-in-a-lifetime chance to shift the balance of British politics to the left. Already, there is a new sense of optimism among activists who note that it was under Corbyn's far more oppositional leadership that government was forced to retreat on cuts to working families tax credits, and later on the government's unwholesome arms deal with the Saudi dictatorship. Labour had been running scared from opposing the government on key policies. Now Corbyn has demonstrated that opposition works.

The strategic problems looming for Labour's nascent new Left, however, are legion. First and foremost, since Labour is in the marrow of its soul a constitutionalist and electoral party, it is naturally built-in to the culture of the party to be obsessed with electoral outcomes to the near exclusion of other considerations. Already, Corbyn's most vitriolic backbench opponents are hoping for a drubbing in upcoming local elections, to expedite his overthrow. A defeat by 2020, which may be unavoidable whatever type of leadership Labour has, will undoubtedly be taken as a defeat for a socialist programme and the basis for a return to right-wing leadership. And yet, Labour was already in decline before Corbyn took the leadership. The sources of decline were deep and worsening over time, and will certainly not be reversed in Scotland, where the decisive damage was done during the independence referendum. If activists are to have any success in their longer-term objectives, they may have to be willing to at least tacitly accept that the short-term is going to be grim in electoral terms and that they are going to have to fight tooth and nail with the party establishment – who are far from innocent of Labour's current weakness – to prevent it from using these weaknesses to restore their dominance. There is no easy, cost-free route to changing the political consensus, much less building a robust left-wing organisation capable of doing so.

Second, as energising as the leadership victory undoubtedly was, and not disregarding the likelihood of left-wing gains at various levels of the organisation such as the NEC, Labour is still a party in which the power is overwhelmingly concentrated at the top. Like other parliamentary parties, it has become far more geared toward state administration even at the cost of its traditional representative functions. This is why thus far, Corbyn's need to reckon with the Labour backbenches, not to mention the dissenters in his cabinet, has arguably done more to shape his policies than the as yet unformed activist base. Quite how they are supposed to deal with this is not clear. Should they seek to deselect MPs who don't represent the membership? If they do, they run the risk of sharpening antagonisms well before they are able to win those battles. Should they attempt to reform the party's structures? Where to begin? If what they want is a genuinely democratic Labour Party, they will be trying to bring about something that has never before existed, and which goes against all the dominant tendencies in parliamentary democracies.

Third, what do they do with electoral victory? If Corbyn is, against all prevailing signals, able to win an election and tries to implement his agenda, that is when his problems will begin for real. There is no precedent in any of the core industrial democracies for success in reversing neoliberalism in this way. Greece is the only country in which a party has been elected to do this, and the result was that party's comprehensive humiliation, a form of waterboarding-by-negotiation at the hands of the Eurozone leaders and finance ministers, resulting in their accepting the agenda of their opponents and – even worse – selling it as victory. The result was utter demoralisation. What do Corbyn's supporters do if they find that the traditional prize of a Labour government is a poisoned chalice? Or, what do they do if they find that Labour is, for other reasons, no longer a hospitable place for them? How do they avoid being churned up in the party machinery or burned out in factional warfare? How do they ensure that they can come out on the other side with a chance of political survival? They would be unwise to get carried away by any illusions as to their current strength, as their opponents will exploit their overreach ruthlessly. They would be concomitantly wise to keep in mind just what kind of party they are trying to change, and the considerable odds against them. Labour, for all its genuine achievements and merits, may not be the kind of party they think it is. The next chapter explains why.

3

Labour Isn't Working: Whatever Happened to Social Democracy?

Labour's history as a parliamentary party is a story of failure far more often than it is a story of success. Labour politicians are certainly justified in boasting about the achievements of the Attlee administration, above all the welfare state, but how many can find anything to boast about in the interwar years, from the underachieving MacDonald-led administrations to the National Government which, to all intents and purposes, pioneered austerity and its 'we're all in it together' myth? Who looks back nostalgically on the Wilson/Callaghan era, from its lame ducks to its stagfla- tion, or from devaluation to the social contract? The Blair/ Brown administrations may have had no reforming ambi- tions to match those of previous eras, but few now think of its hallmark policies – Private Finance Initiatives, the Iraq invasion, low taxes for the rich, regulatory freedom for the bankers – as raving success stories. And not only is the story of Labour overwhelmingly one of failure. It is one wherein the conditions for any success once enjoyed have long since passed. The doctrinal coordinates which once underpinned social democracy everywhere – from the 'mixed economy' to welfarism, from public ownership to Keynesian intervention – will no longer avail, because global capitalism would reject these policy nostrums, much as a body rejects an organ implant.

So many of Corbyn's supporters – admittedly less so the younger variety – want 'real' Labour, 'old' Labour, 'traditional' Labour, what Labour is supposed to stand for. The allure of this idea is difficult to overstate. If there are risks in being too impressed by Corbynism, there is an equivalent danger in being transfixed by an idea of Labour that has never been close to reality. The only remedy for this is a cold, unsentimental look at what 'real' Labour might be (or have been), and why it might not be a satis-factory basis for what is to come. Rather than demonising New Labour as a cuckoo in the nest tearing up the fabric of social democracy, it would be useful to look at where the germs of Blairism were already present, and how they came to the fore. We should at least make space for the possibility that the problem, one way or another, is Labour.

If we are to understand anything about the prospects for Corbynism, we have to consider it as a moment in the degeneration of Labourism. It is the culmination of a series of defeats for a form of political organisation that seems to be inadequate in today's world. And it is prob-ably headed for a defeat of its own. Such a setback, if it is not too demoralising, may ultimately permit the rethinking and regroupment that the Left desperately needs. But only if the nature of the beast is recognised early.

'The advanced wing of Liberalism'

The Labour Party always 'owed more to Methodism', asserts Tony Blair in a critique of Corbyn's leadership, 'than to Marxism'.[1] This shop-soiled cliché is solemnly incanted by Labour loyalists and pundits at every opportunity. If its purpose in Blair's case is to implausibly situate him as a legatee of Christian Socialism, its wider function is to stress the British exception. Labourism is held to have a unique status relative to European social democratic parties, most of which owed something to the Marxism of the Second International in their origins.

There are some elements of truth in the cliché. The Independent Labour Party's foundation in 1893 was accompanied by a Labour Church service attended by several thousand people, expressing the deeply religious, ethical element of the emerging ideology of labourism. Religious nonconformists certainly played a role in Britain's emerging trade union movement in the nineteenth century, and in the formation of Labour's moral ideology when it emerged. Keir Hardie was a Methodist, Ramsay MacDonald the product of a Calvinist sect, George Lansbury was a stalwart Anglican. The Labour Party, meanwhile, was unlike the German Social Democratic Party (SPD) in that, while it had small Marxist currents, it had no party-wide affiliation to Marxism of any variety.[2] Yet, if all that is proven here is that religion had a role in

forming the social life and ideological character of labourism, and that it did not pursue a Marxist agenda from its
inception, this is not to say very much. What seems to have
more enduring significance for the distinctive shape and
trajectory of the Labour Party is its origins in Victorian
Liberalism.

Before it was the basis of a political party, labourism
was the near-spontaneous ideology of a dense network
of labour movement organisations, from cooperatives to
working men's clubs, gardening and brass band clubs to
sports fans associations. In a difficult political environment shaped by the elimination of the Chartist movement
after 1848 and the stabilisation of the British political
system in the relatively affluent latter half of the nineteenth
century, the labour movement had developed in the ruts
and foxholes of working-class life.[3] It provided a defensive
infrastructure in which workers could live and associate
without having to compete for political power. Politically,
this tendency was dependent on the Liberal Party, from
which a few mild reforms could be wrung very slowly, and
which would even stand a few labour movement candidates
known as 'Lib-Labs'. Intellectually, labourism was not
exactly endowed with the most riveting champions – such
a Leftist intelligentsia as existed in Britain at the time was
either anaemically moralistic or redundantly schismatic.
There was little to choose from between the sermons of
the ethical socialists and the braying sectarianism of Henry
Hyndman and his followers (only Britain could offer an
ex-Tory, patrician product of Cambridge as its first leading
Marxist intellectual).

When the franchise was achieved for a substantial number of male workers through the Second Reform Act of 1867, and later extended in a Third Reform Act in 1884, this was arguably more due to the stabilisation of British capitalism in the growth years after 1850 than it was due to persistent organisation on the part of workers. The political establishment was confident in its ability to extend the franchise while managing what Gladstone referred to as 'millions of hard hands'[4] who might otherwise pose a threat to the institution of private property.[5] And in the short-term, the parties of property had considerable success in ensuring that the votes of workers went into their own campaigns. It was a Tory administration led by Benjamin Disraeli which implemented the Second Reform Act, and Disraeli proved to be adept at winning workers to Conservatism on the basis of an appeal to empire and social reform. And if the majority of working class voters cast their votes for the Liberals, this was to little beneficial effect.

In frustration with the recalcitrant, obstructionist attitude of the Liberals, the Labour Representation Committee was founded in 1900 with the support of the Independent Labour Party, the Social Democratic Federation and the Fabians. The wider labour movement was, at this stage, in exceedingly poor repair. By 1888, only one in ten adult men belonged to trade unions. The Independent Labour Party, the precursor of Labour, had attained only ten thousand paid members by 1895, a number that had been cut in half by 1901. Trade unions had suffered a string of defeats, culminating in the damaging Taff Vale judgment of 1901, in which a court found that in common law, unions could be liable to employers for loss of profits incurred by strike action. Even within the Liberal Party, MPs representing organised labour represented only a small minority, amounting to only eleven by 1898, largely due to the obstruction of working-class candidates by constituency associations dominated by middle-class members.[6] The extension of the franchise had also proven to be severely limited, such that in the two general elections leading up to the First World War, only about 60 per cent of adult males were technically allowed to vote – the majority of those excluded being working class.

The purpose of the Labour Party, then, was not to conduct the militant energies of a rising working-class movement into the state. Rather, as it transpired, it was to more effectively lobby the Liberals, a refinement of the existing strategy. Ramsay McDonald had anticipated that 'the advanced wing of Liberalism' would be forced to 'sever itself from an old alliance and form itself into an independent Labour party'.[7] Having done so, the leadership of the new party declared their vehicle 'in the true line of the progressive apostolic succession from the Liberals'.[8] And in practice, as the Victorian era gave way to a more crisis-prone Edwardian regime, Labour proved to be vital in propping up Liberal dominance. Ross McKibbin writes that 'only with the support of the Labour Party and the Irish Nationalists' could the Liberals continue to govern at this point, the 'progressive alliance' being pivoted on the questions of free trade, which Labour defended, and the repeal of Taff Vale, which the Liberals were prepared to support.[9]

It was not until over a decade after the Labour Party was founded, with strike waves upsetting the political order from 1910 to 1914, that the labour movement came into its own. And there, the leadership came not from within the Labour Party – which abjured the strikes with displays of civilised horror – but from syndicalists whose focus was on the development of working class capacities for self-government outside the British state.[10] The indifference of these syndicalists to parliament could hardly be more at odds with the deferential attitude that most Labour politicians held toward the existing institutions of the British state, from the crown-in-parliament to the colonial empire. In fact, whatever else changed about the Labour Party in this era, one of its abiding attributes was to be the priority it accorded to the interests of the 'nation', and the deference it accorded to extant constitutional arrangements and military commitments. Those Labour MPs who, today, find simply unthinkable the break-up of the United Kingdom, the repudiation of Trident, and the end of the 'special relationship' with the United States are in fact authentic legatees of their party's traditions.

But it was through the locust years of the Great War, largely supported by the Labour Party leadership – and by the majority of European socialist parliamentarians, with some notable dissenters – and the epochal rupture of the Russian Revolution, that the Labour Party was decisively formed as a national, centralised political party. Labour, despite its nominal commitment to opposing the coming of war, refuting the nationalist ideology that would justify it, and agitating for a general strike to obstruct it, was

almost automatic in its support for the war once the British
state decided to enter it.[11] Indeed, the fact of war instantly
gave Labour an importance to Britain's ruling class it had
hitherto lacked. Labour had always been in favour of a col-
laboration between classes to secure reform rather than
outright class conflict, and its sociological basis in the trade
union leadership arguably conferred on it a mediating
character – negotiating between the demands of members
and employers was the *raison d'etre* of a union bureaucrat.
By becoming an active participant in the war effort, Labour
in effect institutionalised this mediating role – so that it was
no longer simply registering the demands of the labour
movement in an electorally acceptable format, but also
conveying the demands of the state to the labour movement
in the interests of the war effort.

The party constitution devised in 1918 has been the
source of a 'socialist myth' about Labourism. The call
uttered in Clause IV for comprehensive public ownership
and the recovery for workers of the fruits of their labour,
much eulogised by Labour Leftists once the Blairites
decided to overturn it, was never to be actualised in practice. The trade union leadership had accepted Clause IV
to placate the Fabians and perhaps lend some ideological
coherence to their own limited collectivist objectives, but
they were only prepared to do so because it didn't make
much difference to policymaking.[12] Indeed, the organisation of the party developed through this document was
almost designed to ensure that the clause would not have
to be realised. The sovereignty of the party conference was
a piece of legal fiction, effectively guarded against by the

block votes handed to the union leaderships who would tend to preserve a politically cautious orientation. At any rate, the binding force of conference was only to apply 'as far as may be practicable'. What emerged was an organisation that depended upon the mobilisation of socialists to achieve political power, but which ensured their sidelining in effective decision-making, the better to enable a potential governing elite to emerge. As Gregory Elliott acidly observes, 'The "iron law of oligarchy" announced by Robert Michels in *Political Parties* (1911) did not inexorably and imperceptibly assert itself in the post-war Labour Party. It was enacted at birth.'[13]

Nevertheless, here at last was a mass party of labour, fusing socialists and trade unionists, ready to displace the Liberals and become a party of government. The war had been, in one sense, a shattering blow to European socialism, elevating its nationalist and pro-colonial elements and marginalising its internationalists. The Russian Revolution had introduced a decisive cleavage in the socialist movement, as the left-wing of social democracy largely split to form communist parties. Yet, for Labour, the war had resolved a number of problems, allowing them to decisively break with the Liberals and allowing the leadership to reorganise itself as a potential governing stratum. It had also promoted trade unions to potential helpmeets of the state in its imperial capacities, since the industrial working class was essential to the state's ability to wage war on a modern scale.[14] Finally, with a distinctive mobilising ideology of social reform and public ownership, Labour was ready to take office.

From Zero to Less than Zero:
The First Labour Governments

The sociologist Frank Parkin, looking at the problem of working-class conservatism, suggested that an emphasis on conservatism as a puzzle to be explained was misleading. The real question, given the conservative nature of the dominant institutions – from the church to the military to parliament – was how anyone turned out to be a socialist.

Something similar can be said about the Labour Party. To the familiar Leftist complaint 'Why is Labour so conservative?' we might respond, 'How could we expect them to be anything else?' It is futile to speak of 'betrayal'; this is nothing more than the distress call of the disappointed utopian. Indeed, given Labour's fundamental strategic orientations, its institutional context, and the nature of the system that it seeks to manage, nothing is so utopian as to expect this party to bring about radical transformation. The exception of the Attlee administration is hardly negligible, but that highly unusual moment is not given its due, hardly taken seriously enough at all, unless it is contrasted with Labour's broader record in office.

By the turn of the twenties Labour had converted itself into a party of administration, its leadership integrated into the state and ready to govern. Yet the party of labour, on the brink of taking office, had still not proven to actually *be* a party of labour. In fact, Labour's command of the working-class vote continued to be severely limited. By 1922, with just short of 30 per cent of the vote, it had 'failed to break through' in Birmingham, Liverpool, Bristol, Hull and

Cardiff, and won only nine seats in London. It was a party of urban workers in mining and certain textile areas.[15] The failure to hegemonise even the industrial working-class vote, let alone the votes of rural workers or the middle class, led Labour to moderate its appeal, and stress its long-standing 'national', inter-class thematics.

So it was that in 1923, when Labour finally achieved enough seats to form a minority government with Liberal support, MacDonald reassured both the King and the wider public that Labour would 'not be influenced … by any consideration other than national well-being'.[16] This had both domestic and colonial aspects. As colonial minister, former railway union leader J. H. Thomas offered assurances that he was there 'to see there is no mucking about with the British Empire', and duly proved his mettle in this regard by sending RAF bombers to Iraq.[17] On the home agenda, MacDonald's ministry kept its sights low, noting that a minority government could not be expected to achieve all that much. Such nugatory reforms as it did offer included improvements to housing and welfare provision, and some tax cuts paid for by a budget surplus – including cutting taxes on corporate profits. Given the scale of the problems a Labour government might have been expected to address, such as mass unemployment and deprivation, the rich would have had every reason to expect an attack on their class privileges. Chancellor Philip Snowden, however, was pleased to note that his budget was received warmly by the rich 'who had feared that there might be drastic impositions on their class'.[18] Indeed, Labour ministers seemed to enjoy greatly their chance to mingle with those whom

MacDonald called 'kings and rulers of the earth', on 'terms of equality'.[19]

This first, exceptionally brief, spell in office ended after just over nine months in the squalid scandal of the 'Zinoviev Letter', a forgery sent to the Foreign Office and the *Daily Mail* purporting to describe a Bolshevik policy of subversion in Britain. Labour, already under pressure from the Liberals and Conservatives over their supposed softness on Bolshevism, supported publication of the document – but this, and their consistent opposition to Communism, did nothing to lessen the attacks of their rivals. The chief result of this was not to damage Labour's electoral standing – indeed, while losing seats, it increased its share of the vote – but to finally finish off the Liberals by frightening their anti-socialist voters into the camp of the Conservatives.

Nothing illustrates Labour's parliamentary dilemmas in this era more than the bitter general strike of 1926. The issue at stake was that the coal owners were determined to reduce wages and, while not agreeing to the full extent of the cuts, the Conservative Government was determined to assist them in doing so – even if it meant, as their own Commission suggested, reducing living standards to pre-war levels. To this end, extensive preparations had been made on the government's side to ensure that coal supplies would continue in the event of a strike, while rhetoric against trade unions and 'Bolshevism' was ramped up. And while the union membership became more militant in the face of this, the General Council of the TUC panicked at the idea of such a giant confrontation. J. H. Thomas, acting as the TUC's chief negotiator, 'begged and pleaded' for some form of compromise from the government – 'give us some terms never mind what they are, no matter how bad they are'. But the Baldwin administration, well prepared and in a bullish mood, insisted that the looming strike threatened 'the basis of ordered government'. 'It is not wages that are imperiled,' Baldwin charged, 'it is the freedom of our very Constitution.' MacDonald, though he had pledged to fight the corner of the miners from within parliament, assured the benches that 'with the discussion of general strikes and Bolshevism and all that kind of thing, I have nothing to do at all'.

The Labour leadership thus saw the strike as 'an unmitigated disaster, threatening Labour's claim to be a constitutional party'. The strike, the largest in British history, was adroitly encircled and dismantled by a government having wide recourse to emergency measures, police and military crackdowns and a stentorian campaign of vilification. The Labour leadership may have been reluctant to support outright class warfare; the Conservative government, though invoking the language of the nation, was not. Nor was it above using subsequent legislation, the Trade Disputes Act of 1927, to attack Labour's political levy. These developments, in toto, 'helped to accelerate Labour's rightward drift'.[20]

The Labour minority government that was elected in 1929 was in a much stronger position than the last. It finally had more seats than the Conservatives, and enjoyed the support of a Liberal Party that had radicalised around an agenda of reflationary measures and state intervention. It therefore had more chance of achieving some of its goals than ever.

But what were Labour's goals? Any hope that a Labour government would usher in radical change were squashed given Ramsay MacDonald's conventional cabinet, which comprised 'a familiar mix of moderate politician-trade unionists … middle-class former Liberals … intellectuals … and "mild" ILPers'.[21] Only the appointment of George Lansbury, the left-wing former mayor of Poplar who had led a local rebellion against the payment of rates, edited the socialist *Daily Herald*, and was staunchly pacifist, could be seen as in any sense unconventional. The appointment of the economically orthodox Philip Snowden as chancellor, meanwhile, was the clearest possible signal that the new government would do little to tackle what it identified as its greatest issue, the problem of unemployment. Even before the October stock market crash, Labour had campaigned on this under the slogan, 'The Works Are Closed, But The Ballot Box Is Open.' Yet Labour had few specific policies to deal with it, and the absence of any serious strategy became clearer as capitalism began to enter its worst crisis yet.

This is not to say that the government lacked options. Oswald Mosley, then a Labour minister, proposed a 'Memorandum' endorsing measures to protect industries and support demand through the expansion of credit, increases in pensions and other allowances. There was also the option of a coalition with the Liberals on the basis of their stimulus proposals. The party leadership, desperate for respectability, struggled to form a cross-party consensus, appointing a council of intellectuals, businessmen and trade unionists to hammer out a policy. In the end, chancellor Snowden persuaded the party to endorse the Treasury's orthodoxy that the only responsible economic policy was to allow markets to operate more or less unimpeded.[22]

As was often to be the case in Labour's history, the abstract commitment to 'socialism' was invoked to justify this retreat. In principle, Labour would bring about the supersession of capitalism by winning a 'socialist majority' in parliament and then securing gradual social reform and transitional measures within the context of buoyant capitalist growth. Any policy with an object less far-reaching than said transformation – say, the defence of workers' living standards during recession – could be, where convenient, denounced as mere tinkering. This meant that capitalism had to be allowed to succeed one way or another. Given the cabinet's lack of confidence in any alternative growth formula, and its deference to the Treasury, this meant letting the City of London rule. Parliament, Chancellor Philip Snowden told the Labour Party conference, should not intervene in the financial matters of the nation, since 'Parliament is not a competent body to deal with such highly delicate and intricate matters.' Instead, as Treasury receipts tumbled, Snowden demanded 'drastic and disagreeable measures' to cut public spending.[23] This early austerity project was justified by a familiar 'all in it together' sentiment, but most of the required 'savings' were found in unemployment insurance.

In order to implement these cuts more effectively, MacDonald tendered the resignation of the cabinet and entered into a 'National' government in coalition with the Conservatives and Liberals. The new administration immediately implemented stringent austerity measures, balancing the budget and thereby 'restoring confidence' – that, inevitably, of investors. Having implemented this policy, the government dissolved itself and called a general election. The 1931 general election destroyed all participants in this coalition except for the Tories, who gained an unprecedented 55 per cent of the vote. The Liberals broke up into three factions for the election, whose total vote was barely above 10 per cent. And Ramsay MacDonald's faction, standing as 'National Labour', polled a mere 1.5 per cent. In the wider arc of history, it is clear that the Tories had been on a long upward electoral curve since the late 1800s, a trend that peaked in the 1930s. Baldwin, one of the more astute Conservative leaders, had understood the elements of this shift well; although a growing layer of British society had been moving to the left since the turn of the century, much of the remainder was available to be corralled into an anti-socialist electoral bloc led by the most combative defenders of private property. As such, the subtlety of the Conservatives in this period had been to allow just so much reform – be it pensions or the extension of the franchise to female voters – as would take the edge off any radicalising tendencies, while also banging the anti-communist drum louder than anyone else. Despite the Conservatives' political dominance of the inter-war period, for example, there is some evidence that the growing welfare consensus which Baldwin felt compelled to accept was having some mildly redistributive effects.[24] The Liberals, torn between Victorian nostrums of 'free trade' and fiscal abstinence on the one hand, and a 'new liberalism' enjoining welfarism and state intervention on the other, were unable to lead this bloc, and their period in 'National' government was just as fatal, in its way, as the more recent rose garden nuptials between David Cameron and Nick Clegg. The electoral system produced a clear division between a savvy Conservative Party and a Labour Party that was as yet electorally underdeveloped, strategically vapid and tactically timid.

In coalescing with the Conservatives on an austerity platform, MacDonald's wing of the Labour leadership believed that – against the 'sectional' purposes of trade unionists but consistent with their particular ethical socialist tradition – they were putting 'nation' above 'class', something their critics decried as class treachery. However, the pall of MacDonald's ostensible 'betrayal' may obscure something important here: as if, by putting the problem in moral terms, we can sidestep the strategic problems raised, not just by parliamentary socialism, but even by the limited goal of welfare capitalism in an era of economic depression.

Those of us living through the era of many 'grand coalitions' between social democratic and conservative parties, often in the interests of implementing spending cuts (Greece 2011, Ireland 2011 and 2016, Italy 2013, though not Spain 2016), are in an advantageous position to understand this. Social democratic parties that have funded their welfare commitments on the basis of booming capitalism, or in some cases on the basis of *future* growth (the Greek state's borrowing in the boom years being a case in point), have found themselves compelled in leaner years to pursue austerity policies identical to those of their traditional electoral rivals – even at the cost of losing their electoral base and becoming a mere caste of state managers. The rise of radical-Left parties, from Syriza to Podemos, is at least in part a result of this realignment of social democracy to the neoliberal centre.

For the managers of social democracy, the attempt to resist these cutbacks and gross transfers of wealth to the private sector was hopelessly utopian. Even if they felt the depth and speed of austerity driven by Angela Merkel and conservative technocrats was too severe, there was no working alternative model of growth on the horizon. And even if the private sector was sluggish and investment pitifully low, there was no question of any other sector leading a new round of growth. Certainly, any government which involved the state in taking over the means of invest-ment and attempting to create new growth through public works would face the risk of stiff resistance from business, banks, civil servants, media, and of course European insti-tutions. The legality and constitutionality of their actions could be challenged, and they might face continual crises and challenges from within. They would risk even lower rates of investment, downgrading by the ratings agencies such that borrowing would become impossible, and specu-lative attacks. It should not be so surprising, therefore, if we repeatedly find social democratic leaders, egged on by establishment media, capitulating to the agenda of their opponents with an air of heroic self-sacrifice.

So, if the second Labour government in British history had ended once again in a debacle from which the Conservatives were the primary beneficiaries, it is rather too convenient to castigate the renegacy of a few

short-sighted or corrupt leaders. It is neither an aberra-
tion nor an accident that Labour, from being the 'advanced
wing of liberalism', became the rearguard of reaction: their
means could have no other yield. Nor did the Labour Party,
freed from such renegades, demonstrate renewed efficacy
in opposition. The election as leader of Lansbury, a figure
comparable in many ways to Jeremy Corbyn, confirmed a
turn to the left in the trade unions and party grass roots.
But his period in charge lasted only three years, in large
part because his pacifism and commitment to disarmament
brought him into conflict with the party establishment.
Under neither Lansbury nor his successor, Clement Attlee
– a monarchist from the party's Right – did Labour play a
significant role in organising or supporting the rebellions
of the unemployed. The Jarrow March has entered into
labour movement legend, and it is for this reason generally
forgotten that the Attlee leadership disowned the protest.
And while much of the criticism of Lansbury's pacifism
was justified by the need to defend Europe against fascism,
Labour cheerfully supported the mendacious policy of
'non-intervention' in Spain, where the democracies quietly
endorsed extensive fascist intervention on Franco's side.
Labour in the 1930s did little either to defend its constituencies, to slow the advance of fascism or, concomitantly,
the drift to war: and deviated not one iota from the narrow
electoral path upon which its strategic purview had always
been staked.

In truth, this was not just a problem with the Labour
Party. Social democrats of various ideological hues and
pallors had entered governments across Europe in the

interwar period, and the record was with few exceptions abysmal. For example, as Adam Przeworski writes of this period, despite their ideological commitments to redistribution of wealth and socialisation of the economy, the riches of the upper classes were left largely untouched and not a single industry – barring the French arms manufacturers – was nationalised in this period.[25]

Labour in the 'Golden Age'

How, then, was the Attlee government of 1945–51 so different? For the first time in its history, Labour had won a landslide with almost half of the total vote, and a parliamentary majority of 145 seats. Its manifesto committed it to policies far more radical and far-reaching than any previous Labour electoral programme: a cradle-to-grave welfare state, a national health service, Keynesian economic intervention, extensive public ownership, mass house-building and much more. What is more, its actual accomplishments in these respects – even setting aside the mythopoeic eulogies – can hardly be disdained as trivial. The reformist road to socialism had twice led, in the interwar period, to a sad diminuendo of hopes and a shift to the right. Now, Labour instituted a series of stunning, seemingly irreversible reforms that transferred some of the country's wealth to workers in the form of an expansive social wage. Why?

It is commonly assumed that the war years had accelerated a long-brewing radicalisation in the British public, producing broad popular support for Labour's agenda. Here, surely, was the long-awaited vindication of the

Labourist strategy: popular support for socialism had reached the decisive tipping point, and Attlee's team had only to present their agenda for it to receive broad popular endorsement; and only to win a plurality in order to see those plans realised. Certainly, after the resignation of the pro-appeasement Neville Chamberlain in 1940, there was an overwhelming mood against Conservatism which – given the prevailing electoral winds – would tend to favour a Labour government. This was concurrent with a broad, nebulous 'antipolitical' sentiment aimed at the old governing elites, and support for some substantial reforms.[26] Tory opposition to proposed welfare reforms recommended in a 1942 report by the Liberal economist Lord Beveridge compounded the emerging mood against them. Yet, even if Labour's manifesto declared the party to be 'socialist, and proud of it', it would be exaggerating to call this a 'socialist' consensus. And few anticipated at the time that it would result in a Labour government – sources on both left and right expected a comfortable Conservative majority headed by a popular wartime prime minister who was not personally tarnished by the policy of appeasement.

Just as important as popular disaffection with the Tories was the confidence that Labour had in its reform agenda. Here, Labour gained vital experience from its participation in the wartime coalition government, which used Keynesian stimulus and demand-management techniques to keep production at a pace necessary for the successful prosecution of the war. This shift in statecraft was driven, in part, by the more far-sighted elements of the civil service, who placed liberal reformers in key state apparatuses.[27] The

scarcity of labour during the war had raised the political
power and bargaining leverage of organised labour, and
encouraged the government to use collective bargaining
to manage ongoing struggles over wages.[28] In addition, the
precarious state of British capitalism, like that of many of
its European competitors, was such that a radical government had a unique window of opportunity to reform the
system before the usual business opponents of such reforms
had a chance to become sufficiently organised. It is argu-
able that many of these changes would have been imposed
upon a Conservative administration, and something like
this is suggested by the record of centre-Right governments across Europe in this era. Certainly, once they were
in place, the Tories evinced no appetite for rolling them
back, despite a brief, testerical campaign against 'socialism' in the elections of 1950 and 1951. No doubt this was
in part because, despite exploiting real popular discontent
with rationing and linking such policies to 'socialism', the
Conservatives only gained office in 1951 due to the irreg-
ularities of the first-past-the-post system. Labour had in
fact won slightly more votes than the Conservatives, and
the Tories' polling suggested to them that they needed to
accept existing social democratic policies if they were to
win support among skilled workers.[29] As such, the Conservatives held on to governmental power, once obtained,
by preserving rather than rolling back Labour's reforms.
However, whereas Labour took advantage of its strength
to implement sweeping reforms, the Conservatives would
have resisted them as far as possible, and it is difficult to
believe that anything like the National Health Service

could have emerged from a government led by Winston Churchill.

However, if we are not to buy into maudlin myth, it is also necessary to place these changes in a broader perspective. Labour, having equated the socialisation of industry with public ownership, nationalised important industries such as steel, coal, railways, cars, telecommunications and the Bank of England. A full fifth of industry was taken into public ownership. But most of these firms were incapable of surviving alone at any rate, and their sustenance was necessary for renewed capitalist development. The owners of the firms were generously compensated with public funds and borrowing, so that they could reinvest in the profitable parts of the private sector. Meanwhile, the public corporations were preserved on the model of private industry, with the usual worker–management hierarchies, and their production decisions made on the basis of what was good for private business – their management often drawn from the capitalist class. Once stabilised, the system also proved remarkably resistant to further such encroachments on private ownership.

At any rate, the architects of the nationalisation programme, such as Herbert Morrison, were reluctant to extend it, arguing that Labour had to 'consolidate' its gains before attempting further transformation. Even the Labour Left began to retreat and soften its positions, partially in view of the growing anti-communist climate of the Cold War. Later, post-war social democrats of the Labour Right, such as Anthony Crosland and Hugh Gaitskell, argued that with a 'mixed economy' and some degree of political liberalism,

Labour had actually achieved socialism. Capitalism, if not
in fact done away with, was grievously weakened by the
encroachments on its power by organised labour and the
social-democratic state. Since the Tories pledged to maintain the status quo, there remained only the consensus of
'Butskellism' (named after the Tory and Labour chan-
cellors, Rab Butler and Hugh Gaitskell) to administer.[30]
In some respects, Labour became a prisoner of its own
exaggerations, contributing to an intellectual consensus –
obviously bearing little relation to reality – that Britain's
wealth was being so radically redistributed as to ultimately
lead to what Lionel Robbins bemoaned as 'propertyless
uniformity'.[31] One would hardly know, in the face of such
fantastical assertions, that by the sixties, still some 75 per
cent of personal property was owned by the top 5 per cent
of the population.[32] Even absent such extravagant claims,
the tendency was to treat Britain as an 'affluent society' in
which major social problems had been more or less solved
and poverty had largely disappeared. Such was the mood
music to a long period of Tory dominance – as Macmillan
argued, 'You've never had it so good.'

There is also an unsavoury side to the Attlee administration, inasmuch as such reforms as were achieved were
coterminous with financial orthodoxy, the continuation
of rationing alongside increased exports, a willingness to
use troops to break strikes, and wage freezes. A forgotten aspect of the 'golden age' is indeed this pungently
authoritarian side of Labour administrations. Labour was
in some respects more avid than the Conservatives in prosecuting the war against organised labour and, later, social

movements. Attlee's government repeatedly deployed armed forces against striking workers, invoking wartime anti-strike legislation. Later, it was the Wilson administration of 1964–70 which first deployed the notorious Special Patrol Group in London, while developing legislation to severely curtail the unions' right to strike. In the crisis-ridden 1974–79 Wilson–Callaghan era, Barbara Castle did not hesitate to use armed forces against striking firefighters. Even the famously liberal Home Secretary Roy Jenkins tilted the balance of criminal justice policy in an authoritarian direction with his contribution to Britain's repertoire of 'anti-terrorism' laws, the 1974 Prevention of Terrorism Act authorising internment and jury-less trials in Northern Ireland, while the Criminal Law Act introduced further restrictions on organised labour.[33] The authoritarianism of New Labour was of a different order, but hardly unthinkable in light of the record of social democracy in its heyday.

The post-war consensus was also bought in part with American dollars, which ensured Britain's orientation in a new axis of power which demanded continuity in foreign policy justified by a staunch anti-communist line. Despite manifesto commitments and pre-election insinuations, Labour's Ernest Bevin had promised on election day, 1945, that the new government's foreign policy would not differ from the previous one. His first parliamentary speech as foreign minister made clear that he accepted the policy of his Conservative predecessor, Anthony Eden.[34] He did not dissimulate. Labour had, in 1944, supported the policy of crushing the Greek partisans and supporting monarchist forces. And while it orchestrated the British withdrawal from India, it offered no such relief to Kenya or Malaysia, where brutal counterinsurgency was indicated.[35] Similarly, it would go on to send troops to assist the French restoration in Vietnam, support Nato (despite noisy opposition from the Left), and develop nuclear weapons. Here, then, was the zenith of social democracy: Labour had achieved as much as it was ever likely to, finally establishing the long sought after compromise between the classes, and its commitment to 'nation' never wobbled.

The crucial delusion, common to Labour leaders of the era, was that a new economic formula had been reached for unprecedented, perpetual expansion, which would support an ongoing class compromise. As Stuart Hall wrote in a critical review of the post-war system, they believed that 'the social democratic bandwagon could be hitched to the star of a reformed capitalism: and that the latter would prove capable of infinite expansion so that all the political constituencies could be "paid off" at once: the TUC and the CBI, labour and capital, public housing and the private landlord, the miners and the Bank of England'.[36] To this effect, it is sometimes assumed that the economic controls implemented by Labour were Keynesian in drift. In fact, although the term 'Keynesian' may at times be a convenient marker for the kind of economic controls used in the post-war period, the counter-cyclical measures implemented by post-war Labour governments tended to involve 'taking the economy off the boil' rather than reflationary measures in the down-swing.[37]

The post-war boom had arguably little to do with a uniquely Keynesian policy mix and much more to do with the space for new investment created by the catastrophic destruction of capital during the war. And insofar as the new consensus depended on an unusual period of capitalist dynamism, with close to zero unemployment and growth rates stabilising at 3 or 4 per cent, the first green shoots of capitalist failure were destined to vitiate that consensus. Of course, it was precisely the condition of unprecedented economic growth underpinning Labour's class compromise which began to absent itself toward the late 1960s – catching the Labour Government, then with a solid majority, totally unprepared.

The Collapse of the Consensus

The seeds of downfall were already partially visible when Harold Wilson, then something of a 'bright young thing' by Westminster standards, led Labour to victory in the 1964 election. Most signals were optimistic. Wilson, though he was from the centre, was reviled by the Gaitskellites and able to garner the support of the Left. Thanks to left-wing support, he was able to take the leadership after Gaitskell's death in 1963. He was careful to avoid outright attacks on 'fellow travellers' in the fashion of his predecessor, and evinced an informality and comic turn that went with the grain of popular culture. Labour under his leadership was elected to government on an ambitious project for full employment and public investment, breaking thirteen years of uninterrupted Conservative rule.

At first, everything seemed to be going exceptionally well, despite the tiny parliamentary majority with which the government was formed. Labour began to implement its National Plan for industry, secured agreement with the CBI and TUC, and implemented many of its policies including pension increases, rent controls and the abolition of prescription charges. This may not have been the sweeping transformation of 1945, but with the Tory opposition scattered and in decline, there was reason to be optimistic. Further, despite the enduring influence of Gaitskellite revisionism and the talk of 'affluence', the limits of the post-1945 settlement were becoming visible – the existence of a wide swathe of impoverished people, especially pensioners, was recognised.[38] Even the early attempts by Lord Cromer, the Governor of the Bank of England and a close ally of the City, to force a reverse in policy were seen off. Speculative attacks on the currency – which Cromer advised Wilson signified investors' demands that the government row back from its policy of full employment, use incomes policy to stifle wages and raise interest rates – were not enough to force the government's capitulation at this stage. In the end, Cromer was replaced and returned to the family merchant bank Barings. Labour was confident enough in 1966 to call a new election and extend its mandate, gaining some 48 per cent of the vote compared to the Tories 41.4 per cent. And despite the enduring influence of revisionism, this was clearly a class vote: despite the fact that the Labour leadership was predominantly middle class, it scored the highest share of manufacturing workers' votes in its history, some 69 per cent.[39]

How, then, did the government end up implementing the bankers' desiderata? The underlying problem for the government was that Britain was a declining global power, notwithstanding the efforts – largely supported by Labour – to preserve as much as possible of the colonial empire. As exports fell, Britain was faced with a balance of payments crisis, resulting in further speculative attacks and a choice between currency devaluation and import controls. The Treasury's policy had always been that the currency should be defended at all costs, and Wilson certainly agreed that a strong pound was central to Britain's global dominance. So while Wilson didn't cave in to Cromer's pressure, Labour was certainly determined not to alienate the City. Even the earliest budgets, which did pass some radical measures, tended to be deflationary in effect. Wilson's cabinet therefore overwhelmingly opted for a policy of import controls and deflationary measures to manage the crisis. They did not know, however, that Wilson had negotiated a deal with the Johnson administration in which, for a bail-out of the pound, Britain pledged to deflate the economy and use an incomes policy to restrict wages, while at the same time preserving its East of Suez military commitments and backing the United States in its war in Vietnam. Then, as now, Britain's global role was secured by latching onto the coat-tails of the White House. The National Plan was in effect dead by July 1966, as the government implemented a mandatory wage freeze across the board, the first since 1931, and cut public spending. The wage freeze necessitated one of the government's first fights with organised labour, as seafarers went on strike for a modest pay-rise which, the government claimed, would 'breach the dykes of the incomes policy'.[40]

Finally, in 1967, with the speculative attacks continuing, the government agreed to devalue the pound. The government quickly lost credibility, both among workers who resented growing unemployment and wage restraint, and among the affluent middle classes for whom the episode demolished Labour's economic credibility. The IMF were brought in to manage this process, and it was they who argued for the introduction of prescription charges among other things: a reversal that was implemented, with great embarrassment, in 1968. Dick Crossman asked the Chancellor Jim Callaghan at the time if he might increase family allowances for the poor: 'sorry, old boy, the IMF won't allow it'. Unto which: 'so we're back under the control of the bankers'.[41]

This was not just a case of government going awry. Certainly, Wilson could have devalued earlier and avoided some of the consequences of this protracted dance-off with the speculators. But the forces eating away at Labourism went deeper. The sixties had seen the emergence of two trends that would erode the Labour coalition. The first was the emergence of immigration as a major political issue after the 1962 Commonwealth Immigrants Act which, by enacting the first major restrictions on migration to the United Kingdom from the former colonies, exacerbated a simmering racist anti-immigrant backlash that was effectively harnessed by the Tory Right. The greatest successes for this strategy were enjoyed by the Tories in the West Midlands, where Labour had struggled most to rebuild its vote after a long period of Tory dominance amid relative regional prosperity. There, the right-wing in alliance with local press generated local panics about the arriving migrant populations. By winning the Smethwick seat in the 1964 general election on the slogan, 'If you want a nigger for a neighbour, vote Labour,' the Conservatives found that it was possible to gain working-class support without offering the usual class incentives. Indeed, Enoch Powell acted as a pathfinder for a New Right built on this discovery, that one could build a popular, right-wing coalition as long as racism was at the centre of it.[42] The second development was the growth of Welsh and Scottish nationalisms, coupled with civil strife in Northern Ireland, where the Catholic population was organising against Britain's own miniature version of Jim Crow. The gradual cession of the empire was raising questions about the purpose of the United Kingdom, while Westminster's antiquated institutions alienated growing layers of the middle class in Scotland and Wales. Labour lost its Carmarthen seat to the Welsh nationalists in 1966, then lost its Hamilton seat to the Scottish nationalists in the following year. In 1969, the paramilitary wing of the Ulster constabulary was deployed against Catholic protesters, with bloody consequences.

By the time Labour had lost the 1970 election, the British state to which the party had always deferred was in need of major renovation, while the post-war social-democratic coalition was falling apart. Some voters simply abstained, reflected in a turnout of 72 per cent, the lowest since the war, while others – including many manufacturing workers – decamped to the Tories. Worse than electoral losses, however, was the fact that the economic basis for post-war social democracy was disappearing, and Labour had few means by which to adapt to new circumstances. The post-war corporatist system had confirmed the parliamentary, constitutional route to change as the major strategic orientation of the Left. In this system, governments would use the state to hammer out a compromise between, to borrow a turn of phrase, 'the top floor of the Shell building ... the top floor of the Treasury ... the top floor of the BBC ... [and] the top floor of the TUC'.[43] For mainstream social democracy, the state was the critical actor, holding the ring between rival 'interests'. The task, then, was to elect a Labour government to administer this compromise in a fair way and defend the poorest. But even those in Labour whose objectives were far more radical than the mainstream, tended, for much of the post-war period, to sign up to the essential predicates of this view. The purview of most actually existing socialists involved looking for different ways of using the state to curtail 'the logic of the market'.[44]

This privileging of parliament as the key locus from which change was to be achieved compounded the demoralisation and confusion felt when the corporatist pact began to fall apart, and a New Right espousing a borrowed 'anti-statism' surged. As Britain's underlying economic weaknesses – expressed in declining productivity and profitability – ran confluently into the seventies, leading to rising inflation and unemployment, and as the 1973 OPEC crisis sent the world economy hurtling into the red, the social democratic mainstream, along with a revived Liberal Party, sought to consolidate the role of the interventionist state in securing class compromise. The Labour Left, for its part, did not so much seek to abolish this consensus as effect a sharp shift in the balance of the compromise in favour of workers. Where the corporatist instruments of price and income controls, and the rhetoric of shared sacrifices still prevailed on the Right and centre, Labour's left-wing sought extensive redistribution and nationalisation.

Yet many on the Labour Left and on its periphery also engaged in a thoroughgoing critique of the record of post-war social democracy. As constituency branches and unions moved leftward, members began to critique Harold Wilson's failure to deliver on his manifesto commitments, a fiasco which they blamed for the Conservative's 1970 election victory under Heath.[45] The problem, it was argued, was that Labour had been too timid in confronting concentrated economic and political power. Even where it had nationalised industries, it had left the old guard in charge. In place of deference to parliament and the constitutional settlement, the Left began to advance a critique of the British state and demand democratisation. In addition to extensive nationalisation, and in place of its model of top-down management, they advocated forms of industrial democracy. Tony Benn, a former Gaitskellite who had moved sharply to the left in response to Labour's defeat, played a key role in getting elements of this into Labour's 1974 manifesto. As he argued, his experience as Minister for Technology had shown him the necessity of this as the best means of addressing rising union discontent:

> The old idea of management from the top has got to be looked at again ... the man who actually has to do a job of work on the factory

floor, or in a foundry, or in a shop or office, is the best person to know how his or her work should be organised ... One of the most horrifying experiences of my ministerial life was to walk round factories with management that obviously didn't know what was going on, or who was doing what, and yet quite happily assumed that the right to manage on behalf of the shareholders included the right to tell everybody what to do ... If we can trust the country to democracy, why on earth can't we trust individual firms to the people who work in them? ... And if nationalised industries were seen to be democratically run, and to be distributing incomes more fairly as well as being accountable to the public for the major decisions they make, we could take a massive step toward democratic socialism.[46]

Yet the crisis of social democracy would not yield to parliamentary socialism. Instead, as inflation soared, Labour fell back on traditional corporatist methods to control it. Working on the theory that excessive wages were driving up manufacturing costs, which were being passed on to customers, the Wilson Government elected in 1974 began negotiating a Social Contract with union leaders that would restrain wage growth to no more than 5 per cent a year, while inflation greatly exceeded that increase. While wage growth played a part, not least as organised labour tried to recoup real-term losses incurred during the Wilson-era 'balance of payments' crisis, the actual causes of inflation were considerably more complicated than the solution of wage-restraint implied. Among the major causes were soaring global food and energy prices, coupled with the liberalisation of banking rules under the Heath administration, which had resulted in a glut of cheap credit.

Nonetheless, there were more fundamental problems, above all a secular decline in profitability and productivity in the manufacturing sector. It was logical that business and their allies in the Bank of England and the Treasury would seek a reduction in wage costs by one means or another, as the first condition for freeing up funds for new investment. Heath had attempted to deal with these structural problems at first by chastening the unions, using the whip of market discipline to enforce competition, and steering Britain into Europe. When Heath's solutions didn't avail, only provoking crippling conflict with the unions, it fell to a Labour government to find a way of reducing the cost of labour with the consent of the labour movement. The problem for social-democratic governments therefore became one of how to achieve wage reductions while finding sufficient *quid pro quo* to secure union acquiescence – a problem that became intractable by 1978, as wildcat strikes signalled the withdrawal of labour's consent to the bargain. Aside from wage restraint, the government also severely reduced public spending under an agreement with the IMF. Unemployment remained at approximately 1 million, a situation for which capital was grateful and – initially – inclined to reward with political support.[47] Amid a frenetic anti-communist clamour in parts of the establishment, and with the Labour Right joining in right-wing press attacks on hate figures on the Left such as Tony Benn, civil servants also lobbied Labour leaders to kill off other radical proposals such as Benn's policies for industrial democracy and nationalisation.[48] The centre was falling apart, but the Left singularly lacked the means to take advantage in this hostile terrain.

The Wilderness Years

This is where the New Right found its entrée. As Stuart Hall anticipated in a much-celebrated essay, 'The Great Moving Right Show',[49] the failed attempt to resuscitate the dying body of post-war social democracy merely compounded those aspects of popular discontent with the system that were already destabilising the consensus. The resentments generated by top-down, mandarin control of public industries, by incomes policies, by intrusive welfare bureaucracies and the increasingly authoritarian bent of state interventions may not have been enough by themselves to create a sufficient backlash. But the fact that they manifestly *did not work*, that public enterprises were 'lame ducks', that unemployment still soared, that the consensus had yielded to 'stagflation', and that the social contract broke down with the 'winter of discontent', showed the state to be not merely 'nannying', but also ineffectual. What is more, the leadership of social democracy was increasingly in agreement with the Rightist critique: it was Labour's Denis Healey who effectively introduced the doctrine of 'sado-monetarism' before Thatcher was elected.

In the spaces where social democracy had decomposed, the ideology of Thatcherism began to lay roots. Discovering new energies first unleashed by Enoch Powell, the Conservatives found that a certain 'free market' idiom could gain elements of popular support provided they were linked to the politics of racial backlash.[50] The parlous state of British capitalism could be blamed on an assortment of troublemakers and enemies of order, the migrants, 'muggers' and militants cosseted by a 'creeping socialism': the solution being a dose of old-fashioned British authority, market discipline and, later, firepower. In place of incomes policies and subsidies for lame duck enterprises, Thatcher promised to let crack the whip of the markets. In the car industry, the Tories said, the uncompetitive practices of public ownership and union militancy had led to over-manning and over-priced labour, resulting in cars that could not be sold and rising unemployment. Unions were letting workers down, rather than advancing their interests, while the state supported inefficient industries. Instead, the state should get out of the way, let bad enterprises fail, and let the innovative and industrious succeed. What is more, since the strikes of the era were blamed for inflationary wage claims and had no connection to a wider, popular radical project, their repression could be justified on the grounds that they were narrow, 'selfish' acts harming industrious workers.

Thatcherite discourse struck at a key fault line in social democratic ideology. Social democracy, though emerging from organised labour, cleaved to the possibility of a transcendent national interest, achieved through class compromise and cooperation. This was always going to be difficult to square with the aspirations of its more radical constituents, above all for extensive public ownership of the commanding heights of the economy, in the interests of economic planning. The war state had made a degree of intervention possible, with business happy to cooperate for most of the immediate post-war era, but it was hardly going to persuade the owners of capital to surrender their major sources of profit without a battle. In practice, such aspirations were never on the brink of being realised, but there was at least the prospect that the practice of social democracy would ignite a battle from the other side of the bargain – that of organised labour. This is exactly what had happened in the late seventies, and the New Right seized on this in order to articulate the division in a distinctive way. It was not, they said, a war between classes. The struggle was between the productive and the non-productive. For a 'nation' to be able to afford a welfare system, its productive members had to be taxed, and they would be less inclined to accept this unless the unproductive state and its clients were weaned off the teat.[51]

Thus, the complacent consensus gave way to a belliger-ent offensive led by politicians, intellectuals and institutions largely loyal to the middle-class Right. The flavour of this attack was not to the tastes of the Tory establishment, which largely reacted with horror to Thatcher's vulgar 'retreat behind the privet hedge into the narrow world of class interests and selfish concerns'.[52] Business was also divided over the usefulness of neoliberal nostrums, though a large and dynamic layer of capitalists, led by finance, organised in support of Thatcher's remedies.[53] There was also concern that the ambitious brutality of the government was contributing to an ideological revival of the Labour Left, exemplified by the fact that Tony Benn came within a whisker of defeating Denis Healey in the 1981 election for the deputy leadership. However, whatever excitement Benn was able to generate among constituency activists and a minority of union members, his real support was exaggerated in the election by a system of block voting. A raft of left-wing union leaders had emerged from the previous era of class confrontations, many of whom were inclined to support Benn. But the majority of union members – just like the majority of people – were moving to the right under the pull of Thatcherism. They didn't become Thatcherites, but the gravitational pull was away from the Left. And in the unions that actually balloted all members, Benn was roundly defeated.[54]

The weakness of this Left revival was registered almost immediately when, in March 1981, a faction of the Labour Right organised a split. They had been considering their move for some time. Leading figures in this split, such as Roy Jenkins and David Owen, had been among the pro-government rebels when Heath sought to lead the UK into the European Community. They were infuriated by Wilson's strategy of mediating between the left- and right-wings of Labour, which necessitated that he couldn't campaign for entry on the government's terms. The later calamities of the Wilson/Callaghan government had convinced them that the central problem for social-democratic governance was the power of the trade unions. They argued, just as the Liberals had in the same period, that no party could genuinely govern in the national interest if it was beholden to one class interest. As if this was the only real obstacle faced by the old social-democratic centre. They sought, by ending the Labourist coalition and launching a new party, the Social Democratic Party (SDP), to force an electoral realignment that would draw all the dominant political forces to the centre, and lock the militants and left-wing constituency activists out of power for good.[55]

While the SDP and its Liberal allies were hardly successful in the endeavour to anchor British politics in the centre, the project did build on certain long-term tendencies. The electoral degeneration of the two main post-war parties, the rise of the Liberals and the nationalist parties, and a certain amount of class dealignment in voting,[56] meant that circumstances were ripe for a new electoral calculus. Unfortunately, the immediate beneficiaries were the Conservatives. The popular support for Thatcherism was real enough, however exaggerated by the electoral system.[57] Thatcher had rebounded from the doldrums of 1981 on the basis of a global economic revival beginning in 1982, and in her case linked to martial triumph in the Falklands. But it was the Liberal/SDP alliance which decisively fractured Labour's base, put it on the defensive, ensured that Labour's 1983 vote was the lowest it had gained since 1918, and prevented any recovery until Blair had finally effected the coup de grâce. The 'modernisation' project initiated under Neil Kinnock almost as soon as he was elected leader in 1983, continued by John Smith and consummated by Tony Blair, may have been forced on Labour by other means and in other circumstances. The transformation of social democracy into what has been called 'social liberalism' – a hybrid of traditional social democratic organisation with neoliberal politics – is not peculiar to Britain. It is conceivable that a Left government could have been elected only to see its programme flounder in the face of economic turmoil and resistance from business, thus empowering business-minded 'moderates' to force through a more cautious 'modernisation' agenda. However, without the SDP split, it is difficult to imagine the sweeping scale of the Left's rout in most of its extant quarters of strength, from the miners to municipal socialism. And without the SDP and the victorious Thatcher regime which it enabled, the orchestration of a national witch-hunt and purge of Labour Leftists (above all those said to be tainted by Trotskyism) was not possible.

In the afterglow of the epochal defeats inflicted by Thatcher, it fell to Labour's leadership to detoxify the Labour brand for the liberal middle classes who had deserted it. This project was supported by a union leadership which had swerved sharply to the right, enjoining a 'new realism' according to which unions should seek harmonious relations with all governments, and take a more conciliatory line with employers. This doctrine, unavailing when it was initially unveiled in 1983, proved ideal for a union leadership desperate to avoid conflict after the mauling visited on the miners. And it sufficed for Neil Kinnock, as he and his allies executed an often shambolic, unconvincing retreat from anything which could be considered a left-wing policy, from full employment to unilateral nuclear disarmament.

In a sense, it is difficult to see what else Kinnock could have done. 'Everyone agreed' that these were the steps necessary to make Labour electable, the only worthwhile objective from his point of view. Of course, nothing is ever so simple or so innocent. There were many conceivable ways of being electable, and there was little evidence that the major problem was Labour's core ideological commitments on redistribution, public ownership and welfare. The evidence is that the social attitudes of the majority of people moved significantly *to the left* under Thatcher.[58] Further, the route to electability chosen by the Labour leadership was one congruent with a long-standing strategic perspective on the party's Right, extending back to Gaitskell and company. The problem was that it ultimately meant that Labour dedicated itself to preserving a settlement in which several of the bases of its potential power had been eviscerated. Whatever the 'little caesars of social democracy'[59] may have imagined, Labour's entire basis was the organised working class whom Thatcher had weakened through her fanatical assaults on the industrial base and anti-union laws. Labour and the TUC, however, agreed to accept the majority of the changes wrought by the Tories in the realm of industrial relations. Further, as Labour continued to flounder, it looked for innovative new ways in which it could surrender the instruments of statecraft, ceding one policy area after another to the Thatcherites, such that – accepting the market and competition as the *grundnorms* of any governing politics – it was eventually clear that Labour was left to do little more than humanise what was left to them. Finally, Labour conceded the ideological terrain. In order to explain their electoral difficulties, they began to argue that workers were too comfortably off to support a left-wing programme, too affluent to buy into the language of class solidarity. Left-wing intellectuals who supported the Kinnock leadership fancied that workers had been undergoing a process of 'embourgeoisement'. As Thatcher sought to exclude the very idea of class as a political reference, deriding it as a 'communist concept', Kinnock's team offered a helping hand by replacing such concepts with the market-friendly language of consumers and communities.

By the time Thatcher's reign was finally surrendering to its inner termites, the 'Poll Tax' debacle merely underlining the extent to which her insurgent rightism had become counterproductive for both the business class and her party, Labour's timidity was preventing it from pressing home any advantage handed to it. Thatcher had sought to relieve middle-class taxpayers of as much of the burden of paying for services as possible with the policy of rate-capping. When that initiative reached its limits, the government introduced a Community Charge, a regressive tax that took no account of ability to pay. Here was an issue which suddenly handed Labour majorities, rather than just pluralities, in opinion polls. The voters who had deserted the party to support the SDP–Liberal alliance now appeared ready to return in droves, alongside a swathe of disaffected Conservatives. Labour seemingly had only to remain firm in opposition to the tax in order to preserve the advantage. The problem they faced, however, was that the areas where opposition to the tax was most concentrated were working-class boroughs run by Labour councils. There, the leadership demanded that councils take an unyielding line against non-payment. Just as Neil Kinnock had advocated a 'dented shield' strategy for Labour councils struggling to fund local services in the face of rate-capping, urging that local authorities set strictly legal budgets within the parameters set by the government, so Labour now sought to burnish its constitutionalist credentials by prosecuting non-payers. *The Tribune*, a magazine of the party's soft Left, argued that those Labour members who supported the non-payment campaign represented the 'biggest threat' to Labour's electoral advantage.

Indeed, Labour's commanding poll lead was gradually frittered away, but not because of non-payment. Rather, two developments served to consolidate the Tories' position and allowed alarmed Liberals to return to their party fold. First, John Major replaced Margaret Thatcher as leader, and began to orchestrate a cautious row back from the worst aspects of the Community Charge, while also charting a less confrontational course for the government. While Kinnock attempted to represent Thatcherism-with-a-human-face, he was easily outbid in that necrophilic auction by Major. Second, as in 1982, Britain went to war in Iraq and the response in parliament, the media and much of public opinion was one of jingoistic pride. The majority of Labour MPs, the parliamentary party having rarely passed up on the chance to display its patriotism, were adamantly in favour of the UK's participation in Desert Storm. Only a few opposed with any vim, and the net result was that Major accumulated the political capital of victory in Baghdad without being even slightly inconvenienced by his opposite number.

Labour went into the 1992 election having purged themselves of left-wing policies, centralised power in the hands of the leadership in order to marginalise constituency activists, and embraced modern methods of communication. With Peter Mandelson and Philip Gould's Shadow Communications Agency setting the tone, they sought to spell out a moderate Labour message, highlighting the need for investment in public services, above all health. As recession ate away at the Tories' economic advantage, and the Community Charge continued to provoke resistance, polls tended to put Labour ahead. Everything was surely in place: Kinnock and his allies had cleaned up the party image, expelled the militants, put manners on the Left, dismantled the last trace of 'municipal socialism', displayed loyalty in war and constitutional integrity in peace, and now stood ready to welcome back prodigal voters. The Conservatives once again returned to government, with their vote barely changed at 42 per cent. Nothing Kinnock had done was adequate to make Labour palatable to southern middle classes, nor to win back the chunks of their old electoral coalition who had defected to the Liberal/SDP alliance after 1981. The party saw only a miserly, 3.6 per cent increase in their vote share. This, for a party which had done everything, gone to all lengths, to expunge any trace of radicalism and accept the terms of its opponents, was a defining trauma. The country, most members seem to have concluded, was just too right-wing for even the most timid reform agenda. It was not clear whether Labour would ever govern again. Wallowing in a sump of defeat, the party was easy prey for the coming Blairite takeover.

The Unavoidable Dilemmas of Social Democracy

For most of the twentieth century, Labour was the unrivalled mass party of the British working class. Although it never achieved more than two thirds of the working-class vote, no other party of the Left came close to challenging its dominance. Further, barring the Communist Party, which organised a small minority of militants, Labour was the party where most socialists were organised. As such, if the labour movement and their socialist allies largely failed to achieve their far-reaching objectives, the question must be asked as to how Labour has organised and moulded them, and what opportunities it has given members to challenge the status quo.

Without exception, Labour has cleaved to its constitutionalist, electoral roots. It has disowned the radicalism of its members and union affiliates more often than it has allowed them expression. While it has depended on militant members to build and maintain its social movement base, it has excluded them from effective decision-making as far as possible, and in office it has usually taken the lead from civil servants and business. Insofar as it was a coalition between organised labour, socialists and liberals, it has been the union moderates, Fabians and professional liberals who have usually been dominant. It is too simple to characterise Labour as 'the working-class wing of Liberalism', but the liberal legacy has usually been dominant.

Labour's climax, the high point of post-war reform, was achieved in a quite exceptional set of circumstances that were already breaking down by the time the Wilson era was afoot. The availability of business for a class consensus depended both on its need for extensive government intervention to keep capitalism alive and its ability, in the era of national capitalisms, to accept the state as an interlocutor with organised labour. The ability of social democratic governments to deliver reforms in the interests of workers, moreover, depended on an exceptional period of capitalist growth that will probably not be seen again, short of an economic disaster or war that destroys enough capital to create a space for rapid expansion. As soon as that growth no longer obtained, and once the scale of production was sufficiently institutionalised to expose large corporations to competitive pressures that previously had been experienced only by small business, the post-war compromise was doomed.

If it was to survive as a reforming party, Labour needed to find a way to channel popular discontent with the old order – of which it had become the caretaker – into a project to assail the concentrated and increasingly organised power of business. It needed to outflank a popular media that was increasingly dominated by Thatcherism. And it needed to demonstrate that it could offer a new way of doing politics that shrugged off the domesticating constraints of statecraft. Moreover, with the loss of the colonial empire, the rise of Scottish and Welsh nationalisms and the evident shortcomings in parliamentary democracy, the British state was in need of an overhaul which Labour – being wedded to 'Britishness', and the artificial monopoly on left-of-centre political expression that first-past-the-post gave it – was rarely inclined to consider. The Left, for very brief moments, sometimes had the initiative, but never the adequate power, to impose its own solutions. It could never demonstrate sufficient support within the party, let alone in national electoral terms, to transform Labour into a more radical vehicle. And given that the peak of its strategic perspective was the election of Labour governments, it was necessarily trapped by its own logic – a radical-Left programme rarely has enough support, given normal British psephological realities, to win office. Of course, conditions in Britain today are far from normal. However, even if the radical Left was admitted to government, the evidence is that its real problems would begin at that point. For most of the time, the pressure on Labour has been to move in the opposite direction, not just away from socialism, but increasingly away from the sorts of politics that would once have been mainstream – and that pressure has come from within as much as from without.

The problems that Jeremy Corbyn's team inherits are not just the problems of New Labour's party managers and whips, not just the problems of an enervated 'modernising' project, and not just the problems of a party leadership damaged by the credit crunch. Labour embodies in its make-up and in its traditions a way of doing politics that for the Left has largely been an experience of failure. For Corbyn to take this institution and transform it into a means to make radical inroads on Britain's power systems would require resources, organisation and opportunities that currently don't present themselves. This is not to claim that Corbyn can achieve nothing with this experience, or that his supporters will gain nothing from it. But they are best placed to do so if they are sober about the tremendous obstacles facing them.

4

New Labour and Corbyn's Route to Power

Division among radicals almost 100 years ago resulted in a twentieth century dominated by Conservatives. I want the twenty-first century to be the century of the radicals.

> – Tony Blair, almost a century after
> the foundation of the Labour Party[1]

He's sold out before he's even got there ... Tax, health, education, unions, full employment, race, immigration ... It won't matter if we win, the bankers and stockbrokers have got us already, by the fucking balls, laughing their heads off.

> – Neil Kinnock on Tony Blair[2]

It is, of course, too easy to pin all the blame on the Blairites for the enfeebled Labour Party that Jeremy Corbyn inherited in 2015. But it's nonetheless striking how reluctant they are to take *any* responsibility, or reflect on the fact that they more than anyone else prepared the ground for Corbyn's victory. Asked why she had lost to Corbyn, the Blairite candidate Liz Kendall admitted that her campaign lacked inspiration, suggesting that she had been the 'eat your greens candidate'.[3]

The self-serving nature of such a view is obvious: it says nothing about the record of her political tendency, both in and out of office, and represents the leadership election as a vague battle between sensible moderation and vivid exhortation. But if a relatively unknown candidate from the hard Left can be so rapidly propelled from nowhere to the top, at a minimum this demands scrutiny of the formerly dominant faction and what they left behind.

What sort of beast was New Labour? Led by Tony Blair, effectively an SDP viper in the Labour breast, it seemed neither entirely new, nor entirely Labour. Yet, the speed and facility with which Blair and his allies took over the party machinery during a few months in 1994, gutted its constitution, banished even a nominal commitment to socialism (the 'marketisation' of Clause Four), at least suggests that this tendency had been incubated within the party for some time. The communitarian moralism abetted by the staccato stock of Blairite conjugations ('rights and responsibilities', 'firm but fair', 'fairness not favours' etc.), was not entirely novel. Nor were the 'ethical' pieties, the liberal cynosures or the elevation of 'nation' above 'class'. The Labour Left was outmanoeuvred on every front, resigning itself to the miserable hope that government would at least allow a mitigation of the worst of Toryism, yet it seemed at all points to inhabit roughly the same party as before.

Few left-wingers expected what was to come; that even those policy nostrums with which New Labour defined itself in opposition – for example, opposition to Private Finance Initiatives, resistance to Michael Howard's anti-immigrant legislation, or reversing the sell-off of Air Traffic Control – would be ditched once government was secured. Far less could they anticipate the vindictive attacks on welfare, targeting single mothers and the disabled, or the revival of that old familiar tincture of moral imperialism in alliance with a right-wing US administration. But there was little sign of organised rebellion against these policies within the party. Did that signify that Labour as it had once existed no longer did, or that the party had just returned to some very old, recognisable Labour roots?

There was at least one thing that could be said for the claim of novelty on Blair's part. If Labour's relationship to the working class had always been complicated, New Labour – like the Oedipal child – sought to deny its own vulgar parentage, and disown as far as possible the movement which gave birth to it. Blair often gave the impression that he thought the very formation of Labour as a party separate from Liberalism had been a mistake. He seemed to want to break Labour's founding relationship with organised labour, and to create a party much like the Democratic Party in the United States to whom the unions could plead for favours like any other client. In that sense, New Labour could be seen simply as the triumph of an old, predominantly middle-class liberal current, previously led by Roy Jenkins. Yet, Blair did not succeed in breaking the union link, and the unions did not act against him. Whatever was

new about New Labour, it remained in some vital respects
a very traditional social democratic party.

And what should not be missed is that, however much
New Labour now stands condemned in the eyes of most
Labour members and voters, it once conveyed power and
purpose, and intellectual conviction, something that was
extremely seductive for the traumatised survivors of four
successive Tory election victories. Tens of thousands of
members, and many more voters, appear to have been genuinely enthused by New Labour – easy to forget, in an era
when Blairite MPs look and sound like dull building society
managers.

New Labour in Theory and Practice

New Labour strategists and intellectuals are sometimes
given to borrowing the language and concepts of the
Sardinian Marxist Antonio Gramsci. Among the key ideas
they took from Gramsci was the concept of 'hegemony',
which is a form of power that goes beyond force and violence. A hegemonic group doesn't just dominate, it sets a
moral agenda, it is ideologically persuasive, and it draws
others toward it by taking their interests into account. In
Gramsci's terms, this was intended to be an explanation
for how industrial workers could win leadership in a broad
class alliance with peasants and others. But for New Labour
intellectuals, it came to refer to a narrow party-political
objective, of shaping an electoral agenda and winning a
parliamentary majority. The justifications for New Labour
as a successful 'hegemonic' project[4] coming from the likes

of former health secretary John Reid and former Blair speech-writer Peter Hyman are not, in this sense, a one-off. The intellectual origins of New Labour can be traced, in part, to an assortment of soft-Left intellectuals, many of them either residing in the Communist Party or in its orbit, and usually writing for the journal *Marxism Today*.[5]

These ranged from heavyweights such as cultural theorist Stuart Hall and historian Eric Hobsbawm, to figures such as management guru Charles Leadbeater and policy adviser Geoff Mulgan. Espousing a version of Gramscian Marxism, they tended to argue that the foundations of the old Left – which they derided as economistic, class-reductionist, expecting militant revival at every turn – had been eroded in the post-war world and were now being blown away by global capitalism. Even at the peak of socialist consciousness, they argued, the British working class had never been as unanimously left-wing as its continental equivalents. And now with the rise of consumerist individualism, the decline of trade union organisation and the decay of the old social democratic order, the radical Right was expanding the fill the spaces that neither socialism nor social democracy seemed able to. Thatcherism could tap into certain popular pleasures in the market, while mobilising popular discontent with the social democratic state.

In all, they noted, a great shift in capitalist civilisation had taken place. Economies were now global rather than national, the mass media was increasingly tending toward twenty-four-hour coverage, the working class was fragmenting and identities were increasingly plural. These changes, they collectively labelled 'New Times'.[6] And in these 'New Times', a Left that stuck to the old remedies could not win 'hegemony' in the working class, let alone command across a broad class alliance for socialism. It was on this basis that they led a vitriolic charge against the hard Left, seeking their exclusion in a realignment of forces for a modernised Left.[7]

Though much of what the *Marxism Today* intellectuals said was luminous and prescient, above all when it came with Hall's suave, seductive and assured voice, at least a similar quotient was charlatanry, bullshit and self-fulfilling prophesy. The critique of the Left's cultural oblivious-ness, the theorisation of a new capitalism and the role of consumption and new forms of individualism in it, segued often into a kind of cheerleading for this new state of affairs and the bold energies it seemed to unleash. If Stuart Hall and Martin Jacques could recognise the danger of a Labour Government embracing a 'brand of New Times' that was just a 'slightly cleaned up' version of the radical Right, this was in part because their own intellectual project was a little too entranced by Thatcherite dynamism, and a great deal too scornful of Thatcher's most belligerent opponents. And although these same intellectuals would later reject New Labour as a form of warmed-over Thatcherism, it is well to remember that they had initially welcomed Blair and his reforming zeal.[8]

What became the intellectual foundation of New Labour, then, was in some respects a dilute rip-off of the most vacuous elements of 'New Times' thinking – above all the celebration of designer global capitalism. And indeed, some of the leading figures from that intellectual milieu, such as Mulgan and Leadbeater, were integrated into the New Labour policymaking elite. Another crucial phase of New Labour thinking was pivoted on the ideas associated with the sociologist Anthony Giddens and his prospectus for a 'Third Way', 'beyond left and right'. For Giddens, the centre-Left had to abandon ideas of redistribution, and the traditional uses of welfare. It had to abandon equality for meritocracy, wherein the role of the state would be to attack the forms of exclusion that prevented people from participating fully in meritocratic competition. It had to embrace consumption as a key means by which people organised their identities. It had to accept globalisation as a necessary process, while seeking to manage the risks. Perhaps Giddens's most distinctive contribution was to argue that the relationship between the welfare state and the class structure had fundamentally changed. 'Welfare dependency', that reactionary old cliché, was dusted down in Giddens's account and given a centre-Left gloss. Instead of welfare being a safety net to prevent poverty in the event of market failure, it had increasingly become an impediment to people getting out of poverty, and a means of social exclusion. Welfare thus had to be reformed in order to lever people out of this dependency and into paid work. One of the key ideas embraced by Tony Blair in an effort to stress the novelty of New Labour, therefore, was that of 'workfare' – an idea that came with a distinctive note of moralism, as the emphasis shifted from welfare as a citizenship right, to welfare as a privilege gained in exchange for proving certain moral bona fides such as a willingness to work.

There is also the distinctive formation of Blair himself to take into account. Although he had claimed in correspondence to Michael Foot that he 'came to Socialism through Marxism',[9] it seems rather unlikely that he had ever come within a country mile of either. Nothing he has ever said or done indicates the presence of such formative influences, and the most realistic explanation seems to be Labour historian Martin Pugh's, that Blair entered politics 'as an impressionable and largely non-political young man', that he gravitated to those with power and success, and that his attraction to 'fairly extreme right-wingers' such as Bush, Berlusconi, Aznar and Sarkozy was in part a reflection of his formation in a Conservative family and in part a reflection of his susceptibility to power.[10]

One of the things that was meant by New Labour, moreover, was that it was a fundamentally different kind of party to that which had been known. As the former *Marxism Today* intellectuals astutely argued, Labour had been 'running, ever since Neil Kinnock's election to the leadership, mainly against itself. Key speeches to party and trade union audiences have nearly always emphasised departures from traditional party thinking, and taken the form of public demonstrations ... of how different New Labour was from what had gone before'.[11] The dramatic dropping of one social-democratic nostrum after another was the main policy mood music, culminating in the symbolic change to Clause IV of the constitution, wherein the rigours of the market were to be the main instrument of delivering fairness. But the party itself also had to change.

The centre of power in the Labour Party had never been the constituency membership. In the party's classically federal structure, in which individual members were one component alongside trade unions and various socialist societies, the main power had traditionally been invested in the union leaders. At national conference, after 1918, unions had cast 2,471,000 votes, as compared to 115,000 cast by constituency branches, and 48,000 cast by socialist societies. Through the first experiences of office, the weight of power began to shift to the parliamentary leadership, but this didn't necessarily trouble the union leadership, which understood the need for firm party management, and whose interests were usually congruent with those of the party elite. What is more, managers of both unions and the party tended to converge on their view of the constituency membership as a control problem, being filled with middle-class idealists and unreliable socialists. They were useful to connect to the electorate, but otherwise to be kept away from decision-making.[12] Hence, unions for most of the twentieth century provided the party leadership with a reliable ally, and ensured the unshakeable dominance of the Right and centre over the party machinery.

This was the core of the old Labour Right's power in the organisation. But it had begun to slowly enter into a crisis in the 1960s, in part because the union leaderships began to move to the left, and in part because the social-democratic compact was breaking down. By the 1970s, a section of the party's right-wing was convinced that unions themselves were the problem, rather than their best ally. And by the early 1980s, the party had seen several union leaders line up behind Tony Benn's radical socialist candidacy for deputy leader. Not only that, but thanks to the trade union influence, the National Executive Committee, traditionally controlled by the party's right-wing, had been increasingly populated by the Left – something that the right-wing backlash of the 1980s had only partially succeeded in fixing.[13] The new Labour Right wanted a different kind of power base and, to that purpose, had been enjoying a longing look abroad, at the Democratic Party of the United States. The 'American Tendency' in the Labour Party, as it was dubbed by Robin Ramsay, had always been strong, but it was in the course of early 1990s junkets funded by US businesses that Blair and Brown had begun to forge their alliances with the 'New Democrats'.[14] There was a party in which a dynamic layer of 'New Democrats' was coming to the fore, ready to swing their party hard to the right and bring the grass-roots activists to heel, in order to win. There, the unions had their proper place: as subordinate clients, donors who might be able to buy a few concessions but who had little say in policymaking or internal power struggles. The founders of New Labour convinced themselves and those around them that the union influence in the Labour Party had been a major cause of the party's ongoing electoral difficulties, despite psephological studies providing little evidence for this.[15]

Blair and his allies – Mandelson, Brown, Campbell, and Gould – set about radically reorganising the Labour Party and transferring power to the top and centre of the organisation. The first change was to consolidate the powers of the leadership, which was seen as both an electoral asset insofar as it helped project Blair's telegenic image. It was also construed as being more democratic, insofar as the leadership would be more responsive to popular opinion, as gauged in polls and focus groups, than the unrepresentative party membership. Finally, it would help the leadership secure the support of business and the City, if the membership were seen to be under firm control. The second major change was to the annual conference. Increasingly stage-managed debates took the place of actual policymaking, which was shifted to the National Policy Forum. This was linked to the third change, in which the union block vote was replaced with a voting procedure inaccurately dubbed 'One Member One Vote' (OMOV). In fact, the new system was based on an electoral college in which each MP's vote had the same weight as thousands of members votes. A genuine OMOV system was not used until the 2015 leadership election. Alongside these constitutional changes, the Blairites proved extremely adept at managing and neutralising NEC discussions, and intervening in selection procedures for parliamentary candidates. With the internal lobby group Progress backing them up and with funding from Lord Sainsbury, they successfully parachuted candidates in to safe seats, to ensure that the parliamentary party more closely aligned with the leadership.[16]

The scale of the changes wrought in Labour were all the more remarkable because the actual number of Blairites in the party, even in the parliamentary party, was quite small. The pro-Blair columnist Martin Kettle estimated the number in parliament at perhaps a dozen MPs.[17] They were always operating as a minority vanguard, and would not have been remotely as effective had it not been for the demoralisation of the entire party. Yet, in their way, they merely continued the lines of political and organisational change already signalled under Neil Kinnock, whose hoarding of leadership power and attempt to isolate and disempower the constituency and union base in the interests of 'electability' was the prototype upon which Blair's reign was fashioned.[18]

New Labour in Power

While the Blairites adapted Labour culturally, politically and organisationally to the success of Thatcherism, there had been a growing revolt against it among some of its former supporters, particularly after a major economic debacle in 1992, in which the Major administration attempted to pilot Britain into the European Exchange Rate Mechanism (ERM), only to find it had to support the currency's value with soaring interest rates. This underlined the economic insecurity that the Conservatives had brought even to some traditionally comfortable middle-class layers. Almost nothing in the interim between 'Black Wednesday' in 1992, when the UK crashed out of the ERM, and the general election in May 1997, altered or reversed the huge shift in a critical section of the electorate. The Conservatives languished at around 30 per cent in the polls, while Labour tended to poll in the low forties. Labour's biggest gains in 1997 were among (white-collar and middle-class) AB voters, while it actually saw a small decline in its support from ('unskilled' and unemployed) DE voters.

What New Labour would do with power was not entirely clear at this point. In an era in which the very power of national governments to deliver reforms was under question, the Blairites gainsaid the question. The traditional range of reforms was barely aimed for, while the word 'reform' itself was captured for purposes entirely contrary to social-democratic traditions: for example, the application of market 'efficiency' to even those treasured and sentimentalised achievements of Labour's past. The legacy inherited by the incoming government was bleak. At the foundation was an economy that lacked competitiveness, whose share of global trade had plummeted, and whose manufacturing base was withering. The UK economy was disproportionately pivoted on finance and commerce, something that the Major administration had struggled to rectify but without the requisite policy instruments. In the interstices of economic decline there had arisen unprecedented levels of poverty and, despite the increasingly broad diffusion of multicultural sensibilities, much of it was concentrated among ethnic minorities who had been forced into urban enclaves by a combination of council policy and white racism. Income inequality had risen faster in the UK than in any comparable industrialised country. In the rush to home ownership and sales of council housing, the housing stock had been left to crumble in large areas of the country. The falling value of pensions meant that a growing number of pensioners were in poverty.[19]

New Labour's instrument for dealing with this legacy was what Gordon Brown called 'post-monetarist economics'. This entailed a rejection of Keynesian demand-management techniques, and an acceptance of the doctrine of the 'non-accelerating inflation rate of unemployment' (NAIRU), according to which spending to create jobs was likely to drive up inflation to unsustainable levels. Mainstream economists argued that the 'natural' rate of unemployment was approximately 5 per cent. Brown's strategy was to reduce that level through supply-side measures intended to make hiring more attractive to employers. This could be done by reducing taxes on profits, cutting taxes on employment and even subsidising employment in certain conditions. It also involved maintaining strong anti-union laws to reduce the bargaining power of labour, investing to increase the skills and productivity of workers. Gordon Brown, recognising this, placed particular emphasis on skilling up labour.

Thus, New Labour reduced corporation taxes and small business taxes, kept most of the anti-union laws in place, and introduced various schemes such as the 'New Deal' which were intended to skill-up workers and pay employers to give them work experience. There is not much evidence of success on this front. Employment rose, in general, despite continued low productivity, and expansion was predicated on low-skilled labour.[20] Aside from this, there was little progressive about such supply-side strategies. Improving workers' skills may be a good strategy for business but, on its own, would simply raise the supply of skilled workers and thus depress the cost of labour. And indeed, the imperative to keep labour cheap and flexible shaped and limited many of the measures Labour implemented to satisfy their base – a minimum wage was introduced in the spring of 1999 but at a pitiably low level of £3.60 for adults, some of the worst anti-union controls were repealed but the majority were kept in place, and Labour continued to seek UK opt-outs from EU labour codes.

Spending was also constrained by the promise that taxes on higher income earners and company profits would be kept low, such that corporation tax was cut from the first budget. Further, borrowing was constrained by Gordon Brown's 'golden rule' identified in his first budget – 'over the economic cycle the Government will borrow only to invest'.[21] Given the attempts by Conservatives to claim that Labour 'overspending' produced the deficit – barely contested by Labour – it is important to outline the facts of how Blair and Brown managed spending. In New Labour's first term, from 1997 to 2001, the top priority was not public investment but establishing credibility with financial markets by reducing government debt. The debt was reduced by a total of £34bn in the last year of New Labour's first term – a larger total reduction than all the cumulative debt reduction of previous governments for fifty years. This meant that investment in most government departments fell precipitously for the first years of the New Labour administration. Overall public spending fell from over 40 per cent of GDP in 1997 to 38.1 per cent in 2001. Even with successive fiscal problems in the ensuing years and a subsequent need to borrow to plug black holes, by 2004 Gordon Brown had reduced the debt from 44 per cent of national income to 34 per cent. By 2005, the combined spending on debt interest and unemployment benefits had fallen by a half. In the latter half of the 2000s, public spending would rise to above 40 per cent again, reaching 41.1 per cent in 2007–08. Only with the credit crunch and ensuing recession did it return to levels last seen in Thatcher's first two terms, rising to 47.5 per cent of GDP for 2009–10. The deficit that arose resulted from the reduction in the tax base as unemployment soared and the economy shrank, along with the massive bailouts for the financial sector.[22]

Nor could such investment as was provided be disaggregated from the wider policy framework guiding its use. It was one thing for the government to boast of monies for new hospitals and schools, but the most immediately obvious and visible way that it chose to invest these was in futile semi-privatisation schemes, in which private contractors were given lucrative thirty-year contracts to build and maintain services at greatly inflated cost, and with significantly reduced services.[23] Finally, and most importantly, the entire model of investment depended upon the economic growth provided by a booming financial sector and soaring consumer spending. As soon as that growth model no longer availed, the basis for New Labour's cautious experiments in social democracy was gone.

Work, Flag and Family

The government's economic policy dovetailed with a social moralism that shaped both its welfare and its penal policies. Since, after all, the government was providing 'opportunity' and removing the sources of 'exclusion', any lingering resistance to inclusion on these terms had to be the result of welfare dependency or other behaviours needing discipline. As Gordon Brown put it in his first budget, anticipating the current government's language on workfare, since Labour was offering young people the chance of paid work or training, 'benefits will be cut' for anyone refusing to 'take up the opportunities'. This was also related to the government's obsession with proving its pro-family bona fides. Like any Conservative, Blair tended to locate the blame for social problems in the decay of the family. In Mandelson and Liddle's account of the forma- tion of New Labour, they quote Blair's explanation of the Jamie Bulger killing that it was undoubtedly a result of the 'breakdown in family life'. Later, the government would also add the string of 'Britishness' to its bow, arguing that to be included was to be integrated into a core of – always vaguely defined – British values. This produced a strange effect. On the face of it, New Labour was cosmopolitan, socially progressive and averse to bigotry. Its abolition of Section 28, opposed by Conservatives who would blush to admit it today, seemed to signal the arrival of, dixit John Major, 'a nation at ease with itself'. Yet in many respects New Labour's model of social inclusion, guided by the virtues of work, flag and family, reflected the social values of a provincial fifties suburb.[24]

Social policy under New Labour put a premium on the promotion of 'paid work' as the critical means of social inclusion. The shift on the spectrum from welfare to work- fare, part of a long-developing consensus among governing elites since the 1980s, was necessarily also a shift from safety net to discipline. Surprisingly, despite cleaving to social values more typically liberal than Blair's, the centre-Left press was at times an important ally for New Labour on

this front. For example, when Blair, shortly before his resignation, planned policies cutting welfare for jobless single
parents and introducing agencies to 'nudge' benefits claim-
ants back to work, the *Observer* was there to cast this as
another example of Blair's magic rapport with some mythi-
cal, mysterious creature named 'Asda Woman'.[25] Likewise,
when the government first floated workfare – later implemented fully as a Conservative policy – the liberal columnist
Polly Toynbee was among its most vociferous champions:
'The Tories were right,' she announced, 'workfare really
works.'[26] Nor did Labour stop once it had started. Having
immediately cut benefits for single mothers after being
elected with a landslide, in a policy graciously left to Harriet
Harman to steward through parliament, it was soon going
after the disabled and future retirees. Cynically, one might
applaud such measures if they did 'work' on their own
terms. In fact, where New Labour did succeed in reducing forms of poverty it was through surreptitious forms of
spending and targeted benefits increases.[27] Total employment continually climbed until the credit crunch, but there
is no evidence that benefit cuts or the threat thereof had any
significant impact.

In addition to welfare cuts and inducements to take paid
employment, the government looked for ways to discipline and erase forms of bad behaviour that it claimed were
eroding families and communities and contributing to
social exclusion. With curfews and Anti-Social Behaviour
Orders, the government set about criminalising otherwise
perfectly lawful behaviour. Often the law was strange and
nasty in application: a boy with Tourette's syndrome was

given an ASBO for swearing. Another man was threatened with an ASBO for joking about the death of the Pope. A boy was ASBOd for the grievous offence of wearing a hoodie. And as if to underline just how callous and perverse the law was, a woman with noted suicidal tendencies was given an ASBO forbidding her from going near railway lines or multistorey car parks.[28] The definition of 'anti-social behaviour' was so vague that practically any behaviour could be subject to such an order, and any citizen could thus end up threatened with prison for non-compliance. New Labour developed such confidence in its measures that, toward the end of his reign, Blair began to suggest that the government could pre-emptively intervene to prevent the children of problem families from becoming a 'menace to society' – a form of intervention that could even take place 'pre-birth'.[29] Finally, if parents of children acting 'anti-socially' refused government help, there were to be 'parenting orders' mandating forcible state intervention to nudge them along.[30]

This was linked to two developments, one in the scale of repression, and one in the tenor of popular culture. First, to enforce the new disciplinary order, police numbers, as well as the rate of imprisonment in the UK, both soared under New Labour. Thatcher increased police numbers from just shy of 110,000 to approximately 125,000. Under Major, police numbers remained relatively flat. Under New Labour, police numbers increased from 125,051 in March 1997 to 141,631 in March 2010.[31] The prison population almost doubled from 44,386 in June 1993 to 86,048 in June 2012.[32] One notable result of all this was a surge in prison overcrowding and a dramatic increase in prison riots and

hostage-taking in jails.[33] Second, under New Labour the
consensus on welfare and redistribution shifted sharply to
the right.[34] The demonisation of the poor, the rise of stereo-
types about council estate dwellers, single mothers, 'feral'
teens and 'chavs' was the logical terminus to which New
Labour's ideological thrust moved Britain – and on such
terrain, neither the Tories nor UKIP have had much difficulty making gains.

Logically enough, Blair's particular emphasis on the
institution of the family also segued into a racial authoritarianism, as in his final days in office he decided to leave his
mark by identifying 'black culture' as the cause of a series
of knife and gun murders in the capital: 'we won't stop this
by pretending it isn't young black kids doing it'. In particular, New Labour was concerned that the breakdown of
black family life had given rise to a generation of children
without appropriate parental discipline. Here, the government once again pushed the boundaries of debate to the
right, helped along by some in the race relations industry,
such as the New Labour-friendly Commission for Racial
Equality, who backed Blair's speech.[35] There had developed, since the 1980s, a consensus on multiculturalism and
anti-racism which for all its flaws had constrained previous
Conservative administrations. In an effort to render race
a politically manageable problem, the discourse of multiculturalism sought to create a well-defined representational
space for each 'culture', wherein selected representatives
of each supposedly discrete entity would be given access to
funding and influence in exchange for their role in securing
political quiescence.

Though New Labour had no intention of rowing back from the practice, the cultural consensus it produced posed certain problems for a government seeking to outflank the Tories on the issue of immigration, and subsequently to discipline British Asians following the 2001 northern riots. Jack Straw, as Home Secretary, cheerfully vilified Roma gypsies as troublemakers who 'think that it's perfectly OK for them to cause mayhem in an area, to go burgling, thieving, breaking into vehicles, causing all kinds of other trouble including defecating in the doorways of firms and so on'.[36] Notably, the invocation of misplaced excrement as a symptom of multicultural disorder had previously found its way into Enoch Powell's 'Rivers of Blood' speech.

Later, in setting up a network of detention centres for asylum seekers and replacing cash benefits with stigmatising vouchers, Straw went further than the previous Home Secretary Michael Howard had dared. Those detention centres have notoriously become routine sites of human rights abuses. David Blunkett demanded that British Asians should speak English in their own homes, proposed a 'Britishness test' for immigrants, and signalled that 'multiculturalism' was over. New Labour-friendly intellectuals, such as David Goodhart and Trevor Phillips, gave this ideological shift a neo-Powellite gloss, drawing on the culturalist racism of the New Right. Phillips declared multiculturalism over, demanding of minorities 'integration' to shared values which were always just on the brink of being discovered. Goodhart argued that the existence of wide varieties of people culturally too dissimilar undermined the basis for the welfare state, since few would willingly pay into the pot to help people who were different: 'most of us prefer our own kind'.[37] In place of many cultures, there was to be 'Britishness' and a demand that all 'cultures' assimilate to this core of national being. In place of challenging racism and the disadvantages it brought to minorities, there was to be victim-blaming, and unfounded claims that British Asians were 'self-segregating'.[38] As all of this took place, unsurprisingly, so did a renewed surge in racist violence and harassment. Between 1996 and 1997 and 2003 and 2004, racial incidents more than quadrupled in England and Wales from 13,151 in 1996–97 to 52,694.[39]

Disillusionment and Demoralisation

As Labour approached the 2001 general election, Blair was in a characteristically strident mood. Everywhere, opinion polls told him that his major policy of public sector reform, the Private Finance Initiative (PFI), was deeply unpopular. Analyses suggested that such policies were costly boondoggles giving favoured private enterprises access to grotesque amounts of public money for new hospitals and schools or renovations that were far more cheaply done in the public sector. Worse, they resulted in poorer services, as PFI hospitals tended to have fewer staff and fewer beds. In every conceivable respect, the policy was a disaster.[40] Labour was no longer just running against itself and its own social-democratic instincts. It was also running against the British public, to the extent that they shared those instincts. Blair decided that PFIs were not just another policy, but were the flagship policy for this election, and dared the electorate to oppose him. Of course, given that PFI was originally a Conservative policy, there was little to choose between the big two parties on this issue. Only in one constituency, the marginal Kidderminster seat of Wyre Forest, was a candidate for the makeshift party Health Concern able to capitalise on opposition to PFI and take the seat from Labour. But elsewhere, much of the electorate simply abstained. Turnout plunged to below 60 per cent for the first time since 1918. The biggest drop was in the Labour vote, which fell by just short of 3 million, while the Tory vote dropped by just over a million.

The disillusionment even spread into the quarters of the old Labour Right. Former deputy-leader Roy Hattersley, who can be credited with laying some of the groundwork for New Labour, declared that under Blair the party had not only moved further and ever faster to the right, but had embraced 'an alien ideology'. By replacing the discourse of equality with that of 'meritocracy', it had in effect signed up to 'shifting patterns of inequality'.[41] Urging party members to 'rise up against the coup d'état' against social democracy, he committed himself to an unavailing fight against the Blairites – apparently oblivious of the fact that the battle against the Left, in which he had energetically participated, had also helped decimate the ranks of almost all currents to the left of New Labour within the party. If he now found that old Rightists like him were marginalised, how much more so were the soft Left who had once formed common cause with him? In initiating the reforms of the party structure which centralised more power in the hands of party managers in order to sideline constituency activists, they empowered the clique whose ascension they had done so much to bring about. And in driving out or demoralising some of the most confident and capable militants in the interests of electability, and by forcing through the party's adaptation to Thatcherism, they had compounded the traumas which made the grass roots so susceptible to the Blairite takeover. Unsurprisingly then, none of the grumblings of discontent amounted to a serious challenge to the leadership.

It is quite possible that developments in the trade unions might have led to a rupture in other circumstances. On 11 September 2001, Blair was due to give a speech to delegates at the TUC conference, at which it was expected that he would be given a rough ride over his unseemly determination to force through private sector involvement in public services. There had been, alongside a growing discontent among trade unionists, the beginnings of an ideological radicalisation among a layer of young people, manifest in the anti-capitalist movements. Public opinion, after a series of disasters in the rail network, was overwhelmingly calling for renationalisation.[42] New Labour had failed to secure victory for its London mayoral candidate against the left-of-centre challenger, Ken Livingstone, who was pledged to oppose the Public Private Partnership (PPP) on the Underground.[43] Small chinks in the armour of neo-liberal rule were beginning to open up. Whatever may have happened, however, the attacks on the World Trade Center suddenly shifted the conversation to other matters, and secured a quiet welcome for Blair.[44] While the government remained determined to press ahead with policies that would leave transport, health and education services paying off huge dividends to corporations for decades into the future, the emphasis shifted to the prime minister's allegiance with President Bush, and the wars that were to come.

Public opposition to the first such war, in Afghanistan, was seemingly muted – but already, unexpectedly large public protests signalled what was to come.[45] By the late summer of 2002, as Blair prepared to lead his party to war in Iraq, up to 400,000 people had demonstrated in London.[46] Significantly for New Labour, the build-up to war divided the traditionally pro-Labour press, as the *Mirror* came out against the prime minister while the *Observer* remained fiercely loyalist[47] – even to the point of suppressing explosive stories developed by its leading journalists, such as the news that the CIA considered Bush's 'weapons of mass destruction' line to be a pack of lies, or that the United States had been spying on the UN Security Council. By early February 2003, Blair was faced with the largest popular opposition he had yet faced, with overwhelming opposition to the looming Iraq War signalled by the presence of approximately a million anti-war demonstrators in London.[48] This anti-war movement was remarkable for the fact that, despite the prominence of seasoned Labour left-wingers such as Tony Benn, George Galloway and, of course, Jeremy Corbyn, its massed ranks drew as much from the affluent and professional suburbanites as from the metropolitan Left. Blair drew upon his immense reserves of contumely for public error to issue a counterblast as imperious as it was self-serving. It was, he remarked, wonderful that people could protest in a democracy, much as they could not in Iraq. But in addition to rooting out weapons of mass destruction which Saddam had allegedly concealed in a series of wily desert escapades, the war would bring liberation to an oppressed people. He did not 'seek unpopularity as a badge of honour. But sometimes it is the price of leadership. And the cost of conviction'.[49] As is often the case when political leaders scorn popular will, he evinced a matchless heroism about his purpose, as if true courage was to defend a cause with no more powerful allies than the Ministry of Defence, the major press and broadcasters, the Pentagon, the CIA and the White House.

The presidentialism of Blair's leadership style was exacerbated by his foreign policy belligerence. The role of the prime minister in prosecuting wars is inevitably far greater than in the execution of domestic policy, and Blair did not hesitate to take advantage of this. He was inordinately fond of being seen on the international stage, with world leaders, or among military men, with white shirt-sleeves rolled up, as if he was about to throttle an enemy combatant himself. This Blair, who had proved even more belligerent than a centrist US president in waging Operation Desert Fox in Iraq, and the Kosovo War, who aligned with a hard-Right US president in the invasion of Iraq, and whose astonishing zeal in battling Labour's own supporters now took the form of facing down a mass social movement which went from the inner city estates to the heart of cherished 'Middle England', was the Blair whom much of the commentariat fell in love with.

If there had been any expectation that the dominance

of New Labour would suddenly prove depthless, that the grass roots would rebel, or even that there would be a left-wing split on the model of Continental equivalents – where the senior defections led to the formation of new radical-Left parties – it was disappointed. While Labour Party activists partook fully in the peak of anti-war activity in 2002 and 2003, and Labour banners were even occasionally visible on protests, the party as a whole remained strikingly cohesive. Despite resignations of senior ministers such as Robin Cook, and despite deep unhappiness on the back-benches about the case for war, only one Labour MP would find himself on the outside of the party after the war began. This was George Galloway, who did not choose to leave but was driven out over comments urging Iraqis to fight the invaders and calling on troops to defy orders. Galloway's exit enabled a short-lived alliance of the far Left and Muslim groups to form on an anti-war, left-wing platform, and the political party they formed, Respect, was able to embarrass Labour with a stunning swing in a core East End constituency, while taking sizeable numbers of votes in Birmingham and Leicester. Yet such a ramshackle, fed-eral alliance, overly dominated by certain well-placed egos, was never likely to seriously challenge Labour's heartland dominion on a broader basis, even as its working-class vote eroded.

Meanwhile, the Labour Party conference in 2003 was remarkable for one thing – the absence of Iraq from the discussion, and the torrents of standing ovations for one right-wing speech after another. John Reid was cheered to the rafters for a speech promising to model the NHS on

private health provision. David Blunkett roused conference with a speech attacking the Liberal Democrats from
the populist Right on crime: 'they know just where they
stand. Four square behind the human rights of the perpe-
trator'.[50] And to cap it all, Tony Blair won seven minutes
of applause for a classical strident performance culminating in the line, 'I've not got a reverse gear'. All of this was
manna for the constituency activists, who didn't have to be
hectored into such extraordinary displays of loyalty. Their
fervour was reflected in their votes. As Nick Cohen wrote
in the *Observer*: 'Activists from constituency Labour parties
usually backed Blair by a majority of three-to-one. The
majority never fell below two-to-one, however contentious
the issue. From now on when the whips confront a rebel-
lious Labour backbencher, they will be able to tell him he
isn't standing up for his local party workers but flying in the
face of their express wishes.'[51]

One of the main reasons the war did not enter the formal
debate that year was because the unions played their traditional role in protecting the party leadership on its most
exposed flank, using their block votes to prevent a motion
on the war from being debated. This is not to say that the
unions were happy with the government. The union leaderships acted to spare the government's blushes, because
they saw it as 'their' government. However, New Labour
ministers seemed to take glee in attacking them and inciting
their outrage. Health Minister John Reid was particularly
combative in his speech supporting 'foundation hospitals',
a matter on which he knew the unions would vote against
him. It didn't matter, since conference had long since lost

any serious policymaking authority, and Reid could declare that even if he lost the vote to the unions, he had 'won the argument'. But, while handing the government empty defeats on public sector reform, any motion on war was kept off the agenda, so that Defence Secretary Geoff Hoon could deliver a pro-war sermon to polite applause.[52]

Discontent with New Labour among union leaders therefore bubbled away, with occasional empty threats to withdraw funding or seek out a new political partner, leading to short-lived confrontations which usually fizzled out before a major breach. One such confrontation came to a head in the year after the Iraq War began, over Blair's determination to persist with Private Finance Initiatives and market-based public sector 'reform'. But any chance of this becoming an organised breach between the union leadership and the party leadership was neutralised by the decision of the National Policy Forum in Warwick to offer the unions a series of incentives to remain in the fold. The offer was modest, comprising some employment rights such as restrictions on firing striking workers, and a promised review on the gender pay gap.[53] But this was the classic *quid pro quo* for the unions – squeezing for reforms in exchange for loyalty within the overarching policy framework.

With this agreement under its belt, the anti-war movement still powerful but receding, and the Tories still stuck with an unpopular Thatcher-era relic as their leader, New Labour could go into the next general election with a war treasury supplied by the unions. Despite the localised threats posed by Respect and various anti-war campaigns, the major beneficiaries of Labour's losses, with almost a further million votes gone, were the Liberal Democrats, whose personable and highly regarded leader had taken a wanly anti-war stance for as long as it was convenient.

Brown Fudge

Notwithstanding Blairite obduracy, greatly inflamed in the aftermath of the attacks on London on 7 July 2005 – upon which, Blair gravely informed us, the rules of the game had changed – the beginning of the end of New Labour was becoming gradually visible. There was, for a start, an increasingly broad constituency of left-wingers, liberals, middle-of-the-road Conservatives, and those of a libertarian persuasion, for whom New Labour's statist authoritarianism seemed to be out of control. The extremely broad uses to which anti-terrorist legislation was put, pre-empting the way in which different groups of protesters under Conservative rule were stigmatised as 'terrorist' and 'extremists',[54] was the softer end of a continuum of author-itarian policies that extended through CCTV on Muslim council estates to extraordinary rendition.[55] Twinned with this was a rising arc of Islamophobic provocation from the government and friendly intellectuals. Jack Straw's gra-tuitously public refusal to speak to Muslim constituents in Blackburn who wore the full veil merely punctuated an increasingly febrile climate that led *Guardian* columnist Jonathan Freedland to opine: 'If this onslaught was about Jews, I would be looking for my passport.'[56] In addition, Blair's growing emotional and political affiliation with the hard Right could be seen not just in his friendships with

Bush, Aznar, Berlusconi and Sarkozy, but also in his decision to give wholesale, uncritical support for Israel in its 2006 invasion of Lebanon – a war that was opposed by the majority of Britons. Labour's poll ratings fell to the low thirties for the first time since 1992, while the Conservatives under Cameron had seemingly rebuilt their base to gain the support of about 36 per cent of the voting public.

Blair, who had thus far survived the unprecedented opposition to his decision to invade Iraq, was spared embarrassment at conference over the matter, and suffered no serious parliamentary moves against him through the ensuing years of chaos. Robin Cook, the only anti-war MP with sufficient clout to have a chance of competing for the leadership, died in the summer of 2005. So it was that when conditions finally ripened for Blair's departure, the avowed causes of his ousting were as depoliticised as could be. In 2006, a letter sent by some of the 2001 intake of Labour MPs to Blair suggested that he had been 'an exceptional Labour Prime Minister', but that without a change in the leadership it was 'less likely that we will win the next election'. Tom Watson's resignation letter affirmed the same idea: 'Your leadership has been visionary and remarkable. The party and nation owes you an incalculable debt.' But for the sake of Labour being 're-elected at the next general election', it was time for him to stand down.[57]

Not a single policy or decision of the old regime was criticised by the coup plotters – which was just as well since the man behind the coup, Gordon Brown, was as up to his neck in it as Blair. The turf war between the Blair and Brown factions of New Labour, notwithstanding the vain attempts by pundits and politicians to find an issue of principle between them, seems to have been chiefly about who should lead the project. Brown's oscillation between Hamlet-like procrastination and furious private rages directed at New Labour's co-founder, was a drama without the slightest wider resonance: Brown simply thought that he should inherit the project without debate and without any challenger. And, having worked out a compromise with Blair on the timing of his exit, he was duly inaugurated without any election process, as Labour MPs prevented possible rivals, such as John McDonnell, from even getting on the ballot. Brown's leadership was welcomed with a deep sigh of relief by some ministers, but the relief barely lasted a year. The disillusionment of New Labour apparatchiks with Brown was once more not over any matter of political substance, but had to do with a combination of personal loyalties, ambitions and Brown's apparent strategic blunders. In particular, having failed to call a snap election in 2007, he had seen Labour's poll ratings decline and walked into a major global economic crisis for which Labour had to take responsibility and over which it had limited time to manage. Straw, who had rallied for Brown, later declared that he would have been a better prime minister.[58]

The looming problems with the global economy had not been totally invisible. As early as September 2007, Northern Rock – one of the UK's subprime mortgage lenders – began to appeal to the Bank of England for liquidity support. The sectoral imbalances in the British economy, the weakness of its manufacturing base, pitiful levels of research & development, the ongoing slump in productivity only made up for by long working hours and an expanded workforce, and the housing bubble, had all been apparent for some considerable time before then.[59] All of this, above all the centrality of debt and speculation to the British economic model, made the UK particularly susceptible to the credit crunch when it struck. While the Conservatives are opportunistic in claiming that the economic mess was one made by Labour, their mendacity should not be allowed to obscure the extent to which New Labour created a British haven for banks and speculators.[60] As the crisis struck, Brown's position was suddenly elevated and dignified, whereas it had been increasingly frustrated and diminished beforehand. Having developed his relationships with Washington and Wall Street power-brokers since those hesternal days of the early 1990s, and taken a leading role in negotiating Britain's integration into the Washington Consensus, he was well-placed to take part in the globally orchestrated interventions to prevent a banking collapse and sustain economic demand – a role for which he gained considerable political credit with the electorate. The net effect of these interventions was to heighten the power of the banks: in effect, it was not so much that failing banks were nationalised, as that the Treasury was semi-privatised and put at the disposal of the City.[61] They were to be followed by years of bracing austerity to cover the costs of bailing out the banks, while the underlying financial infrastructure was left more or less intact.[62] Brown at least signalled a mild shift from the New Labour era by raising the top rate of tax for the first time, and declaring the era of fully free markets over. But the phrase 'too little, too late' was rarely more apt: Labour crashed in the 2010 general election, with 29 per cent of the vote, the lowest share it had received since 1918.

As the New Labour project teetered on the brink of collapse, there was one group of people on whom it had made a great impression: the Tory modernisers. *Times* columnist and later Tory minister Michael Gove was one such, who expostulated, 'I can't hold it back any more – I love Tony.' The Cameron wing of the Conservative party into which Gove was inducted became enraptured by Blair, with George Osborne declaring him 'the master'.[63] This Tory faction, having taken the leadership of their party from a recalcitrantly right-wing base, had begun to slowly assimilate Blair's presentational and political lessons. In particular, Cameron had begun to triangulate New Labour on key issues, and even to outflank them to the left on some issues and some local campaigns – for example over Post Office closures or immigration. Initially, he refused to contest Labour on public spending totals, and instead focused on priorities.[64] The volte-face following the banking bailout was a mark of skilled political opportunism but, even as the Tories attacked Labour spending and began to lay the narrative demand for austerity, they were preparing to implement cuts with a 'progressive' facade.

Conclusion: The Miliband Interregnum

For the Blairites who had been plotting to get rid of Brown as soon as he took the leadership, the 2010 Labour leadership election campaign ought to have been their moment of delicious revenge. With a youthful and, by their standards, charismatic candidate in David Miliband, they were confident of victory. But instead, the leadership was taken by the younger, more neurotic Ed Miliband, who gained the support of trade unionists by cautiously letting it be known that he was slightly to the left of his brother, and would be more receptive to the concerns of trade unionists if he won. 'Red Ed' was always a tabloid conceit, but Miliband was at least someone who recognised the need to decisively close the New Labour era, recover lost working-class votes, and ever-so-slightly push at the boundaries of acceptable neoliberal discourse. What is more, he seemed to begin to attract new members, cautiously optimistic about the possibility of pushing Labour moderately to the left.

Why, then, was the period of Ed Miliband's leadership one of general fug and confusion for Labour? In part, the answer is organisational. While Miliband's major allies were on the soft-Left of the party, he was beset on all sides by powerfully positioned Blairites who were outraged that their candidate had been pipped to the post. Miliband was desperate to keep this faction onboard due in part to their entrenched power and their potential to wreak havoc for him. Another part of the answer is societal. The immediate response of British society to the credit crunch and ensuing recession was to freeze, as though caught in the headlights. It was not until late 2010 that the first glimmer of any kind of organised revolt against austerity began to make itself visible in the form of the students' rebellion. And that movement, while culturally very significant and probably laying some groundwork for a general turn to the left among the young, was as short-lived as subsequent public sector pensions campaigns, and the UK's miserably diminished version of the Occupy movement. As such, there was no continuous or generalised shift to the left, and in fact much of the movement after 2011 was to the racist and authoritarian Right. But the most important answer was political. It was an integral part of Ed Miliband's strategy for reviving and rebranding Labour that it should seek a new synthesis of left and right, rather than be seen to move to the left. This was arguably another reason that Miliband needed the Blairites, to counter pressure from trade unionists and constituency activists to move further left than he wished to go.

The 'Blue Labour' shenanigans of the Miliband era can be interpreted in part as an attempt to anchor the response to Labour's problems to the right, with a series of appeals based on 'faith, flag and family'. In essence, while the Blairites wanted to woo middle-class Tory voters, Blue Labour wanted to flatter working-class voters drifting to the nationalist Right. To achieve this, they argued, Labour had to fashion a patriotism that would attract such voters,[65] one that reversed the Left's supposed softness on crime, its indifference to the 'culture of entitlement' on welfare, and its failure to understand anger about immigration. As Blue Labour doyen Maurice Glasman put it, he wanted Labour to be somewhere that members of the far Right rabble, the English Defence League, might feel at home.[66] This was quite at odds with the view of Blairite insider Dan Hodges, who described how the party leadership had attempted to 'ape the language of the BNP' only to succeed in 'boosting the BNP'[67] by driving their obsessions up the political agenda. It also gave Cameron, who was not averse to using a 'muscular' rhetoric on immigration when it suited him, the opportunity to deride Labour's 'Alf Garnett' race politics.[68] Miliband nonetheless cleaved hard to this strategy throughout his reign.

The rightward tilt was not just a question of Labour seeking to co-opt anti-immigrant rhetoric for the centre-Left. Soon, while Shadow Chancellor Ed Balls relinquished his brief flirtation with anti-austerity economics, Miliband was adopting a more rigorously punitive version of welfare policy than his New Labour predecessors had managed, at least at the level of policy. In addition to a welfare cap, Miliband proposed that those who had not worked in the previous five years should have their benefits cut, retirement ages should rise and parents should be forced into work-related training as soon as their child hit the age of three.[69] This was all laid out by Shadow Work and Pensions Secretary Liam Byrne, someone on the Right of the New Labour project with a flair for pugnacious populism – his election campaign, managed by seasoned right-winger Tom Watson, had pledged to 'smash teen gangs' and stop benefits for 'failed asylum seekers'. And indeed, as pernicious as the policy was the rhetoric, which was culpably aligned with that of the populist Right – just as Labour sought to (gently) bash the bankers and call for 'responsible capitalism', so it sought to (harshly) incriminate the poorest as yet another usurping pressure on the 'squeezed middle'.[70]

The British nationalism that Miliband sought to mobilise had another purpose, however. One of the reasons that New Labour had so fanatically pursued its 'Britishness' agenda was to ward off the menace of Scottish independence. The devolved institutions that New Labour had itself created, the better to forestall such questions, had become a terrain in which the SNP consistently outmanoeuvred and out-classed their Labour rivals. By 2011, the SNP, having simply demonstrated a better ability than Labour to defend basic social-democratic rights such as free higher education, had swept the elections at Holyrood with a landslide. By the following year, they had gained an agreement with Cameron that there would be a referendum on independence come 2014. Since the Tories had little in the way of a base or party machine to fight the campaign in Scotland, they left it to the Scottish Labour Party, the bastion of the Labour Right, to take the lead. It was, of course, not compulsory for Labour to wage this fight and, having decided to do so, it did not have to form an open alliance with the Tories. In so doing, Labour merely underlined the extent to which there was a policy consensus at Westminster on essential matters from Trident to spending cuts. While the pro-independence campaign highlighted that Scotland need never again have a Conservative Government like the one which at that moment was privatising the NHS, Labour showed that within the Union, there would be a Tory Government whoever was in office. This not only fatally alienated much of its core vote – with the 'No' vote being concentrated in working-class heartlands like Glasgow – it also set itself up for perverse attacks from the Conservatives for supposed 'softness' on the SNP.

Miliband had always been so terrified of being thought of as in any sense left-wing. He capped his first year as leader by assuring the *Sun* that 'Red Ed Is Dead',[71] while posing with a copy of said paper. Later, when Emily Thornberry posted an apparently disobliging photograph of a St George's Cross-strewn house in Rochester, Miliband forced her resignation so that no one would think he lacked 'respect' for such patriotism.[72] Whenever the shade of 'Red Ed' seemed on the brink of resurfacing, Miliband took pains to ward it off by clumsily veering to the right. The Conservatives duly took this as a sign of weakness on Miliband's part and, despite Labour's self-destructive leadership of the 'Better Together' campaign, they embarked on a campaign to pre-empt any potential Labour–SNP coalition after the election by depicting Miliband as Alex Salmond's puppet. Miliband took fright, and used every available platform to attack the SNP, particularly on the two policies on which it had strongest support: Trident, and austerity.[73] It was both tactically preposterous, since Labour had no idea what sort of *quid pro quos* it may have to engage in after an election, and unconvincing, since the demonstrative attacks were plainly bluster under fire.

Labour went into the 2015 general election faced with the defeat it had been preparing for through the last five years. The hallmarks of its campaign were the farcical 'pink bus' campaign seeking to mobilise female voters – because, apparently, women won't communicate in any other colour – and the 'Edstone' listing Labour's pledges, a fittingly terminal punctuation for a campaign that was dead on arrival. The share of the vote received by both Labour and the Conservatives barely altered: only the distribution of seats changed, as a freshly detoxified Conservative Party took advantage of the Liberal collapse to mop up their seats. This was not, *pace* the Blairites, because Miliband was too much the left-wing firebrand, or because, as Blair predictably claimed, New Labour had been ditched.[74] The Beckett review into the party's electoral failure noted that the left-wing policies were in fact among the popular things about Miliband's Labour.[75] What hamstrung Miliband was that he was invested in the worst legacies of New Labour. These included not just the ill-fated attempt to triangulate the hard Right on race and immigration, the pandering to anti-welfare resentment and the defensive British nationalism, but also Miliband's own control-freakery, his excessively presidential manner of running the party, and his determination to bring US-style campaigning methods into Britain.[76] As a party, Labour seemed to have no coherent purpose: were they out to tame capitalism, as Miliband sometimes claimed, or out to tame welfare? Were they for or against austerity? They had many populist policies which were not difficult to sell by themselves, but these often cut against the grain of the overall policy framework. As an opposition, Labour could barely bring itself to oppose – to the extent that Ed Balls openly declared before the general election that he wouldn't reverse anything from Osborne's latest budget.[77] As tacticians, they couldn't bring themselves to act intelligently, because their strategy was too invested in a way of doing politics that was bringing about Labour's destruction. This was not anti-Blairite Leftism. It was a timorous attempt to reformulate Blairism for a post-credit crunch terrain. New Labour was not dead; it was undead.

5

Two Years Before the Mast: Corbyn's Subaltern Leadership

Day One: Project Despair

If Corbyn won, it would be back to the SDP and 1980s splits. Back to the 1970s. Back to the USSR. Sputnik would triumph again if Corbyn won. Wall to wall, from populist Right to centre-Left, the news was of a coalition of simple-minded, palaeolithic tribalists, Militant thugs, over-emotional hysterics and sun-stroked hippies converging to take over the Labour Party.

Labour MPs were determined not to let it happen. If Harriet Harman didn't stop the plot by cancelling the election, the coup would strike on 'day one' of any Corbyn leadership. He had been warned. Simon Danczuk told LBC radio that Labour MPs would not put up with any 'crazy, left-wing policies'. The coup would come 'as soon as the result comes out', 'if not before'. Talks among Labour MPs, other reports suggested, were taking place as to how soon a no-confidence vote and a leadership challenge could be mustered.[1] Others were more equivocal about the precise timing, with a Labour MP anonymously briefing the *Telegraph*, 'We will have to decide whether he should be removed immediately, or whether it would be better to give him a year or two of being a disaster and get rid of him by 2018.'[2] A great deal depended on the size of Corbyn's margin of victory; a smaller mandate would permit an earlier challenge. Once Corbyn's victory was secured with an overwhelming mandate, placing him 40 per cent ahead of his nearest rival, the arch-Blairite apparatchik Peter Mandelson cautioned against anything too importunate. 'It would be wrong to try to force this issue from within,' he said, 'before the public have moved to a clear verdict.'[3] This caution prevailed, to an extent, but it didn't prevent restless backbenchers from sabotaging, or members of the shadow cabinet from briefing against, Corbyn. After all, it was important that the public move to the correct verdict, one way or another.

The strategy that began to take shape was no longer 'Project Fear'. It was 'Project Despair'. The idea was no longer to terrify people about Corbyn the Red and his Trotskyist interlopers but, through brute force and open sabotage, to cause members to despair of their candidate ever succeeding. To make them give up on their dreams and reconcile themselves to old-school 'realism' and its shopworn mantra: there is no alternative.

In a vicious circle of sabotage and blame, Corbyn's critics were able to both mount damaging public attacks, or leak against him, and then blame him for the effects of this. Thus, for example, a document of unknown provenance, listing Labour MPs according to their degree of hostility toward, or support for, the leadership, was leaked to the press. This trivial incident was, of course, given an extraordinary amount of prominence in news coverage. David Cameron used it to attack Corbyn in parliament, while backbenchers scolded him to 'get a grip on the situation'.

Soon enough, there were calls for Corbyn to resign, with Jamie Reed and John Woodcock, have-a-go heroes of the backbench Right, leading the complaints. 'We should be talking about the chaos and the civil war that is destabilising the Tory Party,' Reed complained. 'If your boss is killing your firm, do you stay quiet?' Woodcock, who had accidentally-on-purpose publicly called Corbyn a 'fucking disaster' on Twitter, added, 'we simply cannot go on like this.' Ex-whip Angela Smith added, 'If Corbyn is not prepared to buckle down and show proper leadership he should just go.'[4]

A logical question at this point would be, why on earth would they expect him to go over such a pathetic non-issue as a leaked list? Why would they expect him to go over *any* of the pathetic non-issues that routinely prompted calls for resignation? *Did* they expect him to go, or were they just trying their luck? Would it have occurred to them that, for many people watching from outside the bubble, the spectacle of Cameron braying and backbenchers hyperventilating might be by far the most embarrassing aspect of the whole incident? Even allowing that for them, Corbyn's failures were cumulative, that Corbyn's way of doing politics was completely at odds with everything they had been educated to believe was effective, that every day of watching him on the job had been painful, that everything he said and the way he said it caused them head-clutching agony. Even allowing that Corbyn made real mistakes which, to those expecting a calamity from the start, must have given them a Cassandra complex. Even allowing for all that, they chose *this* as the issue on which to demand resignation. It only makes sense in light of a wishful assumption on their part that Corbynism was a temporary malfunction, a glitch rather than anything more deeply rooted. It also bespeaks their continued underestimation of Corbyn himself.

The next issue on which Corbyn was to be belaboured was that of anti-Semitism. There had been a few highly publicised allegations of anti-Semitism within Labour. One concerned claims of anti-Semitism at Oxford University Labour Club made by Alex Chalmers. There, a member of the OULC was supposed to have been formally disciplined by their college for having organised a group of students to harass a Jewish student and shout 'filthy Zionist' whenever they saw her. This was, in fact, the only checkable part of the allegations, and it was refuted by the principal of the college. Baroness Jan Royall's inquiry into the allegations, while taking all the claims very seriously and making a number of constructive recommendations, found 'no evidence' of institutional anti-Semitism in the OULC. Another incident involved the views of a sectarian crank, Gerry Downing, who had urged military victory for ISIS against the US, and described Israel as a form of 'the Jewish question'. (What, one wanted to know, was the question?) Downing was immediately expelled. A local Labour vice-chair, Vicki Kirby, had made a number of gratuitously anti-Semitic comments. There were already dark hints that these incidents were 'not isolated' and were part of a wider problem under Corbyn's leadership – but this was hard to sustain when the evidence was thus far so limited.[5]

The false spring of the anti-Corbynites began when a classic online bin-hoking operation by the Guido Fawkes blog showed that Naz Shah MP, who had been working as an unpaid assistant to John McDonnell, had once posted a series of Facebook memes and statuses, which included some outright anti-Semitic statements ('the Jews are rallying') and some at least ambiguous memes. Shah immediately apologised, resigned from her positions, and was suspended by the Labour Party. The following day, a seemingly tired and emotional Ken Livingstone addressed the subject on the radio. He defended Shah, saying she was over-the-top but not anti-Semitic – a defence that, given Shah's contrition and acknowledgement of anti-Semitism, must have been unwelcome. More problematic was the ground on which he made this case, embarking on a historical detour, claiming that Hitler had supported Zionism 'before he went mad and ended up killing six million Jews'.

This inflammatory, bewildering digression referenced the Haavara Agreement between the Third Reich and the Zionist Federation of Germany. But it was historically inaccurate and even a bowdlerisation of his source, which was a critique of the Zionist movement written by Lenni Brenner in the 1980s. The Nazi regime had opportunistically come to an arrangement with the Zionist Federation of Germany, wherein some of the Jews fleeing Germany, and being fleeced of their possessions on the way out, could get some of them back if they moved to British Mandate Palestine. The Nazis were not supporting Zionism, but trying to expedite the expulsion of Jews from Germany by all means at their disposal. Even if Livingstone's rendering had been entirely correct and sensitively expressed, it was an extremely odd moment to raise a recondite historical discussion of Zionism and the Third Reich. Livingstone's stated concern was to distinguish opposition to Zionism on democratic grounds from anti-Semitic dog-whistling. Unfortunately, his intervention, by defending the indefensible and making a hash of history, accomplished the reverse. And provided fuel for a blaze that went on for weeks.

The nature of the claims that now made headlines was not new. Well before the Livingstone fiasco, an anonymously written piece in the *Jewish Chronicle* alleged that Labour was now attracting 'antisemites like flies to a cesspit'. Dan Hodges had trumpeted in the *Telegraph* that 'antisemitism is now firmly embedded in the Labour party's DNA ... Labour is a racist party now'. Jonathan Freedland had written in the *Guardian* that Jewish Britons were 'fast reaching the glum conclusion that Labour has become a cold house for Jews'. The news had spread overseas, with the Israeli liberal daily, *Ha'aretz*, observing that these were 'difficult times to be a Jewish member' of Labour. What was the basis for all this? A number of councillors and members had been suspended in the wake of the furore. Thomas Jones, writing for the *London Review of Books* website, pointed out what the numbers meant: 0.4 per cent of the parliamentary party, 0.07 per cent of the councillors and 0.012 per cent of the membership had been suspended for anti-Semitism. Even assuming that all of these suspensions were fully merited, and that no one was being trigger-happy in the face of an embarrassing scandal, this amounted to a grand total of fifty-six individuals.[6]

The argument was that, as Tom Harris MP and John Mann MP both averred, the main source of anti-Semitism was anti-Israel sentiment on the Left, and that Corbyn's pro-Palestine leadership had made Labour a natural home for this kind of anti-Semitism. Sometimes this was linked to old and discredited smears against Corbyn, whether because he had defended the Arab Israeli Islamist Raed Salah following a failed Home Office attempt to smear and deport him, or because he had met members of the Palestinian group Hamas. This was enough to engage in a kind of nudge-and-wink that Corbyn was, if not anti-Semitic, then certainly not uncomfortable with 'bigots, deniers and exterminationists'.[7] In the early months of Corbyn's leadership, an anonymous Labour source had told the press that 'everyone knows there is a problem with anti-Semitism on the left but they continue with impunity, they have a carte blanche under Corbyn.' The journalist Jamie Stern-Weiner, reflecting on these allegations, wrote of the 'almost comical paucity of evidence' for such claims, and the systematic misrepresentation of such evidence as did exist. Many Jewish critics of Israel expressed alarm at the conflation of opposition to Zionism, or just to Israeli policies, with anti-Semitism, which was, in the words of Independent Jewish Voices, a 'campaign of intimidation ... the battle against anti-Semitism is undermined whenever opposition to Israeli government policies is automatically branded as antisemitic.'[8]

However, as Livingstone had unwittingly offered himself up as a striking example for the critics, he was immediately suspended. Corbyn responded to the scandal by asking Shami Chakrabarti, the respected former head of the civil liberties group Liberty, to investigate anti-Semitism and racism in the Labour Party and recommend appropriate action. As with Baroness Royall's investigation, Chakrabarti found no evidence of systemic anti-Semitism. Labour, despite having suffered an 'occasionally toxic atmosphere' and 'too much clear evidence' of ignorant attitudes, was 'not overrun by anti-Semitism, Islamophobia, or other forms of racism'. The Jewish Labour Movement, which had expressed alarm over Livingstone's remarks and other incidents, argued that the report was 'a sensible and firm platform' which 'accurately diagnosed the nature of the problem'.[9]

In short, while critics had been right to be outraged at specific incidents of anti-Semitism, and some of Corbyn's supporters had been mistaken to adopt a defensive position (by claiming, for example, that Livingstone had said nothing wrong), there was no basis for the claim that Corbyn had turned Labour into a hothouse of anti-Jewish hatred, or that anti-Israel attitudes were *in general* translating into anti-Semitism.

Hard-Boiled Brexit

Other lines of attack unavailing, the issue that would trigger the coup attempt against Corbyn, and signal an acceleration of British political turbulence, was Europe.

This was perhaps surprising, given that Europe had long been a niche concern, and rarely at the top of people's political priorities. But for the middle-class Right it had become a metonym for everything that was wrong with Britain in their eyes: immigration, too many pinko laws and regulations restricting small enterprise, a liberal metropolitan elite running things, political correctness, the decline of British common sense. According to this view, there was a de facto alliance between unpatriotic elites who had sold Britain out and the wretched of the earth, refugees and migrants, who supposedly undercut wages, took British jobs, overburdened public services, and brought crime and terror. This was a story about British decline, one that could be tailored to make sense of a patchwork of diverse life experiences.

And it was UKIP who had achieved this. First, they cut swathes into Tory-voting southern England, where things had never been so good as when Thatcherite estate agents and barrow boys were on the march. Then, they began to draw conservative voters in the rustbelts, where things had never been good and had got worse. UKIP, by this point, was trying to style itself as a party for the discontented working class, which would park its tanks on Labour's lawn. This became, to a degree, a self-fulfilling myth. And insofar as the media and pundits bought into it, it helped UKIP, which did not otherwise have significant roots in working-class communities, to add workers to its base.

Prior to the 2015 general election, UKIP's voters included more large and small employers than employees. The biggest chunk of its vote actually came from professionals and managers. However, its 2015 breakthrough, with 4 million votes, was impossible without adding more working-class voters to the mix. These were disproportionately white, male, and older, and often living in provincial or 'left-behind' areas, cut off from the centres of financial, communication, or political power, as well as from the growth of the 'new economy', and left for dead by the political class. Politically, their background was heteroclite. The biggest chunk of UKIP voters were ex-Tories, followed by Liberals, and 10 per cent came from Labour. But there were also quite a lot of former non-voters, as right-wing voters who had backed the BNP or the English Democrats.[10]

UKIP, with the Left still in abeyance, had become the most dynamic political force in England and Wales. It was setting the agenda every day. But electorally, it had cost the Tories more than it had cost Labour. In the northern rust-belt seats in which UKIP had made gains, it largely did so by hegemonising the local right wing, rather than eroding the Labour vote. By contrast, the Tories found themselves shedding almost as many right-wing votes as they gained centre votes from the Liberals. David Cameron, sick of being sandbagged by middle-class right-wing radicalism within his own party, and voted down by his own backbenchers, decided to gamble on offering a referendum on EU membership. As with the Scottish independence referendum, he raised the stakes, on the assumption that fear of the unknown would help the status quo: it was either 'in' or 'out'.

In line with the 'Project Fear' strategy deployed in the Scottish referendum, the Remain campaign would be focused on the economic dangers of leaving a trading bloc that was, for economic purposes, essentially one country. But when it came to fearmongering, they were going to be outplayed. And when it came to telling a story about the future, theirs was sterile and weirdly oblivious.

Neither the feast of reason nor the flow of the soul, the official cross-party Remain campaign hit every possible wrong note. It chose for its name Britain Stronger in Europe, failing to notice the initials, 'BSE', as in 'mad cow disease'. The 'dangerously uninspiring, complacent' launch at a hipster venue in London featured such luminaries as Tory peer and former M&S boss Stuart Rose, and 'celebrity' June Sarpong. Rose made a number of painful gaffes, and no questions were allowed from journalists.

The group's board included, as well as figures from across the parties like Damian Green and Will Straw, football boss and *Apprentice* star Karren Brady, PR man Roland Rudd, Peter Mandelson, and millionaire businessman Richard Reed. The first 'letters' sent out by the campaign were written by such figures as Alan Sugar and Richard Branson, celebrating the fact that the EU gave them access to huge markets. The campaign's first video featured Branson, easyJet CEO Carolyn McCall, and a range of exporters and CEOs, also cock-a-hoop about the wonders of free markets and deregulation. Plus, a student for whom the EU made it easier to backpack during summers and gap yahs.[11]

The burden of the campaign's message was that the EU's internal market is pretty good for rich people. As if voters didn't already know that. Tacitly, it seemed to rely on the idea that most people admire and respect capitalists, their success granting them a kind of celebrity hero status. And, furthermore, that we all had and felt a stake in their gains. So there was no need for the Remain campaign to be overly politicised, or to address any legitimate sources of unhappiness with the EU and the economic model it represented. If discontents were addressed, it was in the form of rebutting 'lies' that 'exploited legitimate concerns'. At times, the campaign would try to play its own version of the anti-immigrant card, as when it claimed that rapists, murderers, and thieves would be harder to deport if Britain left the EU.[12] But against the resonant, racist imagery of Leave, which exploited accumulated resentments and scapegoated the EU and immigrants for them, Remain's campaign was politically and emotionally hollow.

Paradigmatic of this were two debates between Nick Clegg and Nigel Farage that had been staged before the general election and the EU referendum. Clegg had focused on fact-checking, on accusing Farage – correctly – of misrepresenting the truth. Farage dodged all this with his usual aplomb, depicted his opponent (correctly) as an-of-touch member of the elite, and then reiterated his basic claim that whatever the growth figures said, immigration only worked for the wealthy and not for the workers.

This has become a pattern. Liberals respond to the populist Right with a 'fact-check', to no overall effect other than increasing the smug complacency of their own side. Dodging their own compromised relationship with the truth – Nick Clegg, a paladin of political honesty? – they also take the claims of the racists and nationalists too literally. And then are baffled that people still believe in lies, even when they're exposed. The lies are believed because they're fables, morality tales which seem to explain the bad luck, the social misery, the decline, and the accumulated grievances of millions. Simply correcting a falsehood fails to get under the skin in the way that the original falsehood does. It fails to tell a more truthful story which engages popular desires.

The official Labour Remain campaign, Labour In for Britain, led by Alan Johnson and chaired by Phil Wilson, two of the party's leading Blairites, wasn't much better. In practice, it was a very low-key Labour version of the Britain Stronger in Europe campaign, with a specific emphasis on jobs, workers' rights, and national security. Hence it was launched with a speech by Johnson highlighting such inspiring issues as the European Arrest Warrant. Corbyn, traditionally a eurosceptic, had campaigned for leader of the Labour Party on a 'remain and reform' ticket. He highlighted his reservations about the European Union's lack of democracy, and support for neoliberalism, but, recognising the Left's weakness and seeking compromise with the Labour establishment, argued that it would be better to stay in than leave on the basis of a hard-Right campaign which would strip away human rights, workers' rights, and environmental protections. The thinking of some of Corbyn's team was that this was also the only plausible position for Labour to take during a referendum called to settle a fight between two factions of the Right. A 'critical remain' position gave Labour the flexibility it needed to accept either outcome.

Owing to his lukewarm support – he famously declared himself 'seven out of ten' in favour of Remain – Corbyn played a subordinate role in Labour's campaign. Where he did participate, he stuck to the 'remain and reform' position that he had been elected on. At the launch of the 'Labour In for Britain' battlebus, Corbyn's speech urged people to 'remain and reform the EU', to 'defend investment, defend jobs, defend workers' rights and defend our environment'. But he also stressed the need to obstruct the Transatlantic Trade and Investment Partnership being negotiated between the US and the EU, which he said would damage the 'rights of ordinary people and consumers in this country'.[13] Corbyn also refused to share a platform with David Cameron, saying he was 'not on the same side' as the prime minister who, he said,

> wants a free market Europe. He has negotiated what he believes is some kind of deal over welfare and the ever-closer union, which is apparently legally questionable, according to Michael Gove.
>
> I want to see a Europe that is about protecting our environment and ensuring we have sustainable industries across Europe, such as the steel industry, and high levels of jobs and social protection across Europe. His agenda is the very opposite.[14]

This was not in keeping with the tendency of the media to treat the debate as one between two wings of the Conservative Party, with Labour reduced to shoring up the Cameronites. It was also out of step with the emphasis of Labour In for Britain, which avoided any antagonism with Cameron, or indeed any criticism of the EU. Johnson, who had wanted to campaign under the slogan 'EUphoric', was furious with Corbyn.

Nonetheless, the Labour leader campaigned vigorously. Angela Eagle credited him for travelling 'up and down the country, pursuing an itinerary that would make a 25-year-old tired'. He made a total of sixty appearances in the last sixty days, travelling 2,768 miles. Corbyn also out-performed the Labour 'In' campaign's leaders in terms of media appearances, with a total of 123 appearances, according to a study by Loughborough University. As Angela Phillips, professor of communications at Goldsmiths University, wrote, 'by the end of the campaign, Corbyn had made 6.1 per cent of all media appearances while Johnson figured in less than 1 per cent.'

Corbyn supporters also organised their own 'Another Europe Is Possible' front to distinguish the Left from the official Leave and Remain positions, and to campaign for a 'remain and reform' position. Given the terrible example that had been made of Greece by the EU, a string of campaign appearances by the Greek economist and former Syriza negotiator, Yanis Varoufakis, was scheduled, to persuade sceptical left-wingers to campaign for Remain.[15] It would be easy to take issue with this campaign. Another Europe Is Possible had a perfectly lucid critique of 'Tory Brexit', and understood well enough that it would most likely be the hard Right that would set the terms of any exit. They adopted a principled defence of migrants and free movement, when the official 'In' campaigns refused to do so. They distanced themselves from the official Remain campaign's tendency to infantilise voters. And they had a reasonable case that reform of Europe was necessary. Yet it wasn't clear exactly what these reforms were, or how they were to be achieved. If their campaign wasn't to be a leftier version of the largely defensive, apolitical Remain campaign, it needed to outline a strategy for an offensive. Another Europe was possible – but *how*?

John McDonnell was intellectually the sharpest defender of this case. He used a rally to condemn both the paranoid bombast of Boris Johnson, comparing the EU to the Third Reich, and Cameron's 'Project Fear' approach to Remain. The debate, he said, was a perpetuation of the 'gang warfare of the Eton playing fields', dragging the country 'into the intellectual gutter'. He stressed that many of the issues facing the future were transnational and required trans-national solutions: climate change, financial malfeasance and tax avoidance, refugees. He stressed that the British had been major beneficiaries of free movement of people in Europe. Finally, he added the strategic perspective:

> The question for the Left, then, is whether we can transform the operation of the European Union. It's the same question asked by the Left about any state institution, whether it's the local council, the national government, or any transnational institution. The strategy we pursued on the Left in the past, and now, has been described traditionally as 'in and against the state'. The state isn't just a set of institutions, it's a relationship: usually one of dominance of the institution over the individual. Socialists and progressives have gone within these institutions to try to transform that relationship. That is, to transform it into a democratic relationship, where it is the democratic people's wishes that dominate, not the bureaucracy or the powerful economic interests that the bureaucracy often rep-resents. ... Can we, and how can we, democratically reform our

European institutions? Well, the optimism is based upon this. For the first time in over a generation, there are movements and political forces mobilised and mobilising across Europe to respond to that challenge. But responding to it, increasingly together.[16]

In short, then, McDonnell and his allies hoped that the convergence and cooperation of movements across Europe would put pressure on the EU establishment to accept democratic change. This was one of the few occasions on which this question was seriously put on the Left, which had little history of engaging with the subject of Europe. The trade unions, following the grim defeats of the 1980s, had largely abandoned their critical stance toward Europe, instead relying on it to defend a set of workers' rights against Tory onslaught. Much of the Left, too, had ceased thinking about whether and how to reform, or indeed leave, Europe, and approached the issue from a defensive position. However, the plausibility of McDonnell's solution surely depended on the EU being democratically susceptible to pressure, in a way that it had not been in relation to Greece, Ireland, Italy, Portugal, or Spain. Far from the EU being accountable to pressure, it was national governments which had buckled to the EU. This did not mean that 'Left Leavers' had a more plausible answer. The critique of the EU as an undemocratic bloc committed to neoliberal practices was well founded, but there was, in truth, little strategic calculation about what Brexit would mean in practice, or how it was to be harnessed by the Left.

The bigger problem, however, was that the Left was barely a factor. The media weren't interested in what it was saying. Corbyn arguably only got the coverage he did, which was limited, because he was Labour leader. The top six figures reported in the news were David Cameron, Boris Johnson, George Osborne, Nigel Farage, Michael Gove and Ian Duncan Smith. Of these, four were Brexit campaigners. Taking the entire media into account, and factoring for viewership and readership, the Brexit campaign received 80 per cent of the coverage. Corbyn's campaign focused on trying to outflank the media by building grassroots support, while Labour In for Britain muddled along in obscurity – in a BBC article on the campaign, it was mentioned as an afterthought. On the day of the referendum, in a last-minute effort to reach voters, they hired propeller jets to fly banners over London and other major cities with the tepid slogan, 'Labour says vote Remain'.[17]

The Leave campaign won by a narrow margin of 52–48. Almost immediately, Johnson and Hilary Benn went on the attack against their leader, claiming that Corbyn had 'sabotaged' their campaign. He was taxed with raising the supposedly 'esoteric' issue of TTIP and being 'critical of the EU in tone'.[18] John Mann, MP for Bassetlaw, observed that the high Brexit vote in northern constituencies showed that the party was 'out of touch' with voters. The pro-Remain *Economist*, a magazine for company directors and owners, asserted with characteristic insight into Labour politics, 'Mr Mann's critique must be particularly worrying for Mr Corbyn, as it comes not from his old foes on the right of the party, like the Blairite Lord Mandelson, but from the trade-union core.' The fact that Mann was and is on the right of the party, and had been a voluble, vitriolic, at times volatile opponent of Corbynism from the start, had evidently missed the editors.[19] Indeed, the chorus of complaint that arose from within Labour was the prelude to the long-brewing coup.

Chicken Coup

In the weeks before the European Union referendum, I was touring the UK with the first edition of this book, mainly visiting local Momentum and Labour members. I began to hear from activists that they were expecting a coup against Corbyn in the days after the referendum – no matter what the result was.

This didn't seem to make sense. Corbyn had only been on the job for nine months at that point, while the backbench opposition didn't have either a candidate or a programme or an answer to the crisis of social democracy. The Tories would be in some sort of crisis whatever the outcome, with their majority small. Already, they had been forced to make a number of concessions to Labour. Any attempt to blame Corbyn if the Remain campaign failed would surely look tendentious at best, given that the Blairites had the run of Labour's campaign, and at worst like a gift to the government.

It looked even worse once the results were broken down. As psephologist John Curtice wrote, following the vote, the biggest movement in the final weeks before the referendum was a collapse of the pro-Remain position among Conservatives. Phil Wilson claimed that 'an honourable leader would bear the responsibility for the

failure to persuade Labour voters to vote remain.' But
Labour voters were as pro-Remain as the SNP, with two-
thirds voting to stay in the EU. Peter Mandelson alleged
that Corbyn was 'most of the time absent from the battle',
yet Corbyn was more present in it than Labour's leading
Remainers.[20] Would that have been the case had Corbyn
merged with the Tories as Labour had disastrously done
during #indyref? Could left-wing voters have turned out
to vote for such a campaign with a clean conscience? What
about those Brexit-voting northern seats? Would Corbyn
have appealed to them *more* by being *less* critical of the EU?

Yet, within days of the Brexit result, Labour MPs, led by
members of the shadow cabinet, instigated the planned coup
attempt. Hilary Benn, who had set himself up as a potential
leadership contender during the Syria debate, fired the first
shot. But the resignations were carefully staggered, choreo-
graphed for maximum impact. By and large, the resigners
were people who had never supported Corbyn's leadership, and they were followed by a string of statements from
Labour grandees, including former leaders such as Neil
Kinnock and Ed Miliband, calling on Corbyn to 'do the
right thing'. A vote of confidence was arranged in which
the majority of Labour MPs declared that they had 'no confidence' in their leader. Gloria De Pieiro took to the pages
of the *Sun* to call for mass entryism of the Right to help
defeat Corbyn. Jamie Reed published a letter to Corbyn,
via his Twitter account, in which he accused the leader of
having 'sought to inject an unprecedented poison into our
party', by 'inciting' supporters on social media against MPs
from the party's centre and centre-Right.[21]

This had not been entirely unexpected among the leadership team. While most of the plotting took place on a series of Whatsapp groups, the whispering was loud and stagey enough on the backbenches for left-wing MPs to get wind of it and start spreading the word. Did they understand why it was coming? Marsha-Jane Thompson, currently Labour's campaigns manager, argued at the time,

> They wanted to find a hook, and it didn't matter what it was. We knew it was already planned, we knew that they were just waiting for the nod, and it didn't matter that it was for a really spurious reason ... They'd leaked a number of times before and backed off. But, in going for him this time, they completely underestimated him personally. They thought that if they organised these resignations and put him under pressure, that he wouldn't be able to cope. And it wasn't just that he's an amazingly strong person, but that for every MP who said they didn't have confidence in him, five or six hundred people said they did. People were emailing him, sending him messages on social media supporting him. When we had the first campaign for the leadership, part of the message was welcoming activists home, that this was their party: and that's how they felt, they weren't going to be driven out.

In the early days of the coup, the Corbyn leadership team held a staff meeting at which Corbyn made it clear that he would not resign. He was committed to the project of changing the Labour Party, and understood that if his opponents were allowed to drive him out, there wouldn't be another left-wing candidate on the ballot, and the Left wouldn't get another chance at this project. Corbyn's stolid

refusal to 'do the decent thing' and resign led to speculation about who might be a plausible candidate. Evidently,
the coup plotters had reasoned that Corbyn would collapse
under pressure, and that any left-wing challenger could be
kept off the ballot next time. Finally, after several bluffs,
Angela Eagle let it be known that she was ready to put
herself forward as a leadership contender. At that point, it
was noised abroad that Corbyn could be kept off the ballot
paper by a decision of the NEC. If they ruled that Corbyn
was a challenger for his own incumbent role, he would
need the nomination of 20 per cent of Labour MPs. If the
parliamentary party was given a veto on this scale, which
exceeded even the 15 per cent share of MP nominations
Corbyn needed as a candidate in 2015, Corbyn would not
be elected. Eagle, for her part, indicated that she would not
be unhappy were this to be the ruling.

An extraordinary NEC meeting was convened at the last
moment in circumstances that suggested that a secret ballot
would be used to allow delegates to participate in a stitch-up.
In the final vote, the meeting went in favour of Corbyn
being automatically included on the ballot. However, in a
petty and vindictive gesture, many of those present waited
for Corbyn and some of his supporters to leave the meeting,
and immediately passed a new ruling excluding over a
hundred thousand members who had joined since January
from participating in the leadership election – a move
that ITV reporter Robert Peston said 'looks and smells
like gerrymandering'. This last-ditch effort to fix the vote
was followed up by an attempt by members of the Blairite
'Progress' faction in Labour to illegally mine membership

data for anti-Corbyn canvassing, before the Information Commissioners' Office slapped down the ploy.[22] Perhaps most egregiously, the party management intervened in a number of cases to suspend meetings of constituency parties from Brighton to Manchester during the leadership election campaign on the supposed ground of preventing intimidation and bullying. Finally, all local party meetings were suspended, following an incident in which a brick was thrown through the window of Angela Eagle's constituency office by an unknown vandal. Even assuming that all allegations were true, and as serious as described, it was an extremely odd idea that the solution to some people trying to prevent others from speaking freely was to prevent everyone from speaking freely.[23] All of this only undermined the anti-Corbyn faction further. Their legitimacy had depended on their reputation, cultivated in the media, as sensible, moderate, and working within accepted parameters. No objective observer, witnessing this brazen corruption and partially successful offensive against party democracy, would come away with that impression intact.

The media, just as they had for Hilary Benn only months before, began a pattern of talking up the contender, covering her political past in a largely admiring light, and exploring her suddenly mesmerising personality. This is part of a pattern that is worth briefly commenting on. Throughout Corbyn's leadership, media outlets have eyed numerous possible candidates for his replacement, and each time have larded them with an embarrassment of praise. But this has always been short-lived, and the same outlets have always found at least similarly marvellous qualities in the next big thing. In psychological terms, this is known as 'love bombing', a practice used by pimps, gangsters, and cults to manipulate people and win their confidence. As the expression suggests, what is presented as affection and positive attention is actually an aggressive exercise. It exploits the insecurities and aspirations that most people have, but which ambitious politicians have by the bucketload.

The *Telegraph*, for example, not known for its sympathy to Labour politics, ran a column by former Blair advisor John McTernan arguing that Eagle was 'exactly what Labour needs', and radiating warmth about Eagle's qualities: 'Intelligence. Passion. Eloquence. Humour. Authenticity.' McTernan's praise was patently insincere. Eagle, in one of the only signs she had entered his radar, was among the class of 'career politicians' lacking 'character and charisma' that McTernan had criticised when she was part of Ed Miliband's shadow cabinet. The *Telegraph* for its part began to intersperse its online pieces about the leadership challenge with a video segment titled 'Angela Eagle MPs' best moments'. In a profile box, it affirmed that her 'reputation as a fierce public debater with a quick wit helped her become the unity candidate'.[24]

The *Guardian* offered both Angela Eagle and her sister, Maria Eagle, a predictably soft-soap interview, accentuating their 'working-class roots, their Stakhanovite work ethic and self-confidence to spare'.[25] The *Mirror* carolled her virtues as a 'unity candidate' who was loyal to her party, had 'wiped the floor' with opponents in parliamentary debates, and – crucially – was admired by the Pretenders' Chrissie Hynde.[26] 'Eagle Dares', the *Sun* exulted, quoting a number of MPs supporting her stance and none of her critics. It ran an article by Hilary Benn supporting Eagle's bid which, with borrowed Churchillian tones, repetitively extolled her 'courage'. Not known for being especially supportive of women in politics, the paper also made fun of Eagle for her campaign launch debacle, in which journalists abandoned her to cover Andrea Leadsom's bid for the Tory leadership: 'The Eagle Has Crash Landed'.[27]

The problem with the lionising, whatever elements of truth the praise might have contained, was not just its patent insincerity. It was that Eagle increasingly didn't look like someone who would wipe the floor with anyone. It was hardly her fault that on her campaign launch the media abandoned her, leaving her red-faced. That was just a symptom of how insincere the love bombing was. But she didn't appear to have a coherent critique of Corbyn, or an articulate agenda. She sounded defensive about her politics. When one BBC Radio 4 interviewer brought up her support for the Iraq war, she accused him of pandering to a 'Corbynista meme'.[28] Uncomfortable with specifying political differences, she was more at ease trashing Corbyn's competence. To that extent she merely magnified the mantra coming from the Labour Right, for whom – the cliché went – Corbyn was a decent and honourable man, but not a leader.

Indeed, Eagle's campaign was almost entirely negative. She was surely right to raise the brick thrown through her constituency office window, and the homophobic taunts she had received, but there was an insinuation both on her part and on that of her supporters that this was the work of 'bullying' Corbynistas. The *Sun* went so far as to link the incident to the murder of Jo Cox MP by a fascist.[29] But this approach, while it might galvanise the minority of Labour members discontented by Corbyn's leadership, was hardly designed to win over Corbyn supporters. And the problem with adopting a line of attack predicated almost wholly on personality, as Theresa May would later discover, is that it focuses a very unkind light on your own personal competence. Ultimately, this was ineffectual with Labour members, to the extent that Eagle's own constituency Labour party, Wallasey, issued a statement supporting Corbyn after a motion passed 'with an overwhelming majority'.[30]

At any rate, the press spoke too soon. Eagle was not the 'unity candidate' for the 172 MPs who had voted 'no confidence' in Corbyn's leadership. Owen Smith, positioning himself as a man of the soft Left, untarnished by power, untainted by the past, won the Labour nominations he needed and made it clear he would run. Eagle had no natural base of support in the parliamentary party. She was not a Blairite, or from the old Labour Right. She had come from the party's soft Left, but there wasn't much of a soft Left remaining by this point. To avoid dividing the right-of-Corbyn vote this time, and having had a poor campaign, Eagle stepped down. But if Smith seemed untainted by the past, he also had the monumental disadvantage of attracting headlines such as 'Labour leadership: Who is Owen Smith?' In fact, as Corbyn's social media supporters quickly unearthed, his background suggested he was anything but a Leftist: he was a supporter of austerity, was pro-Trident, had supported the Iraq war, and before he became an MP was a lobbyist for the privatisation of health care as a senior Pfizer employee.

Some pundits were, in fairness, angry about the sudden ditching of Eagle. Anne Perkins, leader writer of the *Guardian*, lamented that while Eagle's 'gender was not exactly a problem', she had 'a bit too much history'. She had made 'hard, real-time decisions' to support the war on Iraq, Trident, and whatever other militarism was on the agenda. Members preferred 'purity' to such 'pragmatism'. But Perkins also averred, although without presenting any evidence, that Eagle had been seen off by the 'lingering backwash of the patriarchal world of industry, trade union-ism and smoke-filled constituency committee rooms'.[31]

Certainly, sexism and homophobia had been part of the picture. John Humphreys, for example, had attacked Eagle for crying over her decision to resign from the shadow cabinet, implying that this did not evince the macho tough-ness needed from a true leader. Smith, for his part, had sought to differentiate himself from Eagle by insisting on what a 'normal' person he was: 'I am normal ... I've got a wife and three children.' He implied, in other words, that if he didn't have children or a heterosexual marriage, he'd be something other than normal. Throughout the campaign, he cut the figure of a Butlin's red-coat act, with a cheap and cheerful humour that was often sexist. For example, in an extremely odd moment, he tweeted at Nicola Sturgeon that he had the 'perfect present' for her, accompanied by a photograph of 'the world's biggest gobstopper'. Challenged about this, which seemed to suggest that the leading woman in British politics should shut up, he offered the standard lad's response that it was 'just banter'. When, on a campaign stop, a member of the public wanted to ask him a 'personal question', he gestured to his penis and said: 'Twenty-nine inches – inner leg measurement of course.'[32]

The signs increasingly were that Smith's campaign was a disaster. It pleased no one. It was off-putting to Corbyn supporters, off-putting to any liberal centrist with remotely feminist politics, off-putting to the old Labour Right. Blairites faulted it for presenting a watered-down, pallid version of Corbyn's policies. Dan Hodges foamed that Smith was running a 'spineless, incoherent, incompetent campaign' whose message was 'I am just like Jeremy Corbyn … Ditch Jeremy Corbyn': 'Amazingly, this "Dump Corbyn, Get Corbyn" line isn't resonating with the Corbynite true believers. For the simple reason that while many of them are stark-staring mad, they aren't stupid.'[33] The one issue on which Smith differed with Corbyn was his position on accepting the referendum result, with Smith arguing that Labour should block Article 50. Corbyn's allies argue that, had Smith won on that agenda, May could have called the election right away and crushed Labour much as she attempted to do in 2017.

There were also signs that, political strategy aside, Smith's everyday tactical judgement was way off. He made strange suggestions, such as proposing peace talks with ISIS. He bragged of his role in the Northern Ireland peace process, when any role he had – as an advisor to Paul Murphy MP – was extremely minor.[34] It would be worth thinking about what the Tories and their supportive media, who hounded Corbyn over fabrications and nonsense about the IRA twenty years after Good Friday, would have made of a Smith leadership given his ISIS slip. Or, indeed, what many more slips he would have made on a daily basis.

As with the 2015 leadership contest, Corbyn ran his campaign like a social movement. Indeed, even if had he not intended it, the movement was there. On 27 June, while Corbyn was holed up in a tense, bitter meeting with Labour MPs, an estimated ten thousand protesters gathered outside in his defence. Thompson, who organised the rally, pointed out that it had been pulled together within the space of nine hours. Another meeting scheduled two days later at Congress House and organised by Momentum had to be postponed due, the organisers said, to 'overwhelming public demand'. Nonetheless, beginning a string of rallies, Corbyn made an ad hoc and rapturously received appearance to thousands of students outside the School of Oriental and African Studies. Protests were held that weekend in Manchester, Liverpool, Exeter, Plymouth, and Penzance.

Importantly, the cross-section of his supporters turning out were, far from the caricature of 'Trots' purveyed by the media and Labour MPs, a mixture of people who supported 'Old Labour', former Greens, people who had voted Plaid or other parties out of desperation for a decent alternative, left-wing journalists like Paul Mason, and leading union officials such as Matt Wrack of the Fire Brigades Union and Jennie Formby of Unite. This was the coalition which had backed Corbyn in the first place. There were also elements of the youth meme culture that would play an important role in the general election. Hilary Benn, whose sacking precipitated the coup, was cheerfully mocked on a placard with the slogan, 'Chat Shit, Get Sacked'.[35]

Soon, Corbyn was touring the country with a red fire truck donated by the Fire Brigades Union. On 2 July, he joined a huge march through Liverpool, before appearing in front of a rally of 20,000 people chanting, 'Tories Out, Corbyn In'.[36] Two days later, he was in Teesside. On 7 July, he was joined by thousands in a rally in the centre of Birmingham. Two days later, he was given a hero's welcome at the Durham Miner's Gala. His tour took him up and down the country from Milton Keynes to York and Harrogate.

Corbyn's support from the constituencies remained strong. A *Newsnight* investigation into fifty of the constituency Labour parties which had backed Corbyn found that at least forty-five of them still would, suggesting that he retained 90 per cent of his old support. The *Guardian*, which supported the coup, conducted a survey of 4,000 of its readers and found that 81 per cent had backed Corbyn, and 95 per cent of those intended to do so again. Crucially, the trade union leaderships did not desert Corbyn, instead turning their fire on the MPs who had orchestrated the coup:

> The current crisis within the parliamentary Labour party is deeply regrettable and unnecessary ... The government is in crisis, but already serious debates are taking place and decisions being made which profoundly affect the interests of working people ... It cannot be right to seek to denude the Labour front bench at this time, when the government more than ever needs to be scrutinised

and held to account by an effective and united opposition that does the job it is paid to do. Jeremy Corbyn is the democratically-elected leader of our party who secured such a resounding mandate less than 10 months ago under an electoral procedure fully supported by Labour MPs.[37]

As Corbyn toured the country, the newspapers continued to ratchet up the warnings of doom if Corbyn won. The *Sun* cheered a report which it said showed that Corbyn had a '0% chance of winning the next general election', and highlighted its former hate figure Neil Kinnock's claim that Labour would not win again 'in his lifetime' if Corbyn won.[38] Even more ominously, the television sofa-friendly Birmingham MP Jess Phillips threatened to resign if Corbyn won.[39]

None of it worked. The ballot finally closed on 21 September, with the result announced on the 24th. To little surprise, Corbyn won the second leadership contest with a marginally higher percentage than before, at 61.85 per cent. Whatever supporters he had lost, he made up for with more to spare, including some who had voted for another candidate in 2015. How did Corbyn's opponents get it so wrong? And how did he survive against such odds?

Above all else, the coup was a shortcut, a resort to brute political force, and as such an admission of failure. Corbyn's critics had all the time in the world to prepare the ground for a better offensive. They had their own supporters within the shadow cabinet. They had the majority of the support within the party apparatus. Most Labour councillors and local notables were not Corbynistas. There were sufficient divisions and weaknesses at the top to allow them time to develop a strategy in which to gradually unwind the hold of Corbyn's supporters through demoralisation. The party membership, even those who had joined after 2015, were far more ideologically open than all the panic-mongering about Militant and Trotskyists let on. It would have been possible to have a series of slow, patient, conversations with them, rather than resorting to ineffectual abuse, Cold War-style grandstanding, and largely symbolic purges.

By acting as they did, without a candidate or a strategy, the plotters effectively admitted that they lacked the vision to persuade people, the resources to bear with a period of marginalisation, or the imagination to hold firm for a future in which they might have something to offer. They let their sense of entitlement to rule drive them to distraction. By acting so quickly and precipitously, and without any idea of what should come after, they made it obvious that they were attacking party democracy. That they also chose to attack around the same time as the publication of the Chilcot Inquiry's findings, which left the *éminence grise* of the plotters bespattered with disgrace, was also suspicious. Many members felt that the coup was at least partly an attempt to avert the fallout from that report.

Corbyn, for his part, was completely underestimated. The conception of 'leadership' that both the backbench belligerati and their media supporters were working with was such that they didn't get how Corbyn was doing what he did. He had an excellent relationship with his base, and understood their power and how to mobilise it. He wasn't as good at handling overwhelmingly hostile media – his critics clearly had a point about this – but what they missed was that he was also not particularly impressed or intimidated by them. A coup predicated on intensive media pressure had worked on Blair, because that was where he gained his strength. Corbyn never depended on the newspapers or broadcasters for anything. These are strengths that the leadership would turn to Labour's surprising advantage in the general election.

'Oh, Jeremy Corbyn …'

No one had expected Theresa May to call the election when she did. On the morning in question, 18 April, Corbyn's team had heard that an announcement would be made later that day, but a snap election was not the first guess as to what it might be.

Rumours in Westminster had suggested that Theresa May was seriously ill, and had been instructed in a meeting with the 1922 Committee of Tory backbenchers to resign sooner rather than later. The *Evening Standard* speculated that there was a royal death. Social media spun into its own characteristic speculations. By quarter past ten in the morning, Labour got the call: May was going for an election. Publicly, she said that the election had to be called because she needed a strong hand in negotiating Brexit and the opposition were trying to hamstring her: 'The country is coming together, but Westminster is not.' Perhaps, in this, there was also a sideways dig at her backbench critics: overwhelming victory would strengthen her hand within her own party and cabinet as much as anything else.

However, purely on its own terms, the decision made sense. The Conservatives, with a popular leader and a clear stance on Brexit, were twenty points ahead in the polls. The triple whammy of Brexit, the chicken coup, and a new Tory leadership had left Labour languishing in the mid-twenties, its leader with negative approval ratings. While, prior to Brexit, the party had been incrementally repairing its base, driving up its core vote in a number of by-elections, it began losing more seats than it won. The decision by centre-Right MPs Jamie Reed and Tristram Hunt to resign their seats forced Labour to fight a couple of urgent defensive battles in Stoke and Copeland, with UKIP and Trident driving the news agenda. Labour lost Copeland and barely held on to Stoke. In local council elections it performed poorly, and lost the West Midlands mayoral contest to the Tories thanks to an abysmal campaign run by the Blairite Siôn Simon on the Brexit slogan 'Take Back Control'. Labour had been divided over the triggering of Article 50, with even Corbyn's ally Clive Lewis resigning from the shadow cabinet in order to vote against the decision. Corbyn's advisors felt it was a case of short-term pain for long-term gain, in that demonstrating acceptance of the result would help prevent it from continuing to be an issue that could damage Labour. But the immediate risk was that by three-line-whipping through Article 50, without achieving any additional concessions, Labour would give the Tories full control of the negotiations. As in Scotland's independence referendum, the EU referendum seemed to have precari-ously realigned politics along nationalist lines, giving the Tories a huge advantage. For May to wait any longer, and risk the negative economic effects of Brexit undermining her support, would have seemed perverse.

When the announcement was made, almost all but Corbyn were pensive. For Corbyn and his advisor Seumas Milne, it was a clarifying moment. They knew what to do, and saw it as an opportunity to get the message out. That afternoon, an emergency meeting was held, and immediately afterwards they hit the campaign trail. One senior advisor explains that they went straight from the meeting to knocking on doors in Croydon. A registration campaign and a social media strategy were embarked upon instantly. Labour, as far behind in the polls as it was, hit the ground running. Meanwhile, in what would be an ill omen for her campaign, as Tory MPs emerged blinking into daylight to greet the news that they were now embroiled in an election, May went AWOL without so much as a cabinet discussion.

Corbyn's cheerfulness must have seemed bizarre to Westminster watchers. Indeed, he began his campaign by pointing out that he had stood for Labour leader as a 200–1 outsider, warning the media not to write him off. Was this just a cute line from a struggling politician, or a genuine admission of the overwhelming odds stacked against him? In fairness to Corbyn, his refusal to panic had already been demonstrated as a strength during the coup attempt. What is more, he had always shown his best side when under pressure, and campaigning.

But this wasn't how his backbench opponents saw it. Many Labour MPs went home to their constituencies and prepared for defeat. As the election began, it was leaked that up to a hundred Labour MPs were preparing to form their own group after the election if Labour got thrashed, presumably as a precursor to a coup.[40] Other plans included the idea of reducing the number of directly elected seats on the National Executive Committee, so that Corbyn's support in the apparatus would be watered down.[41] Several newspapers and journalists speculated on whether Labour could just overthrow Corbyn in a coup before the election. Alas, the *Telegraph* reported, they could not because that would mean rerunning the past, failed coup attempt by triggering another leadership election.[42] Nonetheless, the Labour Right were preparing for a bloodbath and a merciless war against a leadership discredited by awful results.

The type of campaign run by the party's management at Labour HQ, and by local anti-Corbyn MPs, reflected this expectation. The official campaign refused to direct resources and activists into potential target seats, instead waving a defensive struggle to 'save' seats that they assumed were marginal. In Battersea, activists were encouraged to troop up to Westminster North. In North London, activists were asked to campaign for Enfield North MP Joan Ryan. Ryan, one of the most voluble anti-Corbyn backbenchers, and chair of Labour Friends of Israel in parliament, distributed a leaflet to her constituents suggesting that they would have more confidence in Theresa May than in Jeremy Corbyn, but that they could feel safe in voting for her as she was reliably right wing.

Everything from that side of the Labour establishment was predicated on the idea that the Tories were about to annihilate Labour, and the party's job was to save as much as possible and try to survive long enough to depose Corbyn.

Blue Wedge

However, the early signs were that the Tories were fal-
tering. May's disappearance for the first few days of the
campaign, the disorientation of Conservative MPs, and the
failure of the Tory campaign to get off the ground immediately gave Labour an unexpected opening.

Even when May did begin to make appearances, they
were carefully stage-managed, with questions tightly controlled and May seemingly desperate to avoid a spontaneous
interaction with anyone. This was enough to draw negative
publicity from irritated journalists, and it began to explain
why the Conservative establishment had not wanted an
election contest between May and Leadsom, since Leadsom
may well have won. The Tories also increasingly gave the
impression of being a one-trick pony: regarding Brexit as
their trump card, they played it obsessively. For May, the
campaign came down to who the electorate wanted to negotiate for Britain in withdrawing from the European Union.
And, indeed, as long as that was the key issue, the Tories
had a clear advantage. Not just because the stark Tory position on Brexit motivated their supporters, but because May
was personally popular, while Corbyn's personal polling
was abysmal – the index of a very public auto-da-fé (no
smoke without fire).

What is more, the flag-waving and tub-thumping about
Brexit was to be complemented by a relentlessly negative campaign targeting Jeremy Corbyn and his allies
as anti-British oddballs with a soft spot for the nation's
enemies. The themes of 'terror' and 'security' were to

dominate, and this made perfect sense. Security had always been a red line in British politics, and voters were arguably feeling more jittery, more insecure, more precarious in their everyday existence, and perhaps more terrified of the future, than for decades. May, with her autocratic pretensions, was positioning herself as the nation's protector. This was, moreover, the kind of thing that Tory strategist Lynton Crosby specialised in: 'wedge issues' to divide the party form its base, and 'dog-whistling' to motivate hardcore racist voters without offending others. And, surely, May's personal failings aside, in any other context, if the machinery was working as usual, an anti-war socialist with Corbyn's past would have been easy to demonise.

The Tories had prepared the terrain by relentlessly attacking Corbyn for his Hamas 'links', and statements on war and terror, positioning him as a threat to British families. The tabloids had depicted Corbyn as an anti-British oddball unable to display correct decorum at the Cenotaph. The *Sun* ran a notorious story falsely claiming that Corbyn danced a jig before the country's Remembrance Sunday ceremony.[43] And once the snap election was called, the Tories began to tax Corbyn for IRA 'links' dug up by Andrew Gilligan of the *Telegraph*, and repeatedly raked over by broadcasters like Andrew Neil of the BBC. These promised to be particularly potent given that there had been a jihadist attack weeks before the election was called, which was followed by two further such attacks in the course of the campaign.

The substance of the allegations looked a little threadbare to anyone who paid close attention. After all, Corbyn had been elected to his seat as a 'Troops Out' socialist, with a lot of support from Irish constituents. It was no surprise that he would attend republican events; sit in on Diplock hearings (jury-less courts used by the British in Northern Ireland); meet with Sinn Fein leaders; campaign for political prisoners like the Birmingham Six and the Guildford Four; campaign against strip-searching, plastic bullets, and CS gas; and otherwise condemn the British campaign in the six counties. Nor was there anything dishonourable about this. In retrospect, there is even more damning material on the British counterinsurgency available today than there was before, particularly as it relates to the relations between the government and Loyalist death squads. Almost twenty years after the Good Friday agreement, moreover, the idea of talking to Sinn Fein representatives, some of whom have had beaming encounters with the British monarch, looks a lot less controversial.

However, the headline usually counts for more than the content, and the headline insinuation of the coverage was that there was more to it than just ideological socialist republicanism. Corbyn, it was claimed, was on the side not just of the terrorists, but of the terror. As Andrew Neil put it to him, 'Isn't the truth that you've basically supported the armed struggle for a united Ireland, but now you want to be prime minister you have to distance yourself from it?'[44] This line of prosecution was predictably drawn from the right-wing press, with Neil picking his preferred insinuations from an old piece by Andrew Gilligan for the *Telegraph*. Gilligan explained, with pearl-clutching hyperventilation, the details of Corbyn's circulation through the republican scene in the 1980s: he had even attended events run by the Wolfe Tone Society which promoted 'the policies and publications of Sinn Fein'. The same paper worked up a similar surplus of spittle lather over Corbyn's 'three decades of blocking terror legislation'. The paper persisted with an 'exclusive' story showing that MI5 had opened a file on Jeremy Corbyn 'amid concerns over his IRA links'. The piece never explained in simple, precise terms what these 'links' were, nor did it address the natural concern that readers would have about intelligence services using their resources to spy on elected politicians. But it did show that MI5 had opened files on many left-wing politicians and 'infiltrated anti-racist groups'. On the day of the election, the *Telegraph* ran a front-page story by former MI6 boss Richard Dearlove, harrumphing that 'Corbyn would not be allowed into security services, so he's not fit for No 10'.[45] Again, the idea that democracy might take precedence over the desiderata of the spooks seemed not to have occurred to him.

The *Sun*, publishing its hit piece mere hours after a bombing in Manchester in which a jihadist suicide attacker targeted young people and children leaving an Ariana Grande concert, claimed that Corbyn had 'Blood On His Hands'. Its front-page headline was based on an 'exclusive' piece written by a 'former IRA man' who claimed that Corbyn 'might not have planted a bomb, but he made it easier for those who did'. The *Sun* didn't explain that the 'former IRA man' in question, Sean O'Callaghan, was by his own account an Irish Special Branch operative who had been working in the IRA as an informant. Nor did it mention his past record on factual accuracy, such as his attempt to depict the murdered Catholic lawyer Pat Finucane as an IRA man, which was discredited by the House of Commons inquiry into the killing. Nonetheless, any scrupulous reader would have looked in vain in the piece for any specific new information: its sole argument was that by being pro-republican, Corbyn 'boosted the morale' of the IRA.[46] By the same rationale, presumably, those who were pro-Union 'boosted the morale' of the Ulster Volunteer Force, the Ulster Defence Association, and similar Loyalist death squads. The *Sun* had form in this, having previously run a thirty-year-old discredited story about Corbyn funding an 'IRA bomber'.[47]

In another moment of the unfolding media spectacle, a broadcaster criticised Corbyn for refusing to single out the IRA for special condemnation, instead insisting on condemning all the killing. This was an extraordinary criticism: *his refusal to apply double standards* proved that he must be an enemy of the people. By insinuation, if you haven't shown a consistent bias toward the British state, the Union, and the Loyalist paramilitaries defending it, you're as good as one of *them*. That, naturally, segued neatly into the Conservative campaign claiming that Corbyn had, in the words of Security Minister Ben Wallace, 'spent a lifetime siding with Britain's enemies'. Or, as Foreign Secretary Boris Johnson put it, that Corbyn had 'taken the side of just about every adversary this country has had in my lifetime'. The Tories went further in their attack ads, editing pieces of Corbyn's speeches to make it appear as if he refused to condemn IRA violence at all.[48]

The chorus was in synch, the choreography perfectly timed. From the Tory tabloids to Tory ministers to broadcasters who took their lead from both, there was a consensus that this was a crucial issue. And beyond: many Labour MPs had already taken the view that Corbyn's fitness, or otherwise, to lead hung on his ability to convincingly answer these loaded questions. During the attempted coup against Corbyn, Owen Smith's supporters in the parliamentary party had urged him to attack Corbyn over the IRA. Labour's MP for Stoke, Gareth Snell, had previously condemned Corbyn as an 'IRA-supporting friend of Hamas'.[49]

And yet, all of this had already been aired over and over. The leadership team had thought carefully about the kinds of attack they would be exposed to, and concluded that there was no new angle for the media, so the attack dogs have to just go harder on the same lines that they had already used. This meant that Labour, for the most part, had its answers worked out. An example of this was when Sophy Ridge of Sky News confronted Corbyn with one of the nebulous 'links' allegations. This time, the claim was that he was general secretary of the editorial board of Labour Briefing at a time when it ran an inflammatory story about the IRA campaign. Corbyn's withers were unwrung, as he calmly debunked Ridge's claim, and the source for it. But since none of these attacks had proved effective against Corbyn before, what made journalists, or the Tories, think they would avail now? As a senior advisor put it,

They just attacked, attacked, attacked. When there was a coup attempt against Corbyn, we thought it was going to go very badly. But within nine hours, a rally had been organised outside parliament with ten thousand people in attendance. Every attack strengthened Corbyn by motivating people. For every MP who attacked him, fifty people outside supported him. So what they did was strengthen Corbyn. And the Tories thought, 'we'll do the same thing; that's how we're going to run our campaign'. No one learns. Journalists keep thinking this stuff will work. The *Sun* is still running with the IRA smears. Why do they think it's suddenly going to stick?

It didn't stick. As election day loomed it was broadly agreed that Corbyn was mopping the floor with Theresa May on the issue of defence and national security. How on earth did that happen? In the first instance, Corbyn weathered the attacks with the same placid good humour that he had displayed during the Labour leadership coup in 2016. Though occasionally hesitant or slightly stumbling in his speech, he proved impossible to bait into losing his temper. More importantly, he took the initiative in combating the narrative of Theresa May, making a well-poised speech critiquing the role of British wars in generating support for apocalyptic jihadist outfits.

This was subject to the usual barrage of wounded retorts in the British media. The *Telegraph* claimed it was 'blaming the victim', while one of its columnists declared that Corbyn had 'long hated Britain'. The *Spectator* seethed that he had 'always blamed Britain first'. The *Sun* predicted that Corbyn's intervention would provoke 'outrage'. And the *Independent*, while agreeing with the substance of his

speech, pathetically claimed that it was an 'error of judgment' to raise it so soon. The leader column was even
illustrated with a bizarre political cartoon, depicting the
election as a tortoise-and-hare story in which May had
recently slipped on the banana peel of her social care plan,
while Corbyn was about to scupper his own catching up
by slipping on the banana peel of his terrorism speech. But
within days, the polling showed that Corbyn had won the
argument with the general public, and that he was giving
voice to what had long been an unspoken common sense.[50]

Corbyn did not exclusively swing against May from the
Left on this issue. In the aftermath of yet another jihadist outrage, this time involving multiple stabbings in the
London Bridge area, Corbyn made it clear that he supported
the police decision to use lethal force in that situation, and
ran hard on Labour's policy of increasing police numbers.
The idea that increasing police numbers would make the
slightest difference to terrorism seems far-fetched, particularly when there is no conclusive evidence that it even
affects the burglary rate. Nonetheless, representing the
police cuts since 2010 as another aspect of the Tories' sadis-
tic austerity project, Corbyn used the issue to trash May on
what most had assumed was her home turf, thus controlling
the news cycle for a couple of days in which the attacks
were foremost in the coverage. May, having been quite efficiently ruthless in taking on the Police Federation and the
Association of Chief Police Officers, forcing through both
cuts and reforms to the police after years in which uncritical backing for the thin blue line had been bipartisan, was
disarmed.

Manifesto

Thus was the proverbial spanner thrown into the works of the Lynton Crosby spin machine. The centrepiece of Corbyn's aggressive campaign, however, was the Labour manifesto. Almost universally panned in the media, it turned out to be wildly popular. Voters 'overwhelmingly' backed its key policies, including investment in house building; renationalising the rail, mail, and energy; free education; and raising taxes on the richest 5 per cent.[51] This was *entirely predictable* to those who paid attention to anything other than the very narrow media consensus. Polling and social-attitudes surveys had, for years, shown strong support for policies of just these kinds.[52] The difficulty had been getting any major party to offer them. Nonetheless, the public debate continued as if nothing had really changed, and Corbyn was about to be caught short. The response of the media could be divided roughly into the stereotyped right-wing response, which was that Labour's policies were part of a radical attack on middle-class property rights, and the liberal–realist response, which was that the manifesto was an expensive shopping list of policies, laudable in principle but utterly impracticable.

In the liberal–realist category was the *Guardian*, which lamented that while Labour had made certain ideas thinkable, it had done 'too little to make the thinkable seem realistic and practical'. The *Observer* took a similar stance, complaining that the manifesto gave 'no sense of the trade-offs a government would need to make, simply hinting at an unlimited pot of cash'. Andrew Grice of the

Independent scoffed that it was a 'long shopping list' of policies from 'a party that knows it has no hope of power'. Nick Robinson of the BBC agreed, describing Corbyn's manifesto as 'long on passion' and 'short on details. Story of his life.'

This critique, for all that it spoke of feasibility, was not about the technicalities of costing and implementation. Labour had no doubt drafted some of its manifesto in haste, yet it was costed and the Conservative manifesto wasn't. And the sums added up. Moreover, the specific costing mechanisms weren't from Mars – raising taxes on corporations to a level last seen in 2010 surely wasn't breaking the mould. This was a matter of what the journalist class thought was possible in politics. Expectations had been shaped for so long by the bipartisan consensus that the main task in politics, to which every other goal was subordinate, was to streamline government, cut costs, and reduce debts, as though the state was a small business. From this perspective, even the Theresa May–Nigel Farage fantasy of Britain as a 'global trader' – the Del Boy Trotter school of statecraft – looks somehow more realistic than expanding public investment.

On the other side of the political fence, the reactionary press preferred to accuse Labour of taxing 'ordinary working families' (the *Daily Star*) and 'middle-class homeowners' (the *Telegraph*). This was an extraordinary claim given Labour's express pledge, not matched by Conservatives, not to raise taxes for the bottom 95 per cent. The basis of it was the Tory interpretation of Labour's plan to investigate replacing the poll tax with the land value tax. Taking their estimate of the revenue that would be raised by such a tax, they claimed that, averaged out across households, Labour's idea would treble the amount of tax they were paying. But, of course, the point of the land value tax is that it is progressive – most households would pay less, while the wealthiest property barons would pay a lot more.[53] By and large, given the popularity of Labour's manifesto, the Tories and their press supporters preferred to avoid talking too much about it, and keep the fire aimed at Corbyn's record in the 1980s.

By contrast, the Tory manifesto, which turned out to be disastrous, was at first considered a masterful stroke by the press, combining classically Tory policies with some populist feints toward the working class. The *Daily Mail* and *Daily Express* saluted it on their front pages. 'May's plan for a fairer Britain,' the *Express* offered. 'At last, a PM not afraid to be honest with you,' exulted the *Mail*, delighted that May had addressed the 'needs of ordinary working families' without making any big promises. For the *Sun*, it was a 'no-brainer', the manifesto showing a 'grown-up Tory party' which was willing to take 'tough choices' that would even 'make traditional Tories poorer', such as the policy of means-testing the winter fuel allowance, while standing up to 'fatcat corporations' (which in practice simply meant criticising the pensions rip-off artist Philip Green). The front page, headlined 'Blue Labour', lauded 'May's "red Tory" manifesto' with its 'Bold ... bid to win over socialist voters'. Even the *Guardian*, while criticising May's proposals, suggested that it betokened a potentially very popular 'new Toryism': 'Like Tony Blair in 1997, Mrs

May is where the majority of voters are: to the left on the economy and to the right on social issues.'[54]

With the single exception of the tribal *Mirror*, there was a remarkable unanimity that May had redefined politics for the next generation. To an extent, this was a perfectly understandable calculation in the aftermath of the Brexit vote, and in a political culture used to the logic of triangulation. There is always a temptation to think that the surest route to popularity is to come up with a new hybrid of left-wing and right-wing ideologies – 'Blue Labour', 'Red Tories', 'One Nation Labour', and May advisor Nick Timothy's 'Erdington Conservatism' are characteristic failed expressions of this basic strategic conception. And since long-standing polling trends show that most people tend to cleave to the right on social issues, and to the left on economic issues, May's rhetoric about the 'working class' and nationalist, anti-immigration, securitarian rhetoric ought to have worked.

And yet within days, the Tory manifesto was widely agreed to be a disaster. Attacking traditional Tory voters no longer looked so smart. The policy of means-testing winter fuel payments, and making the elderly pay for social care out of the value of their home, was regarded as spiteful rather than popular. It took very little time for it to become obvious that the social care policy – dubbed the 'dementia tax' by Labour – was not aimed at the rich elderly. To qualify, one only had to have, over one's lifetime, accumulated assets worth over £100,000 in a country where the average house price was £215,847.[55] What is more, the Tories bewilderingly insisted on policies that would please only a small number of already committed voters, such as repealing the ban on fox hunting. But perhaps more importantly, May's class rhetoric was a direct response to the potential appeal of Corbynism. The explicit attack on Corbyn had always been *he can't win*. The suppressed fear was *he might actually win*. And since the Corbyn campaign didn't accede to the politics of demoralisation, of there being 'no alternative', and instead pressed ahead with a radical form of class politics, May's rhetoric looked like very thin gruel indeed. Accordingly, the polls began shifting, and the Tory campaign went into meltdown.

Memes and media

If Labour's manifesto was a turning point in the campaign, the second turning point was Corbyn's unexpected appearance before a crowd of concert-goers at Tranmere Rovers football stadium on 20 May.

This almost didn't happen. Many in Corbyn's team were worried that the response was unpredictable. This was not a political crowd. Those in attendance were eighteen-to thirty-year-olds not expecting a politician to show up. There was the risk that they might boo, throw bottles. The appearance might be relentlessly mocked and trolled on social media. It was judged that Labour's campaign was going well, so why spoil it with a big risk like this?

However, there was also an argument that Corbyn had already done the mass meetings outside, and while he would continue to do these – he attended over a hundred events, ninety of them rallies, travelling over 7,000 miles –

he arguably needed to do something new. The bands appearing that night, from Reverend and the Makers to the Libertines, were keen for Corbyn to attend. And so it was agreed that he would introduce Reverend and the Makers. Corbyn gave a short, characteristic speech addressing education, jobs, health, housing, and decent pay, thanked the crowd, and stood back from the microphone. There was some cheering, and then a low noise started up from the crowd. One of those present recalls,

> We heard the 'Ooooh' noise, and for a moment we thought they were going to boo. And Jeremy paused for a minute before he clocked it. They were singing 'Oh, Jeremy Corbyn'. It gave us such a buzz. Then for the rest of that concert, between every single song, twenty thousand people were singing his name. And then it spread. Last week, someone tweeted footage of people chanting it at the Truck Festival, which is between Ed Vaizey and David Cameron's constituencies, right in the middle of Tory country. I thought it would go well, but no one thought it would go that well.

This meme, the most popular of many among Corbyn supporters, popped up in nightclubs, concerts, and football stadiums all over the country, from Newcastle to Liverpool, Camden, and Birmingham. How did this happen? It wasn't because of a Labour plan: you can't script enthusiasm like this. It wasn't because of Corbyn's personal magnetism: the man who went on the BBC's *The One Show* to discuss his allotment and jam-making predilections doesn't exude power and dominance. But arguably, unlike many politicians he approaches young people as equals, and takes them seriously as interlocutors. The same qualities enabled him to reach out to celebrity supporters like JME, who interviewed him for *i-D*. One squirms to imagine, for example, Theresa May or Philip Hammond in a similar setting.

However, none of this would have worked as well or had the reverberations it did, were it not for a profound change taking place. As the Tories discovered to their cost, one reason their strategy wouldn't work was because the media weren't working as usual. Patterns of changing media consumption, long under way, had fundamentally changed politics, and Team Corbyn noticed.

The canary in the coalmine here was the 2015 Labour leadership campaign, wherein Corbyn's social media strategy effectively engaged the broadcasters and press barons in a dispute over the meaning and framing of politics, while also bypassing old media to reach those demographics who had long since stopped paying attention to the print media and television news. By 2017, Labour had improved its game with the traditional media. This involved exploiting May's increasingly apparent weaknesses, including her bewildering refusal to debate Corbyn directly. Corbyn had handled the obstreperous Jeremy Paxman with stoical good humour, exploiting May's weakness and the duty of broadcasters to attempt impartiality by offering equal time to the candidates. But Labour had also rolled out a more sophisticated set of digital operations.

The Tories, reports suggested, were winning the battle in terms of paid-for negative advertising online, targeting marginals with advertising intended to make hate figures out of Corbyn, McDonnell, and – in the 'dog-whistling' category – Diane Abbott. The advertising sent out from Labour HQ, meanwhile, largely avoided mentioning the leader, reflecting the assumption that he would be a negative factor.[56] But paid-for negative advertising is nowhere near as effective as organic, unpaid reach. A paid attack ad is no match for a dozen friends sharing a clickbait article praising Jeremy Corbyn. When it comes to social media, cash is no match for cachet. And Corbyn's team began to win the battle through its official social media accounts, through outriders who voluntarily produced acres of publicity material, and through a mass of users who participated in an emerging online Corbynista culture. The *Evening Standard* reported,

> Mr Corbyn's official Twitter and Facebook pages posted 925 messages over the election campaign, receiving 2.8 million shares. Mrs May's pages posted 159 times, nearly six times less than the Labour leader, and her messages were shared just 130,000 times.[57]

Facebook users were overwhelmingly inclined to share pro-Corbyn and anti-Tory stories, including celebrity endorsements from Stormzy and JME, and stories from Corbyn-supporting websites like *The Canary* and blogs like *Another Angry Voice*, which accounted for 917,000 shares. Stories about Labour's rise in the polls accounted for another 557,600 shares. Labour social media campaigning played a significant role in signing up one million people to register to vote, partly accounting for what would be an improved overall turnout. There were also signs of more focus in its online output. Labour's own pages notably shared fewer stories than in the previous election, but significantly more video content than in 2015. The content it did share was also far more positive than the Tory campaign, focusing on its social promises to build and inspire support.[58]

Labour also invested in some more gimmicky fare. Corbyn was the first leader of a political party to sign up for a Snapchat account. And on election day, Snapchat released a Labour paid-for 'Corbyn' filter for supporters. Supporters also created a 1980s-style arcade game, Corbyn Run, in which the eponymous hero took on Tories, tax dodgers, the ghost of Margaret Thatcher, and Boris Johnson on a zipline. It would be easy to scoff at this kind of thing were it unveiled as a grand leadership initiative, like the 'Edstone', but it worked well as a sideline in a campaign fizzing with energy and confidence.

Beyond the distribution of messages, Labour activists used social media as a mobilising tool. Momentum was able to raise £100,000 from supporters through Crowdpac at the start of the campaign, which it then used to build online tools to help activists. For example, the website mynearestmarginal.com, advertised constantly on social media, directed activists to marginal constituencies where their efforts could make the most difference.[59] And Momentum activists, deploying the characteristic grass-roots methods of street stalls, door knocking, and evening events, were crucial to winning many of the seats taken by Labour. Battersea, for example, would not have even been the target of a Labour effort were it not for Momentum. Derby North, similarly, was won by Momentum. They also contributed to the online buzz, with their videos, along with those created by the 'Jeremy Corbyn for PM' social media account, being shared more than official Labour fare.

By the final week of campaigning, it was clear that Corbyn was far more popular than the coverage had suggested, and that the negative polling didn't tell the whole story. The polling firms couldn't agree on what the actual final result would be. Almost all polling, however, gave the Tories a significant lead. YouGov, which had been one of the most favourable to Labour, put the Tory lead at 7 per cent in its final poll; Ipsos Mori put it at 8 per cent, ComRes at 10 per cent, ICM at 12 per cent, and BMG at 13 per cent. Only Survation came close, putting Labour at 40 per cent and the Tories at 41 per cent. But the mere fact of such a diversity of projections and such disputation over them, coupled with the palpable vibrancy of Labour's campaign on the streets, showed that something unusual was up. Britain was proving to be a more politically turbulent country than it had been for years.

The media and pundits simply refused to believe it. In the *Daily Mail*, Dan Hodges had written confidently that 'Corbyn will struggle to significantly exceed the 31 per cent Ed Miliband achieved in 2015'. In the *Observer*, Nick Cohen had expected the Tories to 'tear' Labour to 'pieces', a 'flaying' that would leave a handful of Labour MPs: 'My advice is to think of a number and then halve it.' The *Independent* front page asserted that May was 'on track' for a 'sweeping win'. Its Blairite political columnist John Rentoul launched an attack on YouGov's election model for projecting a hung parliament. 'Tory lead grows in election's final poll,' celebrated *The Times* on its front page, projecting a majority of up to fifty seats. The *Sun* was less complacent, warning that a 'Marxist extremist' and 'terrorists' friend' could be on the brink of power. It begged readers to 'keep Corbyn and his sinister Marxist gang away from power'.[60]

At just after 10 p.m. on 8 June, the exit poll told the tale. Labour had broken through. May had lost her majority. Corbyn might even have to lead a minority government.

A New Future

As the election results came in at Labour HQ, the atmosphere was something akin to a wild party, gatecrashed by the living dead. As Corbyn's supporters roared excitedly at each confirmation that the exit poll was right, some of his opponents wandered around in a blitzed, uncomprehending daze.

Many of Labour's victories were of a kind that it would only normally get if it was winning the election – the ancient Tory constituencies, the middle-class bellwethers, the shock revolt of working-class voters in the richest borough in London. Unbidden, the ghosts of 1997 resurfaced. For the many, not the few. Things can only get better. Were you up for Portillo? On the Left, abruptly, a sense of pervasive gloom, a foreboding of locust years to be weathered with hard-bitten resilience, gave way to the euphoric realisation that Britain is not just one country, not just the declining, nostalgic, backward-looking cultural sump that incubates racist xenophobia and allows right-wing hatchet men to take out every resentment on the poorest. Another, better country had just announced its existence.

A short video made for the *Guardian* by John Harris illustrated the change. Having gone out to record the political direction of working-class Britain, and largely found the rightward shift of older, white voters angered over Corbyn's 'IRA links', he suddenly found something different. The young celebrating outside pubs and clubs. The Corbyn chant. Asked why they voted Corbyn, they offered various answers: free school meals, the NHS, the politicians ganging up on Corbyn, the *Sun*'s bile. Two young women, clearly delighted, gave this answer: 'We want a new future.'

Beyond the Left, too, the mood changed. While some of the mea culpas from Corbyn's oblocutors were transparently graceless and begrudging, many people expressed a genuine and even moving change of heart. Even Corbyn's hardened opponents, such as Peter Mandelson and John McTernan, began to express a measured respect for him. Even Tony Blair eventually popped his head out of the crypt to own up to Corbyn's success. Those, like Chris Leslie MP, who absurdly tried to claim that the result only showed that Labour could have won with a better leader, were largely laughed at.

It is, in fact, possible that with slightly more time to play, Labour would have won. The momentum clearly favoured Labour, and the Tory strategy had run out steam within the first three weeks. Nothing, not even two high-profile and brutal terrorist attacks in the middle of the campaign, could put the wind back in Theresa May's sails. Labour sources close to the leadership differ on their take about what could have been, with some arguing that perhaps the limits of radical social democracy were reached at 40 per cent of the vote. But either way, it was thanks to Corbyn's leadership and the radical programme it made possible that Labour got as far as it did.

Beyond Labour, the campaign's major achievement was to destroy Theresa May's authority. The Tories, having grovelled before, were suddenly filled with despair and rage. Conservative MPs lined up to savage May. Nigel Evans scathed that she had shot the party 'in the head'. George Osborne gleefully called May a 'dead woman walking'. The Osborne-edited *Evening Standard* took to lambasting May with front-page relish on an almost daily basis. ITV political editor Robert Peston reported a 'senior Tory MP' saying, 'We all fucking hate her. But there is nothing we can do. She has totally fucked us.' According to Ian Katz, editor of BBC *Newsnight*, 'senior Tories' feared going 'to the country any time soon' since Corbyn would be the 'likely winner'. Theresa May struggles on as Tory leader; it is only for as long as her backbenchers are terrified of having a leadership contest, since 'pressure for another election could become irresistible'.[61]

Beyond that, it became immediately clear that the Tories would be unable to govern on a Conservative agenda. The manifesto, lauded on its release, was now a disaster that could not be implemented. Even having negotiated a lash-up with the Democratic Unionist Party, they had to retreat from some of their policies such as pension cuts, means-testing winter fuel payments, and scrapping free school meals. The party's research instructs them that they lost because of their support for austerity, and indeed they had been warned about this before the election. Even so, the Tory chancellor Philip Hammond is determined to keep spending as low as possible on the premise that it will give confidence to financial markets jittered by Brexit, and is resisting attempts to raise public sector pay. All signs currently are that a major civil war is coming within the Conservative Party, with Europe, supposedly a settled issue, at the fore.[62]

'Make June the end of May,' a Labour slogan had said. Barring a freak occurrence, that is exactly what they've done.

6
Prospects: Can Corbyn Win?

Tell no lies; claim no easy victories.
— Amílcar Cabral

The Uses of Crisis, and the Dialectic of Defeat

Two years of Corbyn's leadership have shown us that he thrives in the face of crisis. This isn't just a matter of his unearthly calm and serene good humour when under attack. In another political situation, crisis would mean demise. But in this situation, crises have repeatedly shown themselves to be opportunities.

The chicken coup, which at first appeared to be the beginning of the end, strengthened Corbyn's base and imposed a rapid political clarification on his supporters. Brexit, which looked so devastating to Labour, is now a poisoned chalice for the Tories. The snap election, announced with regal presumption by Theresa May, was a chance for Corbyn to make a once-in-a-lifetime breakthrough for the radical

Left. Some of Corbyn's allies believe that he thrives in such circumstances because he is no longer boxed in by protocol. The journalist Steve Richards had a point when he claimed that power has often left Corbyn 'more trapped as a politician than he has ever been', not simply because of political compromises he has had to make, but rather because of deference to internal procedures and proprieties. Campaigning for political change, rather than smooth continuity, is what he is good at, and it allows him to take risks. Perhaps, though, there is also something else at work. If Corbyn doesn't seem to be afraid of defeat, it might be in part because even defeats have their uses.

In 1861, as the American Civil War raged, the anti-slavery liberal Charles Eliot Norton wrote in praise of defeat.[1] The Union Army had suffered a bitter setback in the first battle of Bull Run, near Washington, DC, its slow and ponderous action allowing an easy victory to the Confederates. The defeat was 'in no true sense a disaster', Norton wrote, and was indeed both deserved and a valuable lesson. Indeed, its 'ultimate consequences' were 'better than those of a victory would have been'. The latter would have rewarded and entrenched complacency and bad strategy, whereas defeat allowed for fast rethinking and regroupment.

Defeat is an underrated experience in political life. It is natural that on the political Left, at least, the scarring experiences of defeat in the 1980s – of the miners and the wider trade union movement, of Militant, of the Greater London Council, of the Labour Left – would lead to a weary cynicism about the possibilities for change in such a reactionary country. This deadly onslaught by the Right has been a primary argument for the ascendancy, within the Labour Party, of a managerial caste hostile to many of its traditions – not just those associated with the Left, but even the old Right defined by the likes of Wilson, Jenkins, and Callaghan.

Indeed, if principle only leads to defeat, why not turn to electoral professionals, media operators, and brutal party managers with at least the virtue of a killer instinct? If nothing else avails, why not at least get some form of electoral revenge on the authors of said defeat by entrusting everything to those who seem to know how to win? And if the Conservative-aligned media are so grossly powerful, why not hand the reins to those who can play the media's game? Surely, those who in such circumstances cleave to doctrine at the expense of exercising power, even if only to mildly temper the excesses of capitalism, are at best political Don Quixotes, and at worst fanatical wreckers. Such is essentially the argument of the Blairites, for whom the project is about making Labour an effective 'party of government' rather than an effective opposition. Forget the policy wonkery, the 'blue-sky thinking', the Geoff Mulgans and Charles Leadbeaters, the Spads and fads, and the passing manias of New Labour triviology. The celebrated cerebral spine of the Blairites was in fact flimsy because it was inessential given the paucity of ambition: it requires little intellectual finesse to leave things more or less as they are. The core of New Labour was its appeal to power. It offered a tempting thrill of success to those who had been so brutally defeated, even if the condition of that success was pre-emptive surrender on all essential questions.

And for some time, at least, the Blairites had everything their way. Through good report and ill; through privatisation, war, and growing inequality; through the tumescence of a billionaire class, the NHS crisis caused by usurious Private Finance Initiatives, and the bankers' pillage, there was barely a simmering reflex of revolt in the Labour Party. The new management ruled with a striking brittleness, defensiveness and paranoia, acting on the basis of a sort of organised distrust of the membership. They used enforcers like Margaret McDonagh to ensure that the leadership line was rarely up for debate, invoking 'unwritten' rules to blockade critical motions, or depending on loyal apparatchiks or trade union allies for diversion. The small remaining left-wing fringe was habitually derided as a coterie of 'Trots'. Loyalists were parachuted into safe seats. When one inconvenient left-winger, Liz Davies, was selected by members as the parliamentary candidate for Leeds North East, Blair and his allies concocted a media smear campaign, and the NEC undemocratically blocked her selection. Those who departed from the loyalist fold over matters of conscience were 'traitors', as Tom Watson dubbed Emily Thornberry when she rejected the government's authoritarian policy of ninety-day detention without trial. Despite their comprehensive triumph over the Left, the leadership clique couldn't trust anyone. Davies, in her memoir of the *haut*-Blairite period, *Through the Looking Glass*, recalls the inability of the leadership to accept responsibility for failure: it was always blamed on 'a lapse in presentation or a conspiracy', or on 'Labour Party members or Labour Party councillors'. Conference speeches, even those of delegates, were written by party staff, and critical delegates systematically prevented from speaking.[2]

Whatever the Blairites lacked in persuasion, they made up for with brute power and with the unanswerable moral trump card: amid sustained economic growth, Labour was winning elections. You can't argue with success and, for as long as this was the case, the Labour Right could couch their agenda in the language of technocracy: 'what matters is what works'. Members voted with their feet, becoming inactive or resigning, while voters began to boycott the polls in unprecedented numbers. It was as if faced with the whole idea of fighting for a party that had become so symbiotically dependent upon the banks, business, the media, and the less liberal wings of the state, a party so crushingly dispiriting, so lacking in promise, millions simply gave up. The brief frisson of victory, the beautiful summer of 1997, when all that mattered was whether you were 'up for Portillo', seemed to have given way to a post-democratic melancholia and a defeat more insidious and disabling than any which Thatcher had inflicted. In 1997, all roads had led to the 'free market'. By 2010, all roads led to austerity. Blyth Valley MP Ronnie Campbell suggested that the major difference between Labour and the Tories was that Labour would 'cut your throat slowly', while the Tories would 'cut your head off'.[3] Given such a choice, approximately 5 million voters – most of them working class – abandoned the party between 1997 and 2010, largely abstaining. Nothing, not even Ed Miliband's neurotic charm, not even the frantic proliferation of new syntheses – 'Blue Labour', 'One Nation Labour', etc. – seemed able to reverse the decline.

Given this dreary history, the understandable temptation among Corbyn's most loyal supporters has been to accentuate the positive, while forgetting the underlying weaknesses that characterise the British Left. However, even in the afterglow of unexpected success, it is worth reflecting on the productive possibilities of defeat. The history of Labourism is, in a way, a dialectic of defeats. Labourism emerged from the setbacks of working-class politics in the nineteenth century, the failure of the 'Lib–Lab' alliance, and the legal impediments to industrial organisation. Corbyn, too, owes his position in a strange way to defeats. Had the British Left and the labour movement not been so comprehensively defeated by Thatcherism in the 1980s, it is more than likely that Blairism would have forced a radical-Left breakaway from the party, as happened to Continental social democracy – thus we would not be talking about a left-wing capture of the Labour leadership. Had the Blairites not been able to force through a series of party reforms reducing union influence, but also ultimately creating 'one-member–one-vote', Corbyn would not have been able to win just by getting the support of most voters. Had Labour not been defeated in 2010 and 2015, the necessary reappraisal of the limits and failures of its recent past would have been postponed, and the sources of degeneration might have continued until it was too late.

Even now, there are many possible ways in which the Corbyn project could suffer setbacks and defeats. The question is what one does with them. To assimilate defeat is to learn the correct lessons from it. One reason why New Labour was able to thrive in the first instance is because the wrong lessons were drawn from past defeats. It was all too easy to focus on the failures of the hard Left – which were real – but the labour movement's impasse was far more deeply structured by the dominant variations of Labourism, the main form that working-class politics had taken for most of the century.[4] How much did the Labour Party foster or constrain the potential of the movements and social forces it sought to represent? How much did post-war social democracy contribute to their de-radicalisation? How might things have been different? While such questions were not exactly ignored, the force of the argument was usually directed against those who, for all their faults, were trying to take the Labour Party away from a repetition of the Wilson/Callaghan debacles. The point of revisiting this is that, in the event of further educational defeats, it is important that activists are not left demoralised, passive, bewildered, and burned out. Corbyn's supporters need to position themselves where they can anticipate and act appropriately on the sources of those defeats.

Jeremy Corbyn is in a strong position. As leader of the Labour Party, he has long enjoyed the support of the great majority of the party's membership. After months of 'Project Despair', YouGov found that 66 per cent of the party's members believed he was doing a good job, an increase on previous polls.[5] The outcome of the chicken coup demonstrated that his support remained firm after a year. And, after a few months of aimlessness following Brexit, the election result has ensured that he now has the overwhelming goodwill of members for years to come. Labour's share of popular support, having incrementally

improved before May's leadership, then fallen back drastically, is now ahead of that of the government and better
than any position Labour has been in since before Iraq.
The drumbeat of attacks from the backbenches has slowed
down and become much more tentative and indirect, with
Labour opponents hoping that, one way or another, Brexit
will give them the opening they seek.

Corbyn has constructed a shadow cabinet more in keeping
with his predilections – something that some of his allies
wish he'd done in the first place – and John McDonnell has
crafted a series of economic policies with proven popular
appeal. These include not just significant expansions of the
social wage, but also a transformation of employment law,
giving workers and unions more rights than they have had
for decades. Labour is no longer compromised by offering
a feeble triangulation on austerity – which, in its Osbornite
version, is broken. Some of the party's traditional bipar-
tisanship on foreign policy has been rolled back. At least
rhetorically, the party has rowed back from simply trying
to offer its own, softer version of Tory migrant-baiting,
although its post-Brexit retreat from free movement continues to be a sore spot for activists. Labour has proceeded
from being an ineffectual opposition, to being an effectual
one, to being a government-in-waiting. Corbyn has out-
stripped the prime minister in terms of approval ratings
and fitness to govern, something that hasn't happened to a
Labour leader since 2008.

Yet for all that, there remain potential sources of weakness.
There is little sign that the media outlets and professionals
who spent two years belittling Corbyn and his supporters

now intend to radically change their ways. In a way, this could be an asset: the more they attack, the more his supporters rally to him. But it also means that they will be continually on the lookout for fresh controversies, however trite. Their power has been shown to be diminished but, for at least some potential Labour voters, not gone. The majority of his supporters in the party have been passive throughout the period of leadership, and the active core has been racing to catch up, and somehow match the organisation, experience, visibility, and power that his opponents have. There is not yet any sign of the broad, popular social movements of the kind that Corbyn has argued a left-wing Labour Party needs, and it is a mistake to think that the party can *be* the social movement. Moreover, supposing Corbyn were to win an election any time soon, he would have to try and implement his programme while negotiating a solution to Brexit. He would have to persuade businesses to invest, financial corporations to stay put (as opposed, say, to moving to Paris, where Macron is planning a range of incentives to attract them), and a range of actors from state personnel to businessmen to make McDonnell's plans for an upgrade of the productive base of the economy work. And he would have to persuade them to accept that a price of this is that workers will be paid more, and will have more rights, and corporations will pay more taxes.

Not for the first time in recent years, the Left has been propelled to a position of influence well beyond its social and political strength, chiefly because of the etiolation of the old guard and the paucity of their analyses of – let alone solutions to – the crisis. But it is rare to catch the establishment with its pants down in this fashion, for so prolonged a period, and it does tend to recover. Neither 'Project Fear' nor 'Project Despair' has availed thus far, but if Corbyn and his allies were unable to use their strength to achieve lasting, hard-to-reverse gains, the opportunity would be lost and another chance would not be likely. So what would success look like?

What Would It Mean for Jeremy Corbyn to Succeed?

Before the 2017 general election, nothing raised the hackles of Labour's 'moderates' more than the idea that they should be reduced to an oppositional rump, a party of activists and street protesters, exerting influence but wielding no power. Tony Blair famously declared that there were two types of culture in Labour: that of protest, and that of government:

> I'm the face on the placard. I'm that bastard, let's get rid of him. The other culture is the guys holding the placard. They don't really want to be in power, they want to make the people in power respond to their concerns.[6]

This raises the question of what sort of power it is that they think they can wield. The history of Labour governments is not such that it inspires one with a sense of their awesome puissance. Rather, one tends to find a scenario much more consistent with Perry Anderson's description,

When a Labour Government is in office, it is an isolated, spotlit enclave, surrounded on almost every side by hostile territory, unceasingly shelled by industry, press, and orchestrated 'public opinion'. Each time in the end it has been overrun.[7]

Of course, no Labour government was as successful as New Labour in shaping public opinion, winning over the right-wing press barons, coalescing with industry, and turning hostile territory into *terra familia*. Even that government was not spared its crises, from the Iraq war to the NHS fiscal crisis to the credit crunch. But these were not the problems of trying to implement reforms from the Left, and by and large they did not incur the opposition of the powerful: they were the problems which arose from accepting the terrain inherited from one's opponents. If this is what is meant by exercising power, the idea seems to have lost a significant part of its meaning.

Yet, because it has been shown that conventional ways of gauging success are less important – headlines, news cycles, poll fluctuations, journalistic ideas about what makes 'leadership' – it would be easy to take refuge in wishful thinking, or in a set of common-sense defaults, without thinking it through. Corbyn's project is in some respects a traditional electoral one, albeit not conducted in a traditional electoral terrain. It will be subject to some of the same logic and limitations of any such project. As such, we need a new way of thinking about success, and power.

One way to define success, of course, is to contrast it with failure. The fundamental condition shaping everything that Corbyn does, or could conceivably do, is the germinal, complicated rebirth of the radical Left, and the concurrent persistence of many weaknesses of the Left and the labour movement. The recent reversal at the level of political organisation, with hundreds of thousands joining Labour to support a socialist leader, has been complemented by a flowering of radical media. Novara Media produces high-quality multimedia content, its personalities making regular, assured appearances on national broadcasters. A range of blogs like *Another Angry Voice* attract phenomenal readerships that at times, and with few resources, outperform the press. Left-wing social media accounts churn out a glut of daily content on Twitter and, more importantly, Facebook. Nonetheless, this is the dynamism of a movement in its fragile upswing, still developing, still maturing, still susceptible to being blindsided by developments. The relative paucity of social movements at this stage, combined with the ongoing decline in the trade union movement, where membership and strike rates are falling year-on-year, also place very high burdens of responsibility on those who are politically organised.

From this perspective, there are several types of benchmark that could be used to think about success. The first is organisational. If Labour is, for the foreseeable future, the agency and vehicle of radical politics, what kind of party need it be? What needs to change so that it enables the creative capacities of members, rather than inhibiting and controlling them? How can the top-heavy distribution of power be changed, and structures democratised? How can the Left, and union members, build a lasting space in Labour, not just as cannon fodder but in the exercise of power? How much compromise with the traditional party management is necessary? How far can Corbyn's supporters go in changing the party, given Corbyn's dependence on the trade union leaderships? Corbyn himself has been reluctant to press for radical change too quickly, in order to avoid heightened conflict with MPs and councillors. And yet the truculent resistance of the party machinery, the jaw-droppingly cynical coup attempt, the suppression of party branches, the vindictive expulsions of members supposedly in breach of the party's 'aims and values', the repeated attempts to sabotage the elected leader and bypass hundreds of thousands of members, must force a change. Particularly now that the election has electrified the party base. Here, a great deal will come down to the activist core organised under the rubric of Momentum.

The second benchmark is ideological. Corbyn won the Labour leadership as a radical socialist, despite the fact that even in name, socialism had been off the agenda of mainstream politics for a couple of decades, if not longer. He immediately began reversing the decades-long trajectory to the right. He not only turned back austerity, but also promised to reverse many of the worst legacies of New Labour, such as tuition fees. There still seems to be broad acceptance of the argument that 'cuts' are necessary to reduce the deficit, which suggests that Labour hasn't yet won all the political arguments about austerity, but it has certainly made a start. Unable to reverse party policy on Trident and NATO, Corbyn nonetheless demonstrated that being anti-nuclear and anti-war was not electoral death in this day and age. And while talking about a 'fair' post-Brexit 'managed migration' system going into the election, Corbyn made a laudable point of refusing to promise to reduce numbers and refuted attempts to blame migrants for social problems. Labour still communicates well with working-class audiences, and Corbyn has used that power to shift the balance of opinion and argument to the left, and change the agenda to one that no longer favours the Right. This is a long game: ideological territories are shaped over generations, not in time for electoral cycles. But the start already made is impressive.

The third benchmark is electoral. Here, Labour's inherited problems were not merely conjunctural but structural. Labour, by 2015, had not only suffered a customary problem with affluent swing voters, but also a more serious problem with working-class voters. The risk was of Pasokification, as these core voters simply stopped turning out, or defected to anyone else offering something similar. This problem has deeper roots than New Labour, and a degree of class dealignment is visible in the votes for most European social-democratic parties, but the problem has radicalised in recent years. Corbyn recognised that a big part of Labour's problem was low turnout among key, would-be-Labour-supporting demographics – young people and poor voters. Given the chance to campaign as he wanted to, he demonstrated against all received opinion that those voters could be mobilised. This doesn't automatically mean that Labour is guaranteed to win the next election. There is a debate in Labour, including in Corbynite circles, over exactly what would be needed to get over the last hurdle.

The final benchmark is policy. This is where Corbyn faces his most difficult test. Of course, the policy lines he develops are necessarily a compromise between the trade union leaderships, the parliamentary party, the party machinery, and the membership. But thus far, the record shows that he has been able to push policy on most issues quite far to the left of where it was. Party colleagues, despite their palpable hostility to him, have mostly wholeheartedly accepted the new anti-austerity politics.[8] They have also largely accepted his direction on more difficult issues like the bombing of Syria, or the triggering of Article 50. The red lines appear to be on issues related to the global power of the British state, its orientation toward militarism, and the alliance with the US – but even these are likely to come into question in the era of Washington's decline. But while Corbyn has secured his party's support for a radical agenda, and has secured a critical mass of public support for it too, the vital question remains whether or not the policy mix would work on its own terms, enough to force the opposition to adapt to it as the new reality, and sustain a prolonged period in government for Labour.

These various ends are often in conflict. How does one reconstitute Labour as a party of the Left without paying a cost in terms of party peace? How does one rebuild the core vote while adding enough swing voters to win? How does one change 'hearts and minds', shift the ideological ground, without paying a short-term cost in terms of media hostility and resistance from the political class? There are necessary trade-offs in the kind of project Corbyn is engaged in, which can't even be evaluated if one focuses narrowly, as the Blairites have traditionally done, on short-range electoral phenomena within a narrow band of crucial 'swing voters'.

Changing the Boundaries of Debate

One of Corbyn's virtues is that he is not overly impressed by that reified category we call 'public opinion'. That is not to say he is indifferent to what people think – but he wants to change opinion, to lead it, rather than merely reflect it in various poll-tested triangulations. On the three main planks of the economy and public spending, foreign policy, and a 'kinder politics', Corbyn's agenda is not exactly the *Communist Manifesto*. It is not even one of the more radical Labour manifestos. In all, it constitutes an attempt to push the boundaries of debate to the left, to open new possibilities, and to push back against some of the nastier forms of right-wing politics. And thus far, by working with the grain of popular discontents, he has been successful.

Much of the raw material for what Corbyn wanted to do was already there when he was elected leader. The bankers were already widely reviled, taxing the rich was popular, spending cuts were unpopular, and most wanted energy firms, rail, and mail renationalised. There was growing discontent about the state of the housing market, with home ownership falling for everyone under the age of sixty-five, and falling sharply for everyone under the age of thirty-five. Even Trident wasn't particularly popular, and nor had Britain had a popular war for decades.[9] British banks and British tanks were not doing most British people any favours, and Labour's bold manifesto skilfully worked with that.

Corbyn also had the advantage that he understood why Miliband-style triangulations wouldn't work:

Ed Miliband made some very good points about zero-hours contracts, about young people's opportunities, about poverty wages,
and so on – very good stuff indeed, but the problem was that the
fundamental economic strategy of the party was a form of austerity-
lite.[10]

Ceding ground in this way had the credibility of Labour's
campaign on living standards (about which it could do little
if it accepted austerity), and also defanged Labour in its
oddly half-hearted attempts to challenge the Tory narrative that Labour had created the national deficit through
public spending.

The Conservatives had been able to profit from the
shared assumption across all parties that the current economic model is the one we have to live with: there is no
alternative. With that framing assumption, it has been
relatively easy to displace attention from Britain's economic dysfunctions onto Labour's supposed overspend or,
as with the Brexit campaign, onto immigration. Labour's
most pressing task has been to weave an answer to many
and various discontents with the existing system into a new
narrative about how British industry could grow, as it was
only on this basis that welfare and public services could
be funded. John McDonnell began work on a modern
version of Harold Wilson's programme for growth
based on technological innovation.[11] He enlisted a series
of high-profile economic advisors whose thinking ran
counter to neoliberal orthodoxy, and argued that growth
based on inequality, debt, and leaving as much as possible
to the private sector was unsustainable.[12] In particular, he

borrowed from Mariana Mazzucato the idea of an 'entrepreneurial state'.[13] Mazzucato's highly praised book of the
same name describes how major growth vectors arise from
extensive public sector investment and experimentation –
the prize example being Apple's global dominion, which
owes its iPod, iPhone, and iPad technology to innovations
first made in the state sector. McDonnell built a case for this
on the pathologies of the British economy. There are, in
fact, few truly dynamic sectors – aside from the City's role
as an historic hub of global finance, a status it has held on to
by becoming, under Major, Blair, and Brown, Wall Street's
'Guantánamo',[14] there are only aerospace and pharmaceu-
ticals. The clamour for 'export-led growth' from the Tories
and the Bank of England was less plausible since without
investment there would be little for Britain to export, its
manufacturing industries having been allowed to shrink
and rust.

Even so, there were impediments. Depending in part
on how the question is put, more Britons have been wary
of state intervention than have supported it.[15] There is
a tradition of support for some limited regulation and
intervention, and a degree of public ownership, but the
embedded assumption that state intervention cannot work
means that a more sustained interventionist thrust has been
opposed by a majority.[16] Corbyn and McDonnell have thus
had to begin to shape and lead opinion in a way that Labour
leaders haven't done for some time. McDonnell took to
promoting a series of public meetings supporting the 'New
Economics' while Labour activists held local events educating activists on economics.[17]

They have also had to counter some of the trends in public opinion, showing a decline in support for the welfare state among the young, in part because of the legacy of anti-welfare rhetoric from the major parties and the widespread belief in claims about exorbitant welfare payments and immigration costing the taxpayer, with no basis in fact. This left British politics increasingly characterised by a form of social sadism, in which the most popular austerity policies were those harming the poorest, such as lowering the benefit cap or cutting housing benefits.[18] The traditional language of 'efficiency' and 'merit', coupled with high popular abstention from voting, meant that the dominant assumptions about the economy favoured the idea that only those whose work was remunerated by employers – unlike, for example, stay-at-home mothers – were truly deserving.

This is merely to indicate just how much Corbyn's Labour has had to overcome in its first two years, and just how precarious its gains may be. Corbyn has necessarily been compromised in waging this battle by the necessity of finding intelligent mediations between what is desirable, what is electorally feasible, what his parliamentary party will tolerate, and what can realistically be implemented in government. And yet it moves. What the election result showed was that, though the weight of received opinion and ingrained assumptions should not be dismissed, they are also no longer decisive. There is an opening.

To ensure that Labour is able to keep moving in this direction, it would be useful to think about a division of labour, wherein the grass roots continually sought to push the agenda farther than Corbyn is able to. Indeed, since ideology is not just about a 'battle of ideas' staged in the national media, but about where those ideas connect with lived experience, activists in their local communities are best placed to win ideological battles. Ideology in this sense is close to what Raymond Williams meant by 'culture', when he argued that 'culture is ordinary'.[19] It is what people take for granted in their everyday practice, the basic axioms they live by and which shape their tastes, their sense of justice and fairness, as well as their sense of the possible. It is also the beliefs, conscious or otherwise, which they take pleasure in, cherish, and are passionately committed to. One reason why it simply isn't good enough to 'win the battle of ideas' is precisely that people take far too much pleasure in their beliefs to give them up for a well-put policy statement.

Put like this, winning ideological space is clearly not something that can be separated from organisation. There is no way of shifting people's beliefs and assumptions without regularly spending time with them. There is no way of winning volunteers, recruits, converts, the sort of people who will proselytise and keep the faith through good and ill, without at least talking to them, and ideally doing something alongside them.

The Church Is Not Brick and Mortar

Christians are apt to say that 'the church is not brick and mortar'. It is, rather, made up of a community of believers. A secular way of putting this is that the party is not primarily its money or its bureaucracy, but its members. Insofar as Corbyn aspires to rebuild the Labour Party, his brief is to recruit active members. Activity aside for a moment, there has been no shortage of success in attracting members to the Labour Party, thus reversing the almost universal trend in party politics in Britain and across most industrial democracies for some decades. The first wave of grass-roots supporters, the potential missionaries of twenty-first-century socialism, were disproportionately young and working class. As Freddie Sayers of YouGov put it in the *Guardian*,

> Corbynmania was a youth movement and a social media movement, but it was also a working-class movement. As a group, the Labour 'selectorate' that voted in the leadership election were more educated and well-to-do than the population at large, but within that the most 'normal' group were actually Corbyn supporters. Only 26% of Corbyn supporters had a household income of more than £40,000, slightly less than the national figure of 27%. (Andy Burnham, Yvette Cooper and Liz Kendall supporters were progressively better off at 29%, 32% and 44% respectively.) So Corbyn got the cool kids and the working-class leftwing.[20]

They were, in short, exactly the sort of people who, as voters, Labour has been losing hand over fist. Subsequent recruits included more older voters, especially ex-members, so that the average age of party membership didn't fall overall. Most of the new members are either party virgins, people who have never joined a political party before (58 per cent), or prodigal members, those who left during the Blair years and came back for Corbyn (31 per cent). They tend to be slightly poorer than the old guard, a lot more female, and a lot more socially liberal. There are also more graduates, but a much higher proportion of university graduates on incomes of less than £25,000. The result is that Labour has more members today than it has had since the late 1970s – and quite possibly well before that, since the Labour Party grossly overstated its individual membership before 1979.[21]

The problem the Corbynistas have faced is that the Labour Party did not suddenly become a democratic organisation just because they got their man elected. The power did not shift to the grass roots. It remained with the party machine, and a largely right-wing parliamentary group. The institutions of Labour have been overwhelmingly ranged against Corbyn and his supporters, and they have had the advantage of their connections to the state, the media, think tanks, and businesses. Nor, for that matter, did parliament become more democratic overnight. The same imperviousness to popular pressure that allowed successive governments to implement unpopular privatisations and pursue unpopular wars persisted. The establishment is ancient, well entrenched, set in its ways, and difficult to shift. And the political class that emerged from the Thatcher era is callous, indifferent to popular will, and determined to cling on. The mere fact of having members, therefore, was never going to be enough. It is a question of organisation.

In an effort to capitalise on the energy of Labour's ranks of new, radical members, some of Jeremy Corbyn's supporters set up the campaigning group Momentum. The idea was that members who had mobilised in the heat of a campaign should not just be ignored and left to their own devices once the election was concluded. The evidence is that Momentum members have been more active than other members of the post-2015 intake, who, research suggests, are overwhelmingly passive and limited to so-called 'clicktivism'.[22]

One difficulty in evaluating the research, however, is that it tends to take for granted the electoralist focus of Labour, focusing on leafleting, canvassing, or party meetings. What if there are party members who are active on other scenes, for example in anti-gentrification, or anti-bedroom tax campaigns? Such people would be deemed politically passive in this kind of research, but that would miss the point. After all, the Labour Party, if it is to become the kind of party Corbyn wants it to be, has to be centrally involved in organising workers, communities, and groups who would otherwise be politically weak and trodden upon. This is something that Labour activists are acutely aware of, and they have been debating how to reorganise the party in order to prevent ingrained electoralism from, as Hilary Wainwright put it, monopolising the energies of activists and thwarting the 'necessary preliminaries of raising and extending socialist consciousness and grass-roots organisation among working people in general'.[23]

Momentum, in this situation, was initially a quite ambiguous organisation. It wasn't clear whether it was to be a lobby, like Progress, or a left-wing version of the Fabian Society, or an activist network. And if it was an activist network, should it be a Labour network, or something that spanned the periphery of activists all the way out to the far-Left groupuscules? Or would it simply become a machinery for getting the right people elected to different parts of the party apparatus? It didn't help serious analysis that the organisation was being constantly demonised in the press, with Tom Watson coming out to denounce it as 'a rabble' and claiming to have 'proof' of 'Trotskyite infilitration', and a huge amount of invective about it being a repackaged Militant Tendency – Owen Smith went so far as to suggest that it wasn't a coincidence that Momentum's name began with an M.[24]

These issues ended up being resolved in the autumn of 2016. It began, in the course of panic over the 'chicken coup', with a power struggle between those who favoured a delegate system for decision-making, and those who favoured an online, one-member–one-vote system. The practical difference between these two positions was that the former lifted an emaciated and politically bunkered far Left to power, by favouring self-selecting activists, while the latter would favour those with some existing semi-celebrity status, or those favoured by the Momentum office. At stake, therefore, was political control over an apparatus with 20,000 members and a much bigger database of supporters and contacts, high media profile, and £20,000 a month income at the time.

But to reduce it to a simple power struggle would be an apolitical travesty. Behind the issue of power was a pair of fundamentally different strategic conceptions. Those who wanted a delegate system were essentially looking for a party-like structure that was both inside and outside the Labour Party, through which an activist cadre could be forged and which would act as a left-wing pressure group within Labour. Unfortunately, they tended to drag local Momentum groups into unproductive factionalism, one symptom of which was an 'anti-Zionist turn' taken by some activists in response to the anti-Semitism scandals, in the belief that Israel had become the key line of attack coming from the Labour Right. Ironically, they merely created new opportunities for attack. Those who favoured an online, one-member–one-vote system wanted a Labour-only group, which would fight to keep Corbyn as leader, secure positions for the Left within the party, campaign for Labour in elections, and wage online publicity battles. This was, in principle, perfectly laudable: it had been demonstrated that Corbyn's position was weak and needed support, and the Corbynistas had been struggling to win their positions in the party as a result of toxic displacement activities.

However, those who favoured an online, one-member–one-vote system ultimately carried out an internal coup, and forced their reforms through. This followed an extraordinary publicity campaign in which, having spent enormous amounts of energy rebutting claims that Momentum was some sort of Trotskyist stalking horse, leading members began claiming that there was a Trotskyist plot to take it over. Owen Jones even appealed to Jeremy Corbyn to intervene and save Momentum from the 'saboteurs'. This, and the undemocratic resolution of the fight, was a reflection of a political weakness. You don't, on the Left, go in for public red-baiting unless you're panicking about being unable to win the argument. And their problem was that they feared they were unable to defeat their opponents in an open contest. The fact that one's opponents are better at manipulating democratic structures (it was often claimed in the prelude to the coup that the destructive sectarians were better at sitting through long, boring, pointless meetings) isn't an impressive justification for cancelling them at will.[25]

Nonetheless, Momentum comes out of the last two years with, particularly after the snap election, tremendous and well-deserved credit. Having decided their remit, as effectively a party faction and an electoral campaigning organisation, they've proved to be exceedingly good at it. Having won seats for Labour, in defiance of Labour HQ's death drive, they are now, with Corbyn, in permanent campaign mode, training thousands of activists for a fight to win more seats from the Tories. They have 24,000 members, and are winning their positions within the party, their activists gaining control of a string of local constituencies in the run-up to conference.[26] The left-wing candidates for the conference arrangements committee, which decides what the annual conference will debate, are well ahead, with three times as many nominations as their Progress- and Labour First-backed opponents. And, as Labour First activist Luke Akehurst complains, with a touch of petulant hyperbole, this would make 'conference a free-for-all where every fantasy politics piece of "resolutionary socialism" gets debated'.[27]

Of course, this leaves a fairly huge gap to be filled. If Labour activists are just defending a left-wing leadership and winning positions within Labour, they're neglecting the organisation of society beyond the party. Whence, then, the 'social movement' upon which a radical Labourism is to be predicated? Beyond Momentum, of course, there are other left-wing groupings, such as the Labour Representation Committee, or Red Labour, but none with the clout and resources that Momentum now has. Nor, of course, are any of them any kind of match for the immense, lordly dominion of the parliamentary party and the electoral-professional caste running daily party life. The foam-flecked scare stories about activists seeking a 'ruthless purge' of Labour, which continue to this day, obscure this basic reality.[28]

What is reasonably clear is that, while activists will always have to prioritise between party-building and movement-building, between electioneering and agitating, they are still wanting a form of organisation that enables them to do this rather than bogging them down in internecine power struggles or sucking them into minutiae. They have, thanks to the unexpected electoral windfall, a unique opportunity to make gains across the Labour Party, and then make choices about how to use that power to make the party more enabling to activists. Whether that means supporting policies like the McDonnell amendment making it easier for Left candidates to stand for party leader, or mandatory reselections for Labour MPs, or changes to the make-up of the NEC so that it is more directly elected, there is a limited period of time in which the party's left-wing has all the political capital it needs to achieve and institutionalise such transformations.

All of this becomes even more urgent if, as now seems to be the case, Labour has a chance of forming a government and trying to implement its agenda. Government imposes pressures and limits on all political parties, but most of all on parties trying to achieve radical change. The only counter-pressure, as Corbyn knows very well, is well-mobilised and empowered grass roots.

Electability: One More Push?

Even in what is increasingly a post-democracy, elections matter. And in a normal political situation, Jeremy Corbyn shouldn't be electable. The 'common sense' of the media and political class should prevail. Too bad for normality. Too bad for common sense. The credibility crunch has destroyed tons of political capital.

At first, it seemed that normality, or what the late Mark Fisher called 'Capitalist Realism', would prevail. Corbyn was polling poorly, unable to expand Labour's base beyond the approximately 30 per cent support that it had had since the 2015 election.[29] He was confronting a centre-seeking Conservative Party, detoxified by the Liberals, and subtle enough to steal Labour's ideas while trashing Labour: whether on the 'living wage' or claiming to represent workers. He had taken over a party widely blamed for the 2008 financial crisis, a theme repeated ad nauseum by the coalition government in preparing the ground for austerity. As a radical socialist, his personal views were those of a size-able minority of the public, but even with the compromises he made, it wasn't clear that he could summon an electoral plurality. As an anti-war Leftist in a country that seemed not to have got over the loss of empire, he was vilified as a threat to 'national security', something the Tories and their press outriders immediately got to work on once he was elected. His efforts to rebuild in Scotland by outflanking the SNP from the Left were falling on fallow ground. With Scottish Labour stretching every sinew to prove that it, at least, wasn't giving in to Corbynism, most voters saw the party as being 'indistinguishable from the Tories'.[30] Corbyn was surrounded on his own benches by those ranging from sceptics to saboteurs.

In the first edition of this book, however, I invited readers to try a different proposition. Supposing this wasn't a normal political situation, that Corbyn's leadership victory wasn't a fluke, and that the old metrics of success didn't hold? What happened if we put all of the reasons why Corbyn is not electable a slightly different way? Labour was polling poorly under Corbyn, but no worse than before he was elected. Part of the reason for its current poor polling was the post-election adjustment made by polling companies, who reacted by weighting heavily against younger and poorer voters. Yet part of Corbyn's brief was to get those voters to turn out en masse. He was confronting a centre-seeking party at a time when the centre was not necessarily as broad as it had been, when living standards continued to decline and parts of the middle class that were dependent on the public sector were declining. As leader, he was far less inculpated by past Labour performance than any of his rivals would have been – above all by the credit crunch, which most voters blamed Labour for, and which was decisive in losing Labour two elections in a row.[31] As a socialist, he was elected to win over and lead people who were not socialists – but it is the task of virtually every political leader, left, right and centre, to assemble coalitions.

Blair did not win office because most of his voters agreed with his politics, but because he persuaded most of them that he was the best deal they were going to get. It was surely not beyond Corbyn to make a more tempting offer than that.

Corbyn's views on war and Trident tended to be closer to the balance of public opinion than his rivals like to pretend, while 'national security' panics were no longer as effectual as they might have been in a Cold War world. Scotland would not return to Labour, but Scotland has rarely in electoral history been key to Labour winning office (ironically, it may have been a Tory surge in Scotland which kept May in office in 2017). And if a coalition with the SNP should prove necessary, Corbyn's stance on Trident and austerity would be an asset. Finally, there were those in Labour waiting to sabotage the leadership, endlessly extolled by the media, but on the most contentious recent issue that Corbyn had faced in the parliamentary party at that point – the vote on bombing Syria – he had carried most of his MPs and even a majority of the shadow cabinet. He had won the very vocal support of Labour big hitters, such as John Prescott and Len McCluskey. The minority who were ceaselessly agitating for a party coup were likely, through their bombast, deluded air of righteous victimhood, and smug sense of entitlement, to powerfully alienate those whom they would need as supporters and allies. (We didn't know the half of it.) On the other hand, with the overwhelming support of the party grass roots, Corbyn could begin to lead a process of democratic reform in the Labour Party, which would put manners on the party's fixers.

All of this was more true than I knew. However, the caveats are worth revisiting too. The Labour Right, though unimaginative and timid even in terms of achieving their own limited objectives, were correct to identify the problem that the existing vote for socialism of the Corbyn variety was not enough to win an election. The metropolitan Left, based in large urban centres and university towns, may be a sufficient source of activists to drive a movement for change. The educated precariat, politicised and with spare time and resources, could take a leading role, insofar as there was a movement for them to lead. And surrounding them were some social groups who never particularly cared for neoliberalism, but were previously silenced because they lacked representation. But beyond that, there were more provincial areas where the concerns of the urban working class were not as visible, where the difficulties with home ownership and renting were not as acute, where a sense of neglect and distance from Westminster wasn't expressed in progressive attitudes. Among these constituencies, it was even quite possible that having a leadership represent a politically correct metropolitan constituency would be just as alienating as a leadership representing economic liberalism.

The results of elections held at that point were not sufficient to make a judgement about how well Corbyn could bridge the gap. Polling had not been good. Labour's poll ratings in the first eight months since the 2015 general election were on average eight points behind those of the Conservatives – the worst performance by Labour after a general election since the Second World War.[32] Corbyn had not impeded the reconstruction of Labour's core vote,

but it had been on the mend since the 2010 defeat. The
increased vote for Labour in Oldham West under Corbyn
was not as big as the improvements Labour experienced in
previous by-elections during the Miliband interregnum.
Elsewhere, the polls indicate a generally poor Labour
vote.[33] Meanwhile in London, the heartland of the metropolitan Left, where Corbyn's support was strongest, he was
denied the chance to take the share of credit he was due for
Labour's victory in London, due to Sadiq Khan's energetic
distancing of himself from the leadership. If one followed
the pattern and stopped the analysis before the snap election, one would have concluded that Corbyn's leadership,
whether through his fault or that of saboteurs, was failing
on electoral terms.

Nonetheless, there was a generational shift taking place
in the UK which, elsewhere, had led to left-wing surges,
from Ecuador to Greece. It was difficult to say when these
tendencies would mature (much sooner than I thought), or
whether millennial voters would be geographically concentrated in the right places (they seem to be). But what should
make Corbyn's opponents pause was the decay of the representative link discussed in the introduction. Everywhere,
there were shocks, sudden surges, and reversals, unpredictable and unpredicted by pundits – who had not discernibly
become more humble in their prognoses as a result. The
old regime was sufficiently lacking in legitimacy and the
political situation in industrial democracies was sufficiently
fissile that, should there be further recessions, eurozone
calamities, or stock market crashes, there was no surety
against another 'government of the Left'.

The possibility of a government of the Left has become a probability. The Tories are in a worse crisis than they have been for years, and the Labour leader looks, even to his most determined opponents, such as deputy leader Tom Watson, like a prime-minister-in-waiting. Long-standing critics, including Chuka Umunna and Stephen Kinnock, both of whom had previously urged Corbyn to resign, and styled themselves possible future leaders, let it be known that they were now willing to serve in the shadow cabinet. His opponent in the 2015 leadership election, Yvette Cooper – who had prepared a press conference for the week after the election, only to be forced to cancel it – also volunteered for a job on the front benches. The *Telegraph* complained, with some justice, that they were 'crawling back to Corbyn' after 'benefiting from Jeremy Corbyn's popularity'.[34]

Even Tony Blair eventually emerged to begrudgingly acknowledge that Corbyn had 'tapped into something real and powerful' and pay tribute to his 'temperament during the campaign', as well as to 'the campaign's mobilisation of younger voters and to the enthusiasm it generated'. Ultimately, of course, Blair was not particularly happy about Labour's breakthrough on a left-wing programme: 'it doesn't alter the judgement about the risks of an unchanged Corbyn programme, if he became Prime Minister and tried to implement it at the same time as Brexit.' But this was merely Blair being true to his long-held position that even if he felt victory was possible by a Leftist route, he would not take it.[35]

But the question now is what it will take for Labour to make the jump from a powerful, energised opposition to a government with a powerful mandate. On this question, figures from the right of the party have begun to promote the idea that, having excited young voters, Corbyn needs to make a determined shift back to the centre in order to pick up another decisive group of voters. And the key issue for them, and the means for a new attack on the leadership, is Brexit. There has been a split between those who want to attack Corbyn for allegedly betraying the hopeful youth vote with 'hard Brexit', and those who want to attack him for abandoning the working-class vote with his pandering to middle-class students. However, both tendencies seemed to agree that, as the *Mirror* claimed, Labour's young voters were 'furious over Brexit'. Robert Ford, the political scientist who had claimed that UKIP's support derived from the 'white working class' who were 'left behind' by globalisation, agreed that the result demonstrated the 'revenge of the Remainers' on the ground that there was a correlation between Labour's gains and the seats with the highest number of Remain voters. The *Telegraph*, in typical fashion, mourned the 'revenge of the liberal metropolitan elite'.

This argument is simply untenable. Brexit mattered a great deal to Conservative voters, but far less to Labour voters, only 8 per cent of whom said it was their main issue. For as long as it was the dominant issue in the snap election, Labour was far behind. But as the campaign went on, and Labour's campaign started to dominate, Brexit became far less important. Had Labour attempted to run a defensive, triangulating campaign focused on that issue – trying to appease anti-immigrant voters on the one hand, and anti-Brexit voters on the other – it would have found it hard to convince anyone, or excite voters. Had Labour run the sort of campaign that the likes of Tony Blair and Alan Johnson wanted him to run, the election result would in all likelihood have been similar to that in recent by-elections, or indeed in the West Midlands mayoral contest, with Labour perceived as weak, and turnout for the party desperately low.

Watson, nonetheless, has argued that Labour, in a future election, must run a 'slightly different' campaign to give 'greater reassurances' to 'traditional working-class voters, some of whom left us on issues like policing and security'.[36] As someone of the traditional Labour Right, he has form on this kind of campaigning. He ran Liam Byrne's successful campaign in Birmingham Hodge Hill in 2005, largely by tacking to the populist Right, with appeals to patriotism and a promise to 'Smash Teen Gangs', and by attacking the Liberals from the right on immigration. Labour's slogan, 'On Your Side', identified an antagonism, but against whom? Criminals and immigrants. He was also closely involved with Siôn Simon's disastrous, failed campaign for mayor of the West Midlands, which used the Brexit slogan 'Take Back Control' and promised to 'fly the flag for English patriotism'.

Phil Wilson has gone so far as to claim that 'working people' 'favoured the Tories' in the election. He went on to add that Labour had become a 'middle-class pastime', wasting money on 'subsidising middle-class kids' (abolishing tuition fees), and winning big largely in university towns and cities.[37] Presumably, what he meant by this was that constituencies which had the largest share of working-class constituents (using those outmoded NRS social grades) had the biggest Tory swing – even though they usually remained Labour. But quite why he thought this was significant is unclear. First of all, constituency-level analysis risked unsafe generalisations: the so-called 'ecological fallacy'. The fact that a swing took place in a largely working-class constituency did not mean that the swing had taken place exclusively among workers. Insofar as there was a working-class swing, this largely reflected working-class conservatives returning to the Tory fold. The story of the election in that respect was that this swing *didn't* produce a blue tide due to a sharply increased Labour turnout. For all the dog-whistling, it was the Brexit dog that didn't bark.

It was even more unclear what Wilson proposed to do about the problem, since he offered no practical proposals other than, seemingly, abandoning the highly successful policy of abolishing tuition fees. It would also be difficult for Wilson to pin his colours too firmly to the mast of Brexit or immigration, since he is a fervent leading supporter of the Remainer group, Open Britain, although he did call for some largely symbolic 'action on immigration' within a single-market system – a particularly ineffectual way of patronising working-class voters. Was Wilson, then, proposing anything different from a Blair/Brown-era policy mix? Gloria de Piero and former chief whip Graham Jones argued that many Labour voters had abandoned the party. Jones added, 'We have to talk about their concerns – counter-terrorism, nationalism, defence and community, the nuclear deterrent and patriotism.'[38]

The thrust of this argument about the working class was clear. Workers could only be appealed to on a right-wing basis: guns and flags, with English rather than Ulster accents. Certainly, there were signs that a layer of older, white, and disproportionately male working-class voters had defected on the basis of Conservative campaigning about Corbyn's nuclear position and IRA 'links'. And although Labour had improved its share of the vote among those classified as 'skilled working class', the C2 vote in the old 'social grades' schema, they had still gone much more strongly for the Tories than for Labour. Even so, the Tories have usually done well among 'skilled workers', and much of their improvement in this stratum was down to the 'UKIP effect'. The fact that it didn't result in sweeping losses across the West Midlands, the North, and Wales is indicative that Labour succeeded in raising the turnout among 'traditional Labour voters' as well as new voters – exactly what Siôn Simon's campaign for West Midlands mayor had failed to achieve.

The weakness in certain working-class constituencies was, moreover, the culmination of long-term trends for which the politics of triangulation bear some responsibility. This is the essence of the problem, and the reason why new Labour hold-outs are split over what direction to take over Brexit. People like Wilson, Umunna and Sadiq Khan want an anti-Brexit campaign, or at the very least a 'soft Brexit'; people like Watson, Piero, and Jones seem to want a harder stance on immigration (as indeed do most on the Labour backbenches). This split is one that, as Chapter 4 suggests, is generic to the New Labour project, which had always embodied elements of both missionary cosmopolitan liberalism and melancholic conservative authoritarianism.

The same party which abolished Section 28 also passed authoritarian legislation targeting non-EU migrants. In recent years, the latter tendency has been more in tune with the *Weltanschauung* winds, but the liberal wing hopes that Labour's disproportionately younger, female, urban, multi-racial, and socially liberal base will break with Corbyn over the question of hard versus soft Brexit.

Those expecting a split in Corbynism are hubristic. Corbyn's preference for leaving the single market and the customs union, and above all for ending the free movement that goes with it, has disappointed some of his supporters. In some ways, the answers that Corbyn and his allies give on this question sound uncharacteristically evasive. The problem is not that McDonnell wants to maintain maximum flexibility in negotiating ('flexit'). That much makes perfect sense. Nor is it with the idea of a 'jobs-first Brexit', however necessarily vague that is. Putting jobs ahead of anti-immigrant prejudice and flag-waving is a good idea. But Corbynite MPs are beginning to offer formulations like, 'with Brexit, freedom of movement will end' and 'leaving the EU means leaving the single market'. Neither statement is literally true. Both are performative in that they intend, by creating a narrative about the meaning of the Brexit vote, to bring about the reality they describe. And the reservation that many of Corbyn's supporters express is that this is being done so that Labour can appease Brexit voters on immigration without accepting any responsibility for it.

However, there is absolutely no evidence that Europe is the most important issue to Corbyn supporters; it was never the central issue on which he campaigned. Still, there is a real dilemma here. In the first instance, there is the question whether to move to the right to win over Tory voters. Chris Williamson, a Corbynite MP elected to Derby North thanks to a vigorous Momentum campaign, argues against it:

> If you trim and start going down the road of triangulating and trying to be all things to all people in order to win over some Tories, what you're gonna end up doing is piss off and effectively disenfranchise a lot of people who have been inspired and got involved for the first time in many years and given the political process a chance. You'll just lose them at the other end. We are never going to win an argument, nor should we even try to win the argument, by trying to out-UKIP UKIP or out-Tory the Tories.[39]

Most of those close to the Corbyn leadership would agree, but that doesn't mean there isn't a problem. There is no doubt that Labour would be able to stack up many more votes if another election was called tomorrow, but a first-past-the-post system has distorting effects – one has to pick up the extra votes from among a small number of geographically decisive voters. Some of those are the 'skilled manual' workers identified by Corbyn's critics.

Trying to reach out to such voters on a right-wing basis would be totally unconvincing, but how does one reach them? What can Labour offer to people who are not exactly affluent, but not doing too badly either? It may well be the case that some of them can be convinced of the left-wing programme. It may be that the fearmongering about the IRA, Hamas, and nukes will be less effective against a party that isn't as openly divided as before. The stigma against Corbyn has certainly been diminished. It may be that the abysmal Tory performance will lead to a collapse in the turnout of their vote. It is even possible that Labour could pick up more seats by extending the Corbyn effect to Scotland.

Ultimately, the party's best resource may not be a tempting new policy offer, or a neat triangulation, but the fact that there are still, even now, millions more potential voters who have not been drawn to the polls – in part because politicians haven't really paid attention to them for years. In this respect, in preparation for a new election before 2022, 'permanent campaign mode' might be the answer Labour is looking for.

Governing from the Left

Ironically, it was Harold Wilson who expressed most concisely what left-wing critics such as Ralph Miliband have long said about the British state: 'Whoever is in office, the Whigs are in power.'

In the now highly plausible event that a Corbyn-led Labour Party won a general election, how is it possible in the twenty-first century to govern from the left? It is not encouraging that the only major examples of relatively successful left-wing government in the twenty-first century are all from the 'pink tide' countries in Latin America, as the circumstances enabling those experiments to broadly work will not be repeated in Britain. The oil boom of the last decade, concurrent with years of high economic growth, was a crucial factor in funding the social programmes of the 'pink tide' governments. It gave them a vital space in which to experiment with ways of redistributing power, progressively reforming the state and engaging in economic intervention.

The point doesn't have to be limited by its parochial frame of reference, however. Radical parties across the Continent, most recently Syriza, have discovered to their cost that to take office is not necessarily to take power. It is not just that there is something about states, senior civil servants, military leaders, Treasury advisors, Bank of England governors, and so on that makes them resistant to radical change. It is not just that to govern effectively requires a minimum of cooperation on the part of businesses and investors, as well as international trade institutions, ratings agencies, treaty organisations, and other powerful economic actors, who use what clout they have to veto reforms implemented by national governments. It is that there is an almost seamless circulation of power between them all. A radical government finds it difficult to wield power precisely because, if left to itself, it is rapidly encircled by those who actually hold power and who are accustomed to exercising it. Should it find a way to win time and space for its own agenda, the next obstacle it faces is that it somehow has to administer capitalism, while making it work for reform. That is, it has to find a formula that makes capitalism grow, and profitably, while also transferring wealth and power to workers and the poor. In the twentieth century, the solution to this dilemma was a 'mixed economy', with public ownership, price and incomes policies, and a mildly redistributive welfare state. But that solution, insofar as it ever worked for radical ends, no longer works at all.

A Corbyn-led government would be in the far less enviable situation of having to *create* the growth from which it could fund and possibly expand its programmes. And it would have to do so at a time when businesses are still hoarding hundreds of billions of pounds rather than investing. And, crucially, it would have to do so in the context of Brexit, with business jittery about the possibility of lost trade. The discussion of Brexit has been dogged by extraordinary hyperbole on all sides, additionally complicated by an increasingly unavailing jargon of 'hard' and 'soft' Brexit. What all sides are missing, crucially, is that the shape of any divorce settlement depends on what the EU is prepared to offer, not mainly on what British politicians would like, and the EU's red lines are already restrictive.

The 'global-trader' idea of the Brexit Right, wherein an emancipated Britannia will be able to strike lucrative deals in a global market, is a fantasy. It's true that the EU has been in relative global decline for some years, despite stabilising the eurozone crisis (at the significant expense of its poorer countries). It's also true that this has resulted in losses in the City, where, for example, the euro currency is traded. The EU may turn out to be unsustainable in the long term, at least in its present format. However, British capitalism, and the City in particular, still gain enormous benefits from EU membership. The ability of financial firms located in the UK to sell their services throughout the EU, likely to be at the very least curtailed after withdrawal from the EU, is one of the sources of the City's current global power. The strongest likelihood is that parts of the City will break off and defect to Dublin, Luxembourg, and Paris. There will be a significant lag in negotiating a new set of trading arrangements with the EU: the two-year Article 50 negotiations are to finalise the terms of divorce, with the real negotiations on a new set of relationships coming afterwards. And even if Britain achieves tariff-free trade with the rest of Europe, which EU negotiators insist will only be possible if the UK remains in the single market, there are likely to be some costs in terms of non-tariff barriers. Most forecasts expect some costs even if Britain were to remain within the European Economic Area and be subjected to single-market rules, with the Treasury estimating that the UK would lose about 3.8 per cent of GDP.[40]

At the same time, the forecasts of doom, where they are not outright false (Owen Smith wrongly claimed that a 'no-deal' Brexit would cost Britain £45bn in terms of GDP), are necessarily tendentious because they depend on all other things being equal. And yet, of course, all other things cannot remain equal. The UK will have to find another growth formula, whatever deal it ultimately strikes. The Conservatives have looked to the Commonwealth to help with this, in keeping with a certain colonial residue in 'global-trader' thinking; the Commonwealth, especially India, has politely looked the other way. They have looked to Donald Trump, artist of the deal, to offer Britain a quick trade pact, perhaps based on the same hawkishly neoliberal terms as the TTIP. But they are dissembling when it comes to how quickly this can be negotiated and how much of a difference it will make. Beyond this, the Tories have opted for what Labour are calling 'bargain-basement capitalism' – rolling back exiguous European constraints on labour and environmental protections, driving down wages and cutting corporation taxes to rock bottom.[41]

Labour is now in a realistic position to offer something else. McDonnell's first post-Brexit speech addressed the future of British capitalism outside the EU, emphasising the need for an industrial growth strategy backed by an 'entrepreneurial state'. The key lever for generating growth would be a National Investment Bank, a Bank of the North, and other regional investments totalling £500bn. This involves the state getting a lot more directly involved in shaping the future of British capitalism and, in particular, shaping it in a way that diminishes the influence and power of the financial sector. It would emphasise targeting investment in infrastructure improvements and in the development of high-technology industries. This can be understood as, in part, an answer to the likely loss of investment coming from the EU's investment bank in Luxembourg.

Can this work? Can it make up for potential losses to trade? Would it, for example, give space for Corbyn and McDonnell to turn down the single market, with its restrictive rules on state aid, given an estimated £6bn a year extra costs to exporters? Would it allow Labour to opt out of any TTIP deal, with all of TTIP's negative consequences for public ownership, worker protections, environmental legislation, and democracy, without it making British capitalism less competitive? Is it, in fact, even radical enough, given the huge investment gap that, uncontroversially, has opened up in the British economy in the years since 2010? Not to mention the chronic shortfall of investment in research and development in the UK, as well as a long-term productivity crisis.[42]

The important thing about the £500bn investment is that it is not free money. Although the idea was initially cast as a People's Quantitative Easing, an alternative to the current framework wherein the Bank of England just prints money and floods it into the financial system, this is mostly borrowed money. Creating a public promotional bank allows one to borrow money off the balance sheet, but it has to be repaid (even if at very low rates of interest). That means the government has to help create viable projects that the money can be invested in, whether it's a new railway line or a digital technology firm. In principle, there's no reason why this can't work: it has been done before. The usual way in which it has been done has been by allowing big centralised banks to channel credit to other banks which handle applications for credit to fund socially beneficial projects. The credit is marginally cheaper than that available in the private sector – but only marginally, in order not to 'distort the market'. But otherwise the bank has little contact with the projects concerned, and little local or specialist knowledge. What Labour is talking about is not all that dissimilar. The National Investment Bank would use a network of local, publicly owned banks, with specific local knowledge, to distribute credit to useful projects. They would not directly compete with existing banks, which puts a limit on how much they can cut credit. Labour is, to be fair, also talking about proactively creating investment projects, and seeking out corporatist partnerships with 'entrepreneurs'. By and large, you could argue that the policy is a shift in the right direction after years of austerity, and yet if it is run like the standard public promotional bank it will be too mild a step.[43]

The policy is also linked to a moderate but nonetheless important tilt toward democratising ownership. Labour's paper on 'Alternative models of ownership', drafted by researchers and presented to McDonnell in early 2017, argues for giving people a 'right to own' that is not Thatcherite or 'free-market' in principle, but collective and democratic. It looks, broadly, at three ways of achieving this. The first and most obvious is nationalised ownership where there is a natural monopoly, in order to deliver services most efficiently (hence the renationalisation of rail and mail). Of course, there is nothing intrinsically democratic about nationalised industries other than that they are accountable to elected governments. This is why Tony Benn used to advocate some share of workers' control in publicly owned industries. The second is local and community forms of ownership, which is what is proposed for energy firms: that a network of locally owned companies, with a green mandate, be implemented instead of a national monopoly. In these cases, profits would be wholly or partially reinvested in the local community. And the third is the cooperative, owned by its workers. Here, the idea is that the state can make it easier for workers to take control of a firm when its owners try to shut it down, by making available cheap credit, among other things. The total effect of this would hardly be revolutionary, but it can be seen as Labour's attempt to develop its own distinctive answer to Thatcherite ideas of ownership – the 'property-owning democracy' – which ultimately speak to a popular desire to have a real stake in the economy, however small.

The overwhelming sense one gets from Labour's policy agenda right now is that it is both very radical and very mild and commonsensical. It represents a shift in priorities and a break from the existing neoliberal policy framework, and just as importantly it represents a shift in rhetoric. It abruptly reverses course on years of underinvestment and dysfunction, and on the ideology justifying it, but it only takes short, baby steps in the opposite direction. It's likely that, in government, to really get to grips with the British disease, it would have to find ways to be more radical, and perhaps this is one reason why McDonnell has spoken of Brexit being an opportunity, since it could increase the freedom of manoeuvre for the government. There also remains the prospect that, despite Corbyn's project being perfectly commensurable with long-term capitalist success, there will be investor resistance. It is a matter of simple sociological realism that left-wing governments are as susceptible to the pressures of trying to wield governmental power as anyone else, and that considerable institutional pressures can be brought to bear to limit one's scope for action. Corbyn has already been compelled to compromise with his own backbenchers and trade union allies over Trident, NATO, and other issues. In government, he would have to compromise with business leaders, civil servants, the media, international institutions, and of course his own parliamentary colleagues. Even if their persuasive powers are ultimately ineffective, Corbyn and McDonnell still face the problem that they cannot *force* businesses to invest.

They can make up for the lack of investment with govern-
ment-funded projects only up to a point. They are still in
the same bind as previous social-democratic governments,
which is that they aim to represent workers and the poor
while necessarily, desperately, needing the cooperation of
business.

Should Corbyn inherit an economy going into recession,
perhaps precipitated and made worse by a bad Brexit, and
with worsening public finances, he would face some difficult choices. Either he would have to radicalise his policy
of public investment, or he would have to break Labour's
borrowing rules (McDonnell has, in an effort to bypass
investor resistance, committed not to borrow to support
day-to-day spending), or he would have to contemplate
austerity and fiscal orthodoxy while trying to humanise its
worst effects. The strongest pressure on him and the government would be to do the latter. It is probably for this
reason that McDonnell is placing more emphasis on 'flexit'
than Corbyn is – keeping the UK's options open is essential
to a government's ability to pay the bills.

The term for a defeat inflicted by capitalist dysfunction
and the cold pressure of neoliberal institutions, following
on from 'Pasokification', is 'Syrizafication'.

Syriza was swiftly chewed up and metabolised by the
institutions it sought to govern, becoming in effect an
instrument of the neoliberal centre that it was elected to displace. Labour's leadership is, of course, far more intensely
historically aware, far more realistic about the powers that
it faces, and far more serious about confronting them,
than most governments would be. This is the 'subjective

factor' which has got Labour quite far despite unpromising circumstances. Yet the pressures of government would be something else, and the only possible counterpoint to potential Syrizafication, and the inevitable unedifying cries of 'betrayal' that it would precipitate, would be a vibrant and mobilised grass-roots Left in the unions and beyond – a political subjunctive that is in no way also an indicative.

Hopes of the Left

So what can Corbyn realistically do with this unexpected windfall? What would it mean for him to succeed? If it is no longer obvious that the old metrics of success hold true, how do we judge whether Corbyn can win?

These questions can only be answered in relation to Corbyn's project, and the wider historical framework. We now know that Corbyn and his allies have been able to rebuild and rejuvenate Labour, from the Left. We also know that they have converted this new strength into electoral power faster than one would have expected. It is also increasingly clear that the Labour Party and its excited periphery are teeming with 'bright young things', filled with ideas about movement-building, organisation, policy, trade unions, and so on. This is beginning – but only beginning – the job of reversing a long course of decline in the size and activity of the union movement, and the organised Left, as well as the ideological profile and resonance of left-wing ideas. None of this was going to be reversed in one miraculous breakthrough. The course of history may be punctuated, as the late Daniel Bensaïd said, by 'Leaps! Leaps! Leaps!' but no single leap does the job. There remains a generation of work of rebuilding, recomposition, and regeneration. To put it like this is to intentionally take the focus away from the customary short-termism of political analysis, in which the horizon of analysis is always this movement, this party conference, this election. The meaning and final success or failure of Corbynism will disclose itself in relation to that longer-term objective, as much as in relation to electoral outcomes, headlines, and polls.

With this in mind, the future seems increasingly open. The odds have been stacked against Corbyn's project from the start, but the consistency with which the odds are being defeated is not an accident. It bespeaks an underlying set of processes of radicalisation on the one side, and the breakdown of the governing class on the other, which means that the way we have calculated the odds has been incorrect. Labour has already begun to shift the balance of opinion on a number of issues, although lamentably it clings to nursey on such matters as police numbers. It is retreating somewhat, if unevenly and with some splendid moments from Corbyn during the electoral campaign, from the initial courage that Corbyn showed on migration and refugees. But it is setting itself up to win a general election on a more radical basis than we have seen for years.

There is also an incipient, as yet politically undecided and open-ended, change in the alignments of global power taking place. The decline of Washington and Wall Street, capably overseen by the Twitter President, coupled with the political crisis for the EU posed by growing Euroscepticism (not least Brexit itself), is weakening the institutional framework and the ideological axioms in which the neo-liberal centre has dominated. The global economy is being politicised, on both the Left and the Right, and that would provide potential opportunities – no more than that – for any Left government to increase its freedom of movement, if it was bold enough.

In the first edition of this book, I thought it most likely that Corbynism would enjoy some successes but fail in its larger, longer-term objectives. My assumption, much as I preferred to think otherwise, was that at some point a variant of the old Labour Right would regain control, while incorporating elements of Corbynism for its own purposes. As such, the hundreds of thousands of new activists ran the risk of being demoralised, driven out, and left burned out and bewildered if they didn't immediately begin to wargame all the possibilities, including failure. It is no longer evident that this is the most realistic reading.

The obstacles before Corbynism remain considerable. And it would still be useful to take the long-term view, dampen down any triumphalism, restrain any knee-jerk loyalism, and think critically about how to react to setbacks, including defeat. Corbyn is still going to have to struggle to outrun the limits of Labourism – the very limits which brought us to this impasse. However, it would be absurd to talk about a crisis of knowing, and point the finger at the media for their illusions, and not acknowledge that the facts have overtaken parts of my analysis. Apart from anything else, this is one of those occasions on which it is a real pleasure to be refuted by history.

Notes

Preface to the Second Edition

1   Quoted in Nikil Saval, 'Globalisation: the rise and fall of an idea that swept the world', *Guardian*, 14 July 2017.

2   James Meadway, 'What if we've reached peak globalisation?', *Guardian*, 28 September 2015; Shawn Doonan, 'WTO warns on rise of protectionist measures by G20 economies', *Financial Times*, 21 June 2016; 'Press release 793: trade statistics and outlook', World Trade Organization, 2017, at wto.org; Kevin Yao, 'China capital outflows stabilized in first-quarter as capital controls bite', *Reuters*, 20 April 2017.

3   Gaby Hinsliff, 'Labour still has to work out how it can speak for England', *Guardian*, 4 February 2016; Vernon Bogdanor, 'As a political force Englishness is on the rise – and Labour mustn't forget it', *Guardian*, 8 July 2013; John Harris, 'Don't let England be rebranded as a nation of bigots', *Guardian*, 10 October 2016; Polly Toynbee, 'Dismal, lifeless, spineless – Jeremy Corbyn let us down again', *Guardian*, 25 June 2016; Andy Burnham, 'Labour needs to take back control of the immigration debate', *Guardian*, 16 December 2016.

4   Anthony Bond and Steve Robson, 'Revenge of the youth! How 18 to 24-year-olds furious over Brexit gave Theresa May a disastrous general election result', *Mirror*, 9 June 2017; Robert Ford, 'The new electoral map of Britain: from the revenge of Remainers to the upending of class

politics', *Guardian*, 11 June 2017; 'Media coverage of the 2017 general election campaign (report 3)', Centre for Research in Communication and Culture, Loughborough University, 2 June 2017.

5   Alan Travis and Caelainn Barr, ' "Youthquake" behind Labour election surge divides generations', *Guardian*, 20 June 2017.

6   Charlotte Catherine Gill, 'Corbyn's promises to under-25s are nothing but a con', *The Times*, 5 June 2017.

7   Rod Liddle, 'Sssh ... let your kids lie in', *Sun*, 7 June 2017.

8   There are better schemes. The British Election Study uses an occupational grading system called NS-SEC, which is more subtle – it allows for the existence of an employer class, and the traditional petty bourgeoisie of lone traders and small businessmen. Unfortunately, this is not widely used.

9   YouGov itself, working on the same premises, offered this analysis. Chris Curtis, 'How Britain voted at the 2017 general election', *YouGov*, 13 June 2017.

10 Laurence Dodds, 'Was this the revenge of the liberal metropolitan elite?', *Telegraph*, 9 June 2017.

11 Bart Cammaerts, Brooks DeCillia, João Magalhães, and César Jimenez-Martínez, 'Journalistic representations of Jeremy Corbyn in the British press: from watchdog to attackdog', Media@LSE report, London School of Economics, 1 July 2016; Dr Justin Schlosberg, 'Should he stay or should he go? Television and online news coverage of the Labour Party in crisis', Media Reform Coalition and Birkbeck University of London, July 2016; Jane Martinson, 'BBC Trust says Laura Kuenssberg report on Corbyn was inaccurate', *Guardian*, 18 January 2017; Justin Lewis, 'Newspapers, not BBC, led the way in biased election coverage', *The Conversation*, 15 May 2015; Tom Mills, 'The General Strike to Corbyn: 90 years of BBC establishment bias', *Open Democracy*, 6 May 2016; Tom Mills, 'Post-democratic broadcasting', *LRB* blog, 18 May 2017; Stephen Cushion, 'The Tories are the big winners in the TV airtime war', *The 650*, 12 May 2017; 'Media coverage of the 2017 General Election campaign', Centre for Research in Communication and Culture, Loughborough University, April–June 2017.

12 Teemu Henriksson, 'World Press Trends 2017: the audience-focused era arrives', World Association of Newspapers and News Publishers, 8 June 2017.

13 'Newspapers: daily readership by age', State of the News Media 2016, Pew Research Centre, 15 June 2016; Jasper Jackson, 'National daily newspaper sales fall by half a million in a year', *Guardian*, 10 April 2015; Roy Greenslade, 'Suddenly, national newspapers are heading for that print cliff fall', *Guardian*, 27 May 2016; Roy Greenslade, 'Popular newspapers suffer greater circulation falls than qualities', *Guardian*, 19 January 2017; David Bond, 'UK newspapers team up to combat falling revenues', *Financial Times*, 23 October 2016; Teemu Henriksson, 'World Press Trends 2017: the audience-focused era arrives', World Association of Newspapers and News Publishers, 8 June 2017; Peter Preston, 'TV news faces a threat familiar to newspapers', *Guardian*, 17 April 2016.

14 Teemu Henriksson, 'World Press Trends 2017: the audience-focused era arrives', World Association of Newspapers and News Publishers, 8 June 2017; Peter Kellner, 'The problem of trust', YouGov, 13 November 2012; James Grierson, 'Britons' trust in government, media and business falls sharply', *Guardian*, 16 January 2017.

15 Tom Mills, *The BBC: Myth of a Public Service*, Verso: London, 2016

16 Matti Littunen, 'An analysis of news and advertising in the UK general election', *Open Democracy*, 7 June 2017; Jim Waterson and Tom Phillips, 'People on Facebook only want to share pro-Corbyn, anti-Tory news stories', *Buzzfeed*, 7 May 2017; Giles Turner and Jeremy Khan, 'U.K. Labour's savvy use of social media helped win young voters', *Bloomberg*, 11 June 2017.

Introduction: Against All Odds

1 David Smith, 'Tony Blair admits he is baffled by rise of Bernie Sanders and Jeremy Corbyn', *Guardian*, 23 February 2016.

2 'Tony Blair: If your heart's with Jeremy Corbyn, get a transplant', *Guardian*, 22 July 2015; Peter Mandelson, 'The Labour Party is in mortal danger', *Financial Times*, 27 August 2015; Rowena Mason and Josh Halliday, 'Gordon Brown urges Labour not to be party of protest by choosing Jeremy Corbyn', *Guardian*, 17 August 2015.

3 Robert Mendick, 'Tony Blair gives Kazakhstan's autocratic president tips on how to defend a massacre', *Telegraph*, 24 August 2014.

4 Tony Benn, *Office Without Power: Diaries 1968–72*, London: Arrow, 1989.

5   Tony Benn, speech to the Engineering Union, AUEW Conference, May 1971. In Ruth Winstone, ed., *The Best of Benn: Letters, Diaries, Speeches and Other Writings*, London: Hutchinson, 2014, Kindle Loc. 621.

6   Hilary Wainwright and Leo Panitch, '"What we've achieved so far": an interview with Jeremy Corbyn', *Red Pepper*, December 2015.

7   Quoted in Nigel Cawthorne, *Jeremy Corbyn: Leading from the Left*, London: Endeavour Press Ltd, 2015, Kindle Loc. 180.

8   Rosa Prince, *Comrade Corbyn: A Very Unlikely Coup: How Jeremy Corbyn Stormed to the Labour Leadership*, London: Biteback Publishing, 2016.

9   Jessica Elgot, 'Jeremy Corbyn caught looking gloomy on night bus', *Guardian*, 1 August 2015.

10   Quoted in Nigel Cawthorne, *Jeremy Corbyn: Leading from the Left*, London: Endeavour Press Ltd, 2015, Kindle Loc. 238.

11   Jeremy Corbyn, 'Building the Social Movement', in Tom Unterrainer, ed., *Corbyn's Campaign*, Nottingham: Spokesman Books, 2016.

12   Hilary Wainwright and Leo Panitch, '"What we've achieved so far": an interview with Jeremy Corbyn', *Red Pepper*, December 2015.

13   Phil Burton-Cartledge, interview with the author, 19 February 2016.

14   Hardeep Matharu, 'Britain could be more left-wing than people assume, study finds', *The Independent*, 15 January 2016.

15   Sam Webb, 'Jeremy Corbyn gets hero's welcome at refugee rally on day he becomes Labour leader', *Mirror*, 12 September 2015.

16   Larry Elliott, 'OECD calls for less austerity and more public investment', *Guardian*, 18 February 2016.

17   Will Dahlgreen, 'British people keener on socialism than capitalism', *YouGov*, 23 February 2016.

1. How 'Project Fear' Failed

1   Michael Crick, @michaelcrick, Twitter, 28 May 2015, twitter.com/michaellcrick/status/603845352727453696.

2   'Labour leadership latest odds: can Jeremy Corbyn really win?', *Week*, 19 August 2015.

3   Cruddas's spin on the findings was reported by the *Guardian*'s resident Blairite, Patrick Wintour, with the following headline: 'Anti-austerity unpopular with voters, finds inquiry into Labour's election loss'. *Guardian*, 4 August 2015. In fact, the research did not 'find' any such thing.

4   Ross Hawkins, 'Ed Miliband did not lose election because he was too left wing – study', *BBC News*, 17 September 2015.

5   Steve Coogan, 'Andy Burnham is Labour's best hope', *Guardian*, 14 August 2015.

6   Interview with Marsha-Jane Thompson, 14 January 2016.

7   Interview with Ben Sellers, 12 February 2016.

8   Interview with Marsha-Jane Thompson, 14 January 2016.

9   Chi Onwurah, 'My nomination for leader of the Labour Party', Chionwurahmp.com, 11 June 2015.

10   Luke Akehurst, 'Why Jeremy Corbyn should be on the leadership ballot', *LabourList*, 9 June 2015.

11   The speech can be viewed at: 'Jeremy Corbyn – End Austerity Now – June 20 2015', YouTube, 20 June 2015.

12   Stephen Bush, 'Why are we so certain that Jeremy Corbyn can't win?', *New Statesman*, 23 June 2015.

13   Helen Pidd, 'Jeremy Corbyn: "Welcome to the mass movement of giving a toss about stuff"', *Guardian*, 30 August 2015.

14   Jon Stone, 'More people have joined Labour since the election than are in the entire Conservative party', *Independent*, 8 October 2015.

15   Interview with Marsha-Jane Thompson, 14 January 2016.

16   Interview with Ben Sellers, 12 February 2016.

17   Statistic quoted in Ben Sellers, '#JEZWEDID: From Red Labour to Jeremy Corbyn: A Tale from Social Media', in Tom Unterrainer, ed., *Corbyn's Campaign*, Nottingham: Spokesman Books, 2016.

18   Interview with Jeremy Gilbert, 19 January 2016.

19   Interview with Ben Sellers, 12 February 2016.

20   Kiran Moodley, 'The video which shows why Jeremy Corbyn is winning in the Labour leadership race', *Independent*, 23 July 2015.

21   Magpie Corvid, 'The Multitude of Fishes', *Salvage*, 3 September 2015, salvage.zone.

22   Interview with Marsha-Jane Thompson, 14 January 2016.

23   Nicholas Watt, 'Communication Workers Union backs Corbyn as antidote to Blairite "virus"', *Guardian*, 30 July 2015.

24   Tom Gordon, 'One year on: will Better Together change their tactics?', *Sunday Herald*, 23 June 2013.

25   Kiran Stacey, George Parker, Mure Dickie and Beth Rigby, 'Scottish

referendum: How complacency nearly lost a united kingdom', *Financial Times*, 19 September 2014.

26 Nicholas Watt, Patrick Wintour and Severin Carrell, 'Scottish independence: Queen was asked to intervene amid yes vote fears', *Guardian*, 16 December 2015; Severin Carrell, 'Civil servants accused of bias during Scotland's independence referendum', *Guardian*, 23 March 2015; John Robertson, 'BBC bias and the Scots referendum – new report', *Open Democracy*, 21 February 2014.

27 Mikey Smith, 'Labour leadership race "should be halted" over hard-left "infiltrators"', *Mirror*, 26 July 2015; Glen Owen, 'Now top Labour MP warns his party is on the brink of catastrophe', *Mail on Sunday*, 8 August 2015.

28 James Lyons and Robin Henry, 'Hard left plot to infiltrate Labour race', *Sunday Times*, 25 July 2015.

29 Dan Hodges, 'Jeremy Corbyn proves the lunatic wing of the Labour Party is still calling the shots', *Telegraph*, 15 June 2015; Dan Hodges, 'Sadiq Khan winning in London will be bad news for the Labour Party', *Telegraph*, 19 January 2016.

30 Andy McSmith, 'Jeremy Corbyn is a stranger to responsibility and will loathe leadership', *Independent*, 25 August 2015.

31 Andrew Sparrow, 'Miliband wins vote on Labour party reforms with overwhelming majority', *Guardian*, 1 March 2014.

32 Andrew Rawnsley, 'Ed Miliband boldly goes where even Tony Blair feared to tread', *Observer*, 2 February 2014.

33 Isabel Hardman, 'Labour "members" object to "purge"', *Spectator*, 20 August 2015; James Walsh and Frances Perraudin, 'Labour leadership election: rejected supporters express their anger', *Guardian*, 20 August 2015; Stephen Bush, 'Is Labour purging supporters of Jeremy Corbyn?', *New Statesman*, 20 August 2015; Oliver Wright and Matt Dathan, '#LabourPurge: Long-time supporters of party claim they have been barred from voting', *Independent*, 20 August 2015; Rowena Mason, 'Labour bans trade union head from voting in leadership election', *Guardian*, 25 August 2015; Peter Taheri and Kapil Komireddi, 'With up to 100,000 now barred, Labour has become less a broad church and more a secret society', *Independent*, 25 August 2015.

34 Louise Ridley, 'Jeremy Corbyn "Systematically" Attacked by British

Press the Moment He Became Leader, Research Claims', *Huffington Post*, 26 November 2015.

35   Peter Dominiczak, Christopher Hope, Ben Riley-Smith and Kate McCann, 'Union bosses threaten to use Jeremy Corbyn's victory to cripple UK', *Telegraph*, 14 September 2015; Janet Daley, 'The hard Left wants to seize power on the streets, not at Westminster', *Telegraph*, 16 August 2015.

36   David Thomas, 'Prime Minister Corbyn… and the 1,000 days that destroyed Britain', *Daily Mail*, 22 August 2015.

37   Philip Stephens, 'Jeremy Corbyn for UK Labour party leader? Blame the bankers', *Financial Times*, 10 September 2015.

38   Editorial, 'The key questions Jeremy Corbyn must answer', *Jewish Chronicle*, 12 August 2015.

39   Eddy Portnoy, 'Simple, Offensive and Out There', *Forward*, 18 December 2008.

40   'Raed Salah Mahajna -v- The Secretary of State for the Home Department', Courts and Tribunals Judiciary, 10 April 2012, judiciary. gov.uk.

41   Dan Hodges, 'Jeremy Corbyn will be cheered by racists and terrorists', *Telegraph*, 25 August 2015; Simon Walters, 'Labour's "Mayor" savages Corbyn: Party star Khan damns leader over anti-Semitism', *Daily Mail*, 20 September 2015

42   Jonathan Freedland, 'The Corbyn tribe cares about identity, not power', *Guardian*, 24 July 2015; Suzanne Moore, 'Corbyn's Labour is a party without a point, led by a rebel with a cause', *Guardian*, 16 September 2015; Anne Perkins, 'Labour party members, please think before you vote for Jeremy Corbyn', *Guardian*, 22 July 2015; Anne Perkins, 'What the trials of Chris Froome can teach us about Jeremy Corbyn', *Guardian*, 23 July 2015.

43   Andrew Rawnsley, 'Why Labour is gravitating towards the Conservatives' dream candidate', *Observer*, 19 July 2015; Andrew Rawnsley, 'Labour downs a deadly cocktail of fatalism, fury and fantasy', *Observer*, 26 July 2015.

44   Ed Vulliamy, 'Why I take issue with the Observer's stance on Jeremy Corbyn', *Observer*, 20 September 2015.

45   Andrew Sparrow, 'Labour donor: Jeremy Corbyn win could cause SDP-style split', *Guardian*, 24 July 2015.

46   Polly Toynbee, 'In Labour's leadership race, Yvette Cooper is the one to beat', *Guardian*, 23 June 2015.

47   Editorial, 'The Guardian view on Labour's choice: Corbyn has shaped the campaign, but Cooper can shape the future', *Guardian*, 13 August 2015; Selma James and Nina Lopez, 'Yvette Cooper supported sexist austerity; Jeremy Corbyn has always opposed it', Letters page, *Guardian*, 18 August 2015.

48   Suzanne Moore, 'As Jeremy Corbyn was anointed leader, not one female voice was heard', *Guardian*, 12 September 2015.

49   Will Dahlgreen, 'With one month to go, Corbyn's lead increases', *YouGov*, 10 August 2015.

50   Daisy Benson, 'If it's truly progressive, Labour will have voted in a female leader – regardless of her policies', *Independent*, 11 September 2015.

51   Michael Wilkinson, 'Has Jeremy Corbyn got a woman problem?', *Telegraph*, 14 December 2015.

52   Cathy Newman, 'Welcome to Jeremy Corbyn's blokey Britain – where "brocialism" rules', *Telegraph*, 14 September.

53   This is reported, albeit grudgingly, in the *Independent*. Matt Dathan, 'Jeremy Corbyn comes out fighting amid sexism row and insists shadow Cabinet positions he has given to women are the real "top jobs"', *Independent*, 14 September 2015.

54   John Elledge, 'Labour chooses white man as leader', *New Statesman*, 12 September 2015.

55   Andrew Grice and Oliver Wright, 'A third of Labour voters less likely to vote for the party with Jeremy Corbyn in charge, with critics already plotting to oust him', *Independent*, 18 September 2015.

56   Allister Heath, 'One Thing Is Clear – Jeremy Corbyn Has No Understanding of the British People', *Telegraph*, 30 September 2015.

57   Rafael Behr, 'In Oldham, Jeremy Corbyn is just another face of "poncified" Labour', *Guardian*, 2 December 2015.

58   Roy Greenslade, 'The Times counts the cost of spinning against Labour in Oldham', *Guardian*, 4 December 2015.

59   John Harris, John Domokos and Dan Susman, 'Oldham byelection: Corbynmania collides with reality – video', *Guardian*, 2 December.

60   Asa Bennett, 'Oldham by-election: did Muslims worried about war in Syria save Jeremy Corbyn from doom?', *Telegraph*, 4 December 2015.

61   Kate McCann and Rosa Silverman, 'Revealed: Jeremy Corbyn had a second relationship with a Labour politician', *Telegraph*, 18 September 2015.

62   Janet Daley, 'I've lived under Jeremy Corbyn's rule – it turned me into a Tory', *Telegraph*, 25 July 2015.

63   Anne Perkins, 'The National Anthem May Stick in Corbyn's Craw, but It Is His Job to Sing It', *Guardian*, 16 September 2015.

64   Aubrey Allegretti, 'The Sun's Front Page Smear Story On "Hypocrite" Jeremy Corbyn Revealed As False', *Huffington Post*, 15 September 2015.

65   Liam Young, 'Why is the Sun so determined to destroy Jeremy Corbyn? Because he could be prime minister', *New Statesman*, 9 December 2015.

66   Roy Greenslade, 'Rightwing press mounts assault over Jeremy Corbyn's Cenotaph nod', *Guardian*, 9 November 2015.

67   Rowena Mason, 'Corbyn urged to disband Momentum after Labour MPs report bullying and abuse', *Guardian*, 3 December 2015; Charlie Cooper, 'Syria air strikes: Pro-war MPs bullied by extremists, say Labour figures', *Independent*, 2 December 2015; Cathy Newman, 'Showing Corbyn how it's done: The war Britain's bullied female MPs are determined to win', *Telegraph*, 3 December 2015; Roy Greenslade, 'Stella Creasy crushes story about protest outside her house', *Guardian*, 4 December 2015.

68   Rowena Mason, 'Corbyn urged to disband Momentum after Labour MPs report bullying and abuse', *Guardian*, 3 December 2015.

69   Tom Tugenhat MP, 'Jeremy Corbyn is no pacifist – he wants to see Britain defeated', *Telegraph*, 18 January 2016.

70   Caroline Mortimer, 'British Army "could stage mutiny under Corbyn", says senior serving general', *Independent*, 20 September 2015.

71   Rowena Mason and Patrick Wintour, 'Trident: military chief will not be disciplined over Corbyn remarks', *Guardian*, 9 November 2015; Andrew Sparrow, 'Corbyn to complain to MoD about army chief's "political interference"', *Guardian*, 9 November 2015.

72   Philip Collins, 'Am I angry at vain, arrogant Ed? Hell, yes', *Times*, 15 May 2015.

73   Tim Stanley, 'Labour didn't lose because it was too Left-wing. But it will lose again if it becomes too Right-wing', *Telegraph*, 15 May 2015.

74   Tony Blair, 'In conversation with … Tony Blair: opening remarks', *Progress*, 22 July 2015.

75   Dan Hodges, 'Sadiq Khan Winning in London Will Be Bad News for the Labour Party', *Telegraph*, 19 January 2016.

76   Peter Hyman, 'This Is an Existential Moment in Labour's History. It May Not Survive. And It May Never Win Again', *Guardian*, 20 December 2015.

77   Polly Toynbee, 'Dear Labour, split the party and you'll regret it. Love from an sdp candidate', *Guardian*, 26 January 2016.

78   Jon Rentoul, 'Daily catch-up: Will the Labour Party split? Will there be an SDP Mark II?', *Independent*, 14 December 2015.

79   Mark Mardell, 'Is "King Jeremy the Accidental" on the up?', *BBC News*, 21 January 2016.

80   Robin De Peyer, 'Noel Gallagher launches scathing attack on Jeremy Corbyn's Labour leadership', *Evening Standard*, 10 January 2016.

81   Peter Hyman, 'This is an existential moment in Labour's history. It may not survive. And it may never win again', *Guardian*, 20 December 2015.

82   Interview with Jeremy Gilbert, 14 January 2016.

83   Peter Mandelson, 'Peter Mandelson's memo on how Labour's modernisers lost their way – and where they go next', *New Statesman*, 25 September 2010.

84   This is not to deny that New Labour generated a degree of positive support among some voters – especially among ex-Conservative voters on economic issues. However, Labour's biggest asset was the 'new equilibrium' reached by Tories in the polls after the ERM crisis. Peter Kellner, 'Why the Tories Were Trounced', *Parliamentary Affairs*, vol. 50, no. 4, 1997.

85   Rowena Mason, 'Jeremy Corbyn is most popular among voters from all parties, poll suggests', *Guardian*, 15 August 2015; Joe Murphy, 'Left-winger Jeremy Corbyn is "first choice for Londoners"', *Evening Standard*, 14 August 2015.

86   Roy Hattersley, 'Labour's moderates have a duty to serve in the shadow cabinet', *Guardian*, 13 September 2015.

87   John McDonnell, 'How Labour will secure the high-wage, hi-tech economy of the future', *Guardian*, 19 November 2015.

88   Even Paul Kenny of the GMB, who is otherwise sceptical of Corbyn, insists that the Blairites should accept Corbyn's victory or quit the party. Jon Craig, 'Union Leaders Say "Accept Corbyn Or Quit"', *Sky News*, 12 September 2015.

89   When New Labour first promoted the replacement of Trident, an over-whelming majority of the public opposed renewing it. See 'Nuclear Deterrent', *Populus*, 21–22 February 2007. In subsequent polls, a major-ity of the public favoured getting rid of Trident to save money. See: 'Published Voting Intention Figures', *ComRes*, 4–6 September 2009; Glen Owen, 'Here's £37bn of cuts to get you started, voters tell PM', *Mail on Sunday*, 13 June 2010. More recent polling suggests that opinion is at least an even split on Trident. Andrew Grice, 'Trident: Majority of Britons back keeping nuclear weapons programme, poll shows', *Independent*, 24 January 2016. Meanwhile, a number of leading ex-generals have publicly called for the scrapping of Trident. 'Generals in "scrap Trident" call', *BBC News*, 16 January 2009; Helen Pidd, 'Trident nuclear missiles are £20bn waste of money, say generals', *Guardian*, 16 January 2009; Kate Hudson, 'Trident's an outdated waste. Even the military say so', *New Statesman*, 24 June 2015.

2. The Crisis of British Politics

1   Oliver Milne, 'Momentum sweeps board at Labour party youth elec-tions', *Guardian*, 19 February 2016

2   I am grateful to Simon Hewitt for these points. Interview with the author, 13 January 2016.

3   Quoted in Ian Dunt, 'Ed Miliband: We need our working class vote back', *Politics.co.uk*, 16 August 2010. Although, in fact, this argument was slightly over-simplified. Millions of those who had voted Labour in 1997 would have died by 2010. The question is why those voters weren't replaced. The biggest reason is that voters who might tend to support Labour – largely poor and largely young – stopped turning out. For a more conventionally Blairite take on the numbers, see Peter Kellner, 'Labour's lost votes', *Prospect*, 17 October 2012.

4   Jon Trickett reaffirmed this argument after the 2015 election defeat. 'It was the working class, not the middle class that sunk Labour', *New Statesman*, 13 May 2015.

5   Toby Helm, 'Labour's lost voters may never return again, study finds', *Guardian*, 18 July 2015.

6   Ross Hawkins, 'Ed Miliband did not lose election because he was too left wing – study', *BBC News*, 17 September 2015; Rowena Mason, 'Beckett

report: Labour lost election over economy, immigration and benefits', *Guardian*, 14 January 2016.

7   Alberto Nardelli, 'Party membership in the UK is tiny', *Guardian*, 29 September 2014; Hugh Pemberton and Mark Wickham-Jones, 'Labour's lost grassroots: the rise and fall of party membership', *British Politics*, vol. 8, 2013.

8   John Moylan, 'Union membership has halved since 1980', *BBC News*, 7 September 2012; Brian Groom, 'UK trade union membership holds steady', *Financial Times*, 20 May 2014; Michael J Morely, Patrick Gunnigle, David G Collings, G*lobal Industrial Relations*, Routledge, Abingdon, 2006, p. 226; also Robert J Flanagan, *Globalization and Labor Conditions: Working Conditions and Worker Rights in a Global Economy*, Oxford University Press, Oxford, 2006.

9   Richard Hyman, 'Strikes in the UK: withering away?', *EurWork:* European Observatory of Working Life, 27 July 1999.

10 James Doran, '5 Things You Need to Know About "Pasokification"', *Novara Media*, 5 January 2015.

11 The loss of ethnic minority voters was apparent well before Corbyn took the leadership. See Tim Wigmore, 'Is Labour losing the ethnic minority vote?', *New Statesman*, 5 January 2015. The evidence of polling, however, suggests that Corbyn's leadership is less popular among these groups than Labour is as a whole. Aaron Bastani, 'Corbyn's declining popularity?', *LRB blog*, 3 December 2015.

12 Colin Crouch, *Coping with Post-Democracy*, Fabian Society, 2000; Colin Crouch, *Post-Democracy*, London: Polity, 2004; Colin Crouch, *The Strange Non-Death of Neo-Liberalism*, London: Polity, 2011.

13 Peter Mair, *Ruling the Void: The Hollowing Out of Western Democracy*, London: Verso, 2013, Kindle Loc. 367.

14 Peter Mair, *Ruling the Void: The Hollowing Out of Western Democracy*, London: Verso, 2013, Kindle Loc. 437–67.

15 Armin Schäfer and Wolfgang Streeck, 'Introduction: Politics in the Age of Austerity', in Armin Schäfer and Wolfgang Streeck, eds., *Politics in the Age of Austerity*, Cambridge: Polity, p. 16.

16 Peter Mair, *Ruling the Void: The Hollowing Out of Western Democracy*, London: Verso, 2013, Kindle Loc. 665.

17 Peter Mair, *Ruling the Void: The Hollowing Out of Western Democracy*, London: Verso, 2013, Kindle Loc. 623.

18 Pippa Norris, 'Apathetic Landslide', *Parliamentary Affairs*, 54, 2001, pp. 565–89.

19 Pippa Norris, 'Apathetic Landslide', *Parliamentary Affairs*, 54, 2001, pp. 565–89; Ron Johnson and Charles Pattie, *Putting Voters in Their Place: geography and elections in Great Britain*, Oxford: Oxford University Press, 2006, p. 246.

20 David Garner, 'Why do so few people vote in UK elections now?', Department of Politics, University of York, 20 June 2005.

21 Emma Ailes, 'Election 2015: Who are the non-voters?', *BBC News*, 6 May 2015.

22 Roger Mortimore and Kully Kaur-Ballagan, 'Ethnic Minority Voters and Non-Voters at the 2005 British General Election', Ipsos-Mori, Paper for EPOP Conference, University of Nottingham, September 2006; 'General Election 2015 explained: Turnout', *Independent*, 4 May 2015.

23 On these origins, see Daron Acemoglu and James A Robinson, 'Why Did the West Extend the Franchise? Democracy, Inequality and Growth in Historical Perspective', Cambridge, MA: MIT Press, 1998, web.mit.edu.

24 Wolfgang Streeck, *Buying Time: The Delayed Crisis of Democratic Capitalism*, London: Verso, 2014, pp. 77–9.

25 On the relationship between neoliberals, democracy and the far right, see: William E. Scheuerman, *Carl Schmitt: The End of Law*, Lanham MD: Rowman & Littlefield, 1999; Renato Christi, *Carl Schmitt and Authoritarian Liberalism: Strong State, Free Economy*, University of Wales Press, Cardiff, 1998; Perry Anderson, 'The Intransigent Right' in *Spectrum: from right to left in the world of ideas*, Verso, 2005, pp. 15–16; and Renée Sallas, 'Friedrich von Hayek, Leader and Master of Liberalism', *El Mercurio*, 12 April 1981. On the role of neoliberals in the Pinochet dictatorship, see David Harvey, *Neoliberalism: A Short History*, Oxford: Oxford University Press, 2005, pp. 7–9; Naomi Klein, *The Shock Doctrine: The Rise of Disaster Capitalism*, New York: Metropolitan Books, 2007, pp. 77–87; Greg Grandin, 'The Road from Serfdom: Milton Friedman and the Economics of Empire', *Counterpunch*, 17 November 2006. And on the underlying assumptions of neoliberal thought with regard to state and economy, see: Philip Mirowski, *Never Let a Serious Crisis Go to Waste: How Neoliberalism Survived the Financial Meltdown*, London: Verso, 2013; Philip Mirowski, 'On the Origins (at Chicago)

of some Species of Neoliberal Evolutionary Economics', in Robert van Horn, Philip Mirowski and Thomas A Stapleford, eds., *Building Chicago Economics: New Perspectives on the History of America's Most Powerful Economics Program*, Cambridge University Press, 2011.

26   James M. Buchanan, *Public Finance in Democratic Process: Fiscal Institutions and Individual Choice*, Chapel Hill, NC: UNC Press, 1967; William A. Niskanen, Jr., *Bureaucracy and Representative Government*, AldineTransaction, 2007; William A. Niskanen Jr., *Bureaucracy and Public Economics*, Edward Elgar Publishing Ltd., 1996.

27   Rarely a year goes by when some scandal does not befall Serco, by far one of the most useless corporations in the world, and also the government's favourite. Richard Whitell and Emily Dugan, 'Services provider established by outsourcing giant Serco overcharged NHS by millions', *Independent*, 27 August 2014; 'Prisons privatisation cancelled amid Serco probe', *BBC News*, 22 November 2013. Competition in the NHS was found to have driven up overheads to 15 per cent of total costs by 2007. See Steffie Woolhandler and David U. Himmelstein, 'Competition in a publicly funded healthcare system', *British Medical Journal*, 335, 2007.

28   Colin Crouch, *Coping with Post-Democracy*, Fabian Society, 2000.

29   Mark Mills, 'British Businesses Are Hoarding Billions That Could Be Invested in SMEs', *Huffington Post*, 3 January 2014; Adam Davidson, 'Why are Corporations Hoarding Trillions?', *New York Times*, 20 January 2016.

30   An extended version of this argument can be found in Richard Seymour, *Against Austerity: How We Can Fix the Crisis They Made*, London: Pluto Press, 2014.

31   Peter Mair, *Ruling the Void: The Hollowing Out of Western Democracy*, London: Verso, 2013, Kindle Loc. 367 & 1327.

32   Frances Perraudin and Rowena Mason, 'Include Lib Dems in coalition or face second election this year, says Clegg', *Guardian*, 5 May 2015.

33   Emma Ailes, 'Election 2015: Who are the non-voters?', *BBC News*, 6 May 2015.

34   'Building Public Engagement: Options for Developing Select Committee Outreach, First Special Report of Session 2015–16 (House of Commons Papers)'. House of Commons Liaison Committee. November 2005

35   Polly Toynbee, 'Every vote counts – to waste yours would be

near-criminal', *Guardian*, 7 May 2015; Iain Sinclair, 'Polly Toynbee, Jeremy Corbyn and the limits of acceptable politics', *Open Democracy*, 29 June 2015.

36   In the Iowa primary, which was unexpectedly a near draw, Sanders defeated Clinton 6–1 among under thirties. See Aaron Bastani, 'Young Americans', *LRB blog*, 10 February 2016.

37   Gerassimos Moschonas, *In the Name of Social Democracy: The Great Transformation 1945 to the Present*, London: Verso, 2002, pp. 190–204. On the struggle throughout the 1980s to defend a non-neoliberal set of institutional commitments, see Göran Therborn, *Why Some People Are More Unemployed Than Others: The Strange Paradox of Growth and Unemployment*, London: Verso, 1986.

38   This analysis draws extensively from Paolo Chiocchetti's as-yet-unpublished PhD thesis, 'Filling the Vacuum?: The Development of the Partisan Radical Left in Germany, France and Italy, 1989–2013', Department of European and International Studies, King's College London, 14 November 2013. I am also grateful to the author for explaining his thesis in personal conversation. But see also: Dan Hough, Michael Koß and Jonathan Olsen, *The Left Party in Contemporary German Politics*, London: Palgrave Macmillan, 2007; Dan Hough, Michael Koß and Jonathan Olsen, *Left Parties in National Governments*, London: Palgrave Macmillan, 2010; Kate Hudson, *European Communism since 1989: Towards a New European Left?*, Palgrave Macmillan, 2000; Kate Hudson, *The New European Left: A Socialism for the Twenty-First Century?*, Palgrave Macmillan, 2012; Valeria Camia, 'Social democrats, Europe and the radical party factor', National Centre of Competence in Research (NCCR), *Challenges to Democracy in the Twenty-First Century*, Working Paper No. 54, July 2012; Daniele Albertazzi, Clodagh Brook and Charlotte Ross, 'Italy's radical Left in the Age of Berlusconi', *Radical Politics Today*, July 2009; Luke March and Cas Mudde, 'What's Left of the Radical Left? The European Radical Left After 1989: Decline and Mutation', *Comparative European Politics*, 3, 2005; Luke March, *Contemporary Far Left Parties in Europe*, Berlin: Friedrich-Ebert-Stiftung, 2008; Luke March, *Radical Left Parties in Europe*, London: Routledge, 2011.

3. Labour Isn't Working: Whatever Happened to Social Democracy?

1   Tony Blair, 'In defence of Blairism, by Tony Blair', *Spectator*, 9 December 2015.

2   On the role of religious ideas in the formation of Labour, see Mark Bevir, *The Making of British Socialism*, Princeton, NJ: Princeton University Press, 2011.

3   Though not the disappearance of the Chartist idea. See Keith Flett, *Chartism After 1848: The Working Class and the Politics of Radical Education*, Pontypool: Merlin Press, 2006.

4   Quoted in John Saville, *The Labour Movement in Britain: A Commentary*, London: Faber & Faber, 1988, p. 9.

5   Maurice Cowling, *1867: Disraeli, Gladstone and Revolution: The Passing of the Second Reform Bill*, Cambridge University Press, 2005, pp. 48–52; Paul Foot, *The Vote: How it Was Won and How it Was Undermined*, Viking, 2005, pp. 125–9; John Ramden, *An Appetite for Power: A History of the Conservative Party Since 1830*, HarperCollins, 1998, p. 93.

6   Gordon Phillips, *The Rise of the Labour Party: 1893–1931*, London: Routledge, 1992, p. 7.

7   Gordon Phillips, *The Rise of the Labour Party: 1893–1931*, London: Routledge, 1992, p. 9.

8   Gregory Elliott, *Labourism and the English Genius: The Strange Death of Labour England?*, London: Verso, 1993, p. 27.

9   Ross McKibbin, *Parties and People: England 1914–1951*, Oxford: Oxford University Press, 2010, pp. 3–5.

10 Paul Mason's description of the syndicalist milieu, from 1899 to 1914, is apt: 'All over the world, "labour of the humbler kind" was getting organised. If the Paris Commune had closed the door on the era of street revolutions, the dock strike had opened an era of workplace revolutions. The trade union itself could become a mini-commune: training and educating workers for self-government'. Paul Mason, *Live Working or Die Fighting: How the Working Class Went Global*, London: Vintage Books, 2007, p. 117.

11 Ralph Miliband, *Parliamentary Socialism: A Study in the Politics of Labour*, New York: Monthly Review Press, 1964, p. 43.

12   Tudor Jones, *Remaking the Labour Party: From Gaitskell to Blair*, London: Routledge, 1996, pp. 4–5.

13   Gregory Elliott, *Labourism and the English Genius: The Strange Death of Labour England?*, London: Verso, 1993, p. 33.

14   Ross McKibbin, *Parties and People: England 1914–1951*, Oxford: Oxford University Press, 2010, pp. 29–30.

15   Andrew Thorpe, *A History of the British Labour Party: Third Edition*, Basingstoke: Palgrave Macmillan, 2008, pp. 59–60.

16   Ralph Miliband, *Parliamentary Socialism: A Study in the Politics of Labour*, New York: Monthly Review Press, 1964, pp. 103–4.

17   Gregory Elliott, *Labourism and the English Genius: The Strange Death of Labour England?*, London: Verso, 1993, p. 38.

18   Ralph Miliband, *Parliamentary Socialism: A Study in the Politics of Labour*, New York: Monthly Review Press, 1964, p. 108

19   Ralph Miliband, *Parliamentary Socialism: A Study in the Politics of Labour*, New York: Monthly Review Press, 1964, p. 112

20   Ralph Miliband, *Parliamentary Socialism: A Study in the Politics of Labour*, New York: Monthly Review Press, 1964, pp. 128–36; Andrew Thorpe, *A History of the British Labour Party: Third Edition*, Basingstoke: Palgrave Macmillan, 2008, p. 66.

21   Matthew Worley, *Labour Inside the Gate: A History of the British Labour Party Between the Wars*, London: IB Tauris, 2009, p. 123.

22   Donald Sassoon, *One Hundred Years of Socialism: The West European Left in the Twentieth Century*, London: IB Tauris, p. 57; Matthew Worley, *Labour Inside the Gate: A History of the British Labour Party Between the Wars*, London: IB Tauris, 2009, pp. 123–5.

23   Gregory Elliott, *Labourism and the English Genius: The Strange Death of Labour England?*, London: Verso, 1993, pp. 43–5.

24   See Ross McKibbin, *Classes and Cultures: 1918–1951*, Oxford: Oxford University Press, 2000, pp. 38–40.

25   Adam Przeworski, *Capitalism and Social Democracy*, Cambridge: Cambridge University Press, 1985, p. 33.

26   Steven Fielding, 'What Did 'The People' Want?': The Meaning of the 1945 General Election', *The Historical Journal*, vol 35, no 3 (Sep., 1992), pp. 623–39; Ralph Miliband, *Parliamentary Socialism: A Study in the Politics of Labour*, New York: Monthly Review Press, 1964, pp. 272–4; Henry Pelling, 'The 1945 General Election Reconsidered',

The Historical Journal, vol. 23, no. 2 (Jun., 1980), pp. 399–414.

27   On the wartime reconfiguration of the state, see Paul Addison, *The Road to 1945: British politics and the Second World War*, London: Pimlico, 1994.

28   Kevin Jefferies, *The Churchill Coalition and Wartime Politics, 1940–1945*, Manchester: Manchester University Press, 1995, pp. 60–3.

29   Ina Zweiniger-Bargielowska, 'Rationing, Austerity and the Conservative Party Recovery after 1945', *The Historical Journal*, vol. 37, no. 1, 1994; David Seawright, 'One Nation', in Kevin Hickson, ed., *The Political Thought of the Conservative Party Since 1945*, Basingstoke: Palgrave Macmillan, 2005.

30   On the revisionist current, see Tudor Jones, *Remaking the Labour Party: From Gaitskell to Blair*, London: Routledge, 1996.

31   Quoted in John Saville, *The Labour Movement in Britain: A Commentary*, London: Faber & Faber, 1988, p. 105.

32   Figure quoted in John Saville, 'The Labour Government (1967)', in David Coates, ed., *Paving the Third Way: The Critique of Parliamentary Socialism*, London: The Merlin Press Ltd, 2003.

33   On this, the most concise background is given by Paul Gilroy and Joe Simm, 'Law, order and the state of the left', *Capital and Class*, 9 (Spring, 1985), pp. 15–55.

34   Peter Weller, 'British Labour and the Cold War: The Foreign Policy of the Labour Governments, 1945–1951', *Journal of British Studies*, vol. 26, no. 1, England's Foreign Relations (Jan., 1987), pp. 54–82.

35   John Newsinger, *British Counterinsurgency: From Palestine to Northern Ireland*, Basingstoke: Palgrave Macmillan, 2002.

36   Stuart Hall, 'The Battle for Socialist Ideas in the 1980s', *Socialist Register*, 1982.

37   Two Keynesian economists offer an acerbic critique of the post-war record of Labour. See Larry Elliott and Dan Atkinson, *The Age of Insecurity*, London: Verso, 1999. On the greatly exaggerated role of 'planning' in post-war Britain, see Nigel Harris, *Competition and the Corporate Society: British Conservatives, the State and Industry 1945–1964*, Abingdon: Routledge, 2013.

38   Martin Pugh, *Speak for Britain!: A New History of the Labour Party*, London: Vintage Books, 2011, p. 359–60.

39   Andrew Thorpe, *A History of the British Labour Party: Third Edition*, Basingstoke: Palgrave Macmillan, 2008, pp. 169–170.

40   Gregory Elliott, *Labourism and the English Genius: The Strange Death of Labour England?*, London: Verso, 1993, pp. 75–6.

41   Richard Crossman, *The Diaries of a Cabinet Minister: Lord President of the Council and Leader of the House of Commons, 1966–68*, Hamilton, 1976, p. 587.

42   On the 'new racism' pioneered by Powell and others, see Martin Barker, *The New Racism*, London: Junction Books, 1981.

43   Stuart Hall, 'Thatcherism – Rolling Back the Welfare State', *Thesis Eleven*, vol. 7, no. 1 (February 1983), pp. 6–19.

44   This opposition between 'state' and 'market' has always been highly misleading. Markets are not, and never have been, self-generating or self-sustaining: they are politically and legally constituted. Their spread and their global connectedness has been expedited by strong, interventionist states. See Leo Panitch and Sam Gindin, *The Making of Global Capitalism: The Political Economy of American Empire*, London: Verso, 2013. At any rate, it is not quite correct to speak of 'the market' as if this exhaustively described the capitalism which Labour governments have sought to reform. And if, following Marx, we depart the noisy sphere of circulation and trade, and enter the hidden abode of production, we tend to find the state's fingerprints everywhere. From tax breaks to subsidies to diplomacy and espionage, much of modern industry would be impossible without the continual coddling, nurturing and leadership of national states. The Apple corporation would, for example, be considerably less of a global giant were it not for the technologies made available to it by years of public sector investment and research, and the markets in labour and goods opened to it by aggressive US diplomacy. Mariana Mazzucato, *The Entrepreneurial State: Debunking Public vs. Private Myths in Risk and Innovation*, London, New York: Anthem Press, 2013. In short, the issue is never 'state intervention or not?', but always 'what kind of state intervention?'. This has been obscured both by Thatcherites, who claim an 'anti-statist' mantle, and Blairites, who try to distinguish their programme from Conservatism by reference to their acknowledgement of the role of government.

45   Patrick Bell, *The Labour Party in Opposition 1970–1974*, London: Routledge, 2004; Martin Pugh, *Speak for Britain!: A New History of the Labour Party*, London: Vintage Books, 2011, p. 370–1.

46 Tony Benn, Speech to the Engineering Union, AUEW Conference, May 1971. In Ruth Winstone, ed., *The Best of Benn: Letters, Diaries, Speeches and Other Writings*, London: Hutchinson, 2014, Kindle Loc. 621–733.

47 Wyn Grant, 'Business Interests and the British Conservative Party', *Government and Opposition*, vol 15, no. 2, 1980.

48 The idea of enforcing workers' representation in company boards was supported by the Bullock Report of 1977, one of the first major turning points in the conversion of business to Thatcherism, but the plans were never likely to be implemented. In fact, moreover, Benn also had difficulty in gaining the support of trade unionist for industrial democracy, on the grounds that they felt such methods of inclusion were intended to obstruct or replace the exercise of real, rank-and-file power. See David Powell, *Tony Benn: A Political Life*, London: Continuum, 2003, pp. 122–3.

49 Stuart Hall, 'The Great Moving Right Show', in Stuart Hall and Martin Jacques, eds., *The Politics of Thatcherism*, London: Lawrence & Wishart, 1983.

50 Stuart Hall, Chas Critcher, Tony Jefferson, John Clarke and Brian Roberts, *Policing The Crisis: Mugging, The State, and Law and Order*, London: Macmillan, 1978.

51 Andrew Gamble provides an authoritative account of Thatcherite ideology and what might be called its 'rational kernel' in *The Free Economy and the Strong State: The Politics of Thatcherism*, London: Palgrave Macmillan, 1994.

52 Sir Ian Gilmour, quoted in Eric J Evans, *Thatcher and Thatcherism*, London: Routledge, 2004, p. 14.

53 Neil Rollings, 'Cracks in the Post-War Keynesian Settlement? The Role of Organised Business in Britain in the Rise of Neoliberalism Before Margaret Thatcher', *Twentieth Century British History*, vol. 24, no. 4, 2013, pp. 637–59.

54 Martin Pugh, *Speak for Britain!: A New History of the Labour Party*, London: Vintage Books, 2011, p. 365.

55 Martin Pugh, *Speak for Britain!: A New History of the Labour Party*, London: Vintage Books, 2011, p. 371.

56 A general tendency, if culpably exaggerated by the centrist intellectuals and politicians, in European social democracy. See Gerassimos

Moschonas, *In the Name of Social Democracy: The Great Transformation, 1954 to the Present*, London: Verso, 2002.

57 First-past-the-post converted 42 per cent of the vote in 1983 and 1987, into 62 per cent and 58 per cent of the parliamentary seats, respectively.

58 As Tim Bale put it, Thatcher won not because she persuaded a majority of people of her views, but because the macroeconomic conditions were sufficiently congenial for a sufficient plurality of people at just the right times. Tim Bale, *The Conservative Party: From Thatcher to Cameron*, London: Polity, p. 24. On shifting social attitudes under Thatcher and their electoral manifestations, see Anthony Heath, Roger Jowell, and John Curtice, 'Understanding Electoral Change in Britain', *Parliamentary Affairs*, Oxford University Press, 1986.

59 Stuart Hall, 'The 'Little Caesars' of Social Democracy', *Marxism Today*, April 1981.

4. New Labour and Corbyn's Route to Power

1 Quoted in Samuel Beer, 'Liberalism Rediscovered', *The Economist*, 7 February 1998.

2 Quoted in Martin Pugh, *Speak for Britain!: A New History of the Labour Party*, London: Vintage Books, 2011, p. 419.

3 Jon Stone, 'Liz Kendall says she lost the Labour leadership election because she was the "eat your greens" candidate', *Independent*, 26 January 2016.

4 John Reid is quoted lauding 'Labour hegemony' at the moment of the Iraq invasion in Andrew Pearmain, *The Politics of New Labour: A Gramscian Analysis*, London: Lawrence & Wishart, 2011, Kindle Loc. 235; Peter Hyman describes the rough contours of this 'hegemony' in 'This is an existential moment in Labour's history. It may not survive. And it may never win again', *Guardian*, 20 December 2015. As Pearmain points out, these ways of construing Gramsci's concept of hegemony are bowdlerised and narrowly focused on electoral party politics in a way that has little to do with any rigorous use of the idea.

5 By far the most historically and theoretically detailed account of these origins is Andrew Pearmain, *The Politics of New Labour: A Gramscian Analysis*, London: Lawrence & Wishart, 2011.

6 A fairly typical settling of accounts with the Left over its failure to

recognise these changes can be found in Stuart Hall, 'The Culture Gap', *Marxism Today*, January 1984; and Stuart Hall, 'The Meaning of New Times', in David Morley and Kuan-Hsing Chen, eds., *Stuart Hall: Critical Dialogues in Cultural Studies*, Abingdon: Routledge, 1996. Hall would later recant on some of this line of argument, arguing that 'there was that odd moment, when the critique went overboard, when we almost hero-ized consumption and designer capitalism'. Quoted in Pearmain, *The Politics of New Labour: A Gramscian Analysis*, London: Lawrence & Wishart, 2011, Kindle Loc. 1597.

7   The case for realignment, to exclude the hard-Left, was put by Hall in characteristically mollifying tones. It was not about trying to expel enemies or create a monolithic culture, but about repudiating 'the "hard-Left" as a peculiar and distinctive political style, a set of habits, a political-cultural tradition, stretching right across the actual organisational sub-divisions of the Left'. The results were, of course, quite other. Stuart Hall, 'Realignment – for What?', *Marxism Today*, December 1985.

8   Pearmain notes that Marxism Today in the eighties was 'mesmerised and on occasions plainly excited by what Martin Jacques still calls its "power and strength"'. *The Politics of New Labour: A Gramscian Analysis*, London: Lawrence & Wishart, 2011, Kindle Loc. 1597–628. Once Blair took the helm of Labour, a sign of its forced adaptation to Thatcherism's 'power and strength', Hall saluted the 'necessary' changes that New Labour signalled for the Labour Party. Stuart Hall, 'Parties on the verge of a nervous breakdown', *Soundings*, no 1, Autumn 1995. As late as 1996, Hall et al. were inclined to cautiously welcome New Labour's policy developments. Editorial, 'What is at stake?', *Soundings*, no. 2, Spring 1996; by the following year, the disillusionment had thoroughly set in, and was explored in a series of brutally pessimistic analyses, beginning with a pre-election piece written by Hall and Jacques on New Labour for *Guardian*, 'Tony Blair: The Greatest Tory since Margaret Thatcher?'. Later pieces theorised the changing analysis in a distinctively Gramscian idiom. Stuart Hall, 'New Labour's Double-shuffle', *Review of Education, Pedagogy, and Cultural Studies*, vol. 27, no. 4, 2005; and Stuart Hall, 'New Labour has picked up where Thatcherism left off', *Guardian*, 6 August 2003.

9   Martin Pugh, *Speak for the People!: A New History of the Labour Party*, London: The Bodley Head, 2010, p. 412.

10 Martin Pugh, *Speak for the People!: A New History of the Labour Party*, London: The Bodley Head, 2010, pp. 413–15.

11 Editorial, 'What is at stake?', *Soundings*, no. 2, Spring 1996.

12 Lewis Minkin, *The Blair Supremacy: A Study in the Politics of the Labour Party's Management*, Manchester: Manchester University Press, 2014, Kindle Loc. 372–467.

13 On this backlash, see Dianne Hayter, *Fightback!: Labour's Traditional Right in the 1970s and 1980s*, Manchester: Manchester University Press, 2005.

14 See Frances Stonor Saunders, *Who Paid the Piper?: CIA and the Cultural Cold War*, Granta Books, 1999; and Hugh Wilford, *The CIA, the British Left, and the Cold War: Calling the Tune?*, Frank Cass Publishers, 2003; Robin Ramsay, *The Rise of New Labour*, Pocket Essentials, 2002; Andy Beckett, 'Friends in high places', *Guardian*, 6 November 2004; Anthony Seldon, *Blair*, The Free Press, 2005, pp. 119–137.

15 The major factor in Labour's defeats continued to be the historic split in its coalition initiated with the defection of the SDP faction in 1981. See Anthony Heath, Roger Jowell and John Curtice, 'Exclusive: How did Labour lose in '92?', *Independent*, 28 May 1994; and Anthony Heath, Roger Jowell and John Curtice, *Labour's Last Chance?: the 1992 election and beyond*, Dartmouth, 1994, p. 285.

16 Lewis Minkin, *The Blair Supremacy: A Study in the Politics of the Labour Party's Management*, Manchester: Manchester University Press, 2014; Liz Davies, *Through the Looking Glass: A Dissenter Inside New Labour*, London: Verso, 2001. Len McCluskey was sufficiently irritated by the Labour leadership's anti-union drive in 2013 to publicly blow the whistle on the Blairites' selections strategy. See Len McCluskey, 'Yes, Labour's selection process has been abused, but not by the unions', *Guardian*, 8 July 2013.

17 Lewis Minkin, *The Blair Supremacy: A Study in the Politics of the Labour Party's Management*, Manchester: Manchester University Press, 2014, Kindle Loc. 2788.

18 Colin Leys, 'The British Labour Party's Transition From Socialism to Capitalism', in David Coates, ed., *Paving the Third Way: The Critique of Parliamentary Socialism*, London: The Merlin Press, 2003.

19 David Coates, *Prolonged Labour: The Slow Birth of New Labour*, Palgrave Macmillan, 2005, pp. 3–23

20   David Coates, '"Darling, It Is Entirely My Fault!" Gordon Brown's Legacy to Alistair and Himself', *British Politics*, no. 3, 2008, pp. 3–21.

21   'Plan to Reduce Budget Deficit', *BBC News*, 2 July 1997.

22   David Coates, *Prolonged Labour: The Slow Birth of New Labour*, Palgrave Macmillan, 2005, pp. 64–5; Simon Rogers, 'UK public spending since 1963', *Guardian*, 26 June 2010; for some background on New Labour policy on spending and employment, see Richard Seymour, *The Meaning of David Cameron*, Zero Books, 2010, pp. 57–8; David Coates, 'A different double shuffle', *Renewal: A Journal of Social Democracy*, vol. 15, no. 2/3, 2007.

23   The first serious exposé of this remarkably corrupt arrangement between state and privileged sectors of capital was George Monbiot's *Captive State: The Corporate Takeover of Britain*, London: Pan Books, 2001

24   Peter Mandelson and Roger Liddle, *The Blair Revolution: Can New Labour Deliver*, London: Faber & Faber, 1996, p. 48.

25   Gaby Hinsliff, 'Jobless single parents to face benefit cuts', *Observer*, 4 March 2007; Mary Riddell, 'Why Asda Woman matters to Tony Blair', *Observer*, 4 March 2007.

26   Polly Toynbee, 'The Tories were right: workfare really works', *Independent*, 27 February 1997.

27   The analysis of the Institute for Fiscal Studies, not unsympathetic to New Labour, chiefly credits benefit increases and tax credits for falling child and pensioner poverty. Robert Joyce and Luke Sibieta, 'Labour's record on poverty and inequality', Institute for Fiscal Studies, 6 June 2013, ifs.org.

28   Steven Morris, 'Asbo bars suicidal woman from rivers', *Guardian*, 26 February 2005; 'Council withdraws Asbo against boy with Tourette's', Press Association, 28 December 2005; Vikram Dodd, 'Asbo call over jokes about the Pope', *Guardian*, 9 April 2005; Debbie Andalo, 'Teenager handed hoodie ban', *Guardian*, 26 May 2005.

29   'Blair to tackle "menace" children', *BBC News*, 31 August 2006.

30   'Blair "respect" speech in full', *BBC News*, 10 January 2006.

31   See 'Police Service Strength, England and Wales: 31 March 1997 to 30 September 2000', House of Commons Library, Research Paper 01/28, 16 March 2001; and also 'Police workforce, England and Wales: March 2011 supplementary tables', data.gov.uk.

32   In fairness, the prison population had been steadily rising for some time, but the growth very suddenly accelerated from the mid-1990s due to harsher penalties. See 'Story of the prison population 1993–2012', Ministry of Justice, March 2013, gov.uk; and Gavin Berman and Aliyah Dar, 'Prison Population Statistics', House of Commons, 29 July 2013, parliament.uk.

33   'Most prisons are overcrowded – Prison Reform Trust', *BBC News*, 28 August 2012; Jamie Doward, 'Fears that Britain's prisons are at crisis point after growing unrest', *Observer*, 28 March 2015

34   Anushka Asthana, 'New Labour pushed Britain's beliefs to the right, says academic', *Guardian*, 24 January 2010.

35   Patrick Wintour and Vikram Dodd, 'Blair blames spate of murders on black culture', *Guardian*, 12 April 2007.

36   Jack Straw, Interview with Annie Oathen, Radio West Midlands, 22 July 1999; Straw's defecation comments were reported in Vikram Dodd, 'Anger after Straw lets fly at travellers as "crooks"', *Guardian*, 1 September 1999.

37   Rebecca Omonira-Oyekanmi, 'UK immigration detention: the truth is out', *Open Democracy*, 5 March 2015; 'Blunkett names 'Britishness' chief', *BBC News*, 10 September 2002; 'New UK citizenship testing starts', *BBC News*, 1 November 2005; Gaby Hinsliff, 'Speak English at home, Blunkett tells British Asians', *Guardian*, 15 September 2002; Arun Kundnani, *The End of Tolerance: Racism in Twenty-First-Century Britain*, London: Pluto Press, 2007; David Goodhart, 'Too diverse?', *Prospect*, February 2004.

38   The Cantle report, undertaken in response to the northern riots which pitted largely young Asian men against police and the far Right, blamed the 'parallel lives' led by minorities and considered that immigrants should make an oath of national allegiance in future. 'The Cantle Report – Community Cohesion: a report of the Independent Review Team', Home Office, January 2001.

39   'Statistics on Race and the Criminal Justice System – 2004', Home Office, 2005.

40   Charlotte Denny, 'Privately financed revolution', *Guardian*, 3 October 2002; see Allyson Pollock, *NHS Plc: The Privatization of Our Healthcare*, London: Verso Books, 2004; Allyson Pollock, 'The exorbitant cost of PFI is now being cruelly exposed', *Guardian*, 26 January 2006.

41   Roy Hattersley, 'It's no longer my party', *Observer*, 24 June 2001.

42   Even the editorial page of the right-wing London paper the *Evening Standard* gave its backing to 'a full-blooded return to nationalisation'. Editorial, 'The State must step in to save our railways', *Evening Standard*, 12 May 2002.

43   Livingstone failed to block the PPP by legal means, but the sheer fiscal inefficiency of the system led to its eventual collapse, as debt-laden companies ended up selling their stake back to Transport for London. 'Mayor loses bid to block PPP for tube', *Guardian*, 30 July 2001; Alexandra Wynne, 'Why the Tube PPP collapsed', *New Civil Engineer*, 20 May 2010.

44   'US attacks stun TUC', *BBC News*, 11 September 2001.

45   '20,000 join anti-war protest', *Guardian*, 13 October 2001.

46   'Anti-war protests under way', *BBC News*, 31 October 2002.

47   On the *Observer*'s lamentable record of reporting in this period, see Nick Davies, *Flat Earth News: An Award-winning Reporter Exposes Falsehood, Distortion and Propaganda in the Global Media*, London: Vintage, 2009.

48   'Anti-war rally makes its mark', *BBC News*, 19 February 2003; Euan Ferguson, 'One million. And still they came', *Observer*, 16 February 2003.

49   '"Unpopularity is the price of leadership"', *Guardian*, 17 February 2013.

50   'Full text: David Blunkett's speech', *Guardian*, 2 October 2003.

51   Nick Cohen, 'Going nowhere fast', *Observer*, 12 October 2003.

52   Benedict Brogan, Toby Helm and George Jones, 'Union chiefs give Blair bloody nose', *Telegraph*, 2 October 2003.

53   John Kampfner, 'The Warwick watershed', *Guardian*, 2 September 2004.

54   Shiv Malik, 'Occupy London's anger over police "terrorism" document', *Guardian*, 5 December 2011; Daniel Evans, 'Police cracking down on Bristol rioters and extremists', *Bristol Post*, 13 September 2013.

55   John Kampfner, 'Labour's steady path to authoritarianism', *Telegraph*, 19 October 2007; Paul Lewis, 'Birmingham stops Muslim CCTV surveillance scheme', *Guardian*, 17 June 2010.

56   '"Remove full veils" urges Straw', *BBC News*, 6th October 2006; Jonathan Freedland, 'If this onslaught was about Jews, I would be looking for my passport', *Guardian*, 18 October 2006.

57   Andrew Rawnsley, *The End of the Party: The Rise and Fall of New Labour*, London: Penguin Books, 2010, pp. 1397–98; 'In full: Tom Watson's resignation', *BBC News*, 6 September 2006.

58   Toby Helm, 'Disillusioned Jack Straw plotted against Gordon Brown in bid to take over No. 10', *Observer*, 21 February 2010; Decca Aitkenhead, 'Jack Straw: "I would have done a better job than Gordon Brown"', *Guardian*, 31 January 2014.

59   Stephen Nickell, 'The Assessment: The Economic Record of the Labour Government since 1997', *Oxford Review of Economic Policy*, vol. 18, no. 2, 2002; David Coates, *Prolonged Labour: The Slow Birth of New Labour*, Palgrave Macmillan, 2005, pp. 17–184.

60   Gordon Brown, all too late, acknowledged his role in this. Patrick Wintour and Nicholas Watt, 'Brown: I should have done more to prevent bank crisis', *Guardian*, 17 March 2009.

61   Julie Froud, Michael Moran, Adriana Nilsson, Karel Williams. 'Wasting a crisis? Democracy and markets in Britain after 2007', *Political Quarterly*, vol. 81, no.1, 2010, pp. 25–38

62   Ewald Engelen, Ismail Erturk, Julie Froud, Sukhdev Johal, Adam Leaver, Michael Moran, Adriana Nilsson and Karel Williams, *After the Great Complacence: Financial Crisis and the Politics of Reform*, Oxford: Oxford University Press, 2011.

63   Quoted in Jim Pickard, 'Conservatives: the party of business?', *Financial Times*, 3 February 2016; Tim Ross, 'Michael Gove aims to be the heir to Tony Blair', *Telegraph*, 15 May 2013.

64   Simon Lee and Matt Beech, eds., *The Conservatives Under David Cameron: Built to Last?*, London: Palgrave Macmillan, 2009, pp. 13 and 21–2; especially Stephen Driver, '"Fixing Our Broken Society": David Cameron's Post-Thatcherite Social Policy', in Simon Lee, and Matt Beech, eds., *The Conservatives under David Cameron: Built to Last?*, London: Palgrave Macmillan, 2009.

65   Jon Cruddas and Jonathan Rutherford, 'Labour must fashion a new patriotism', *Guardian*, 1 July 2011.

66   Don Paskini, 'Blue Labour founder: "Labour should involve EDL supporters"', *Liberal Conspiracy*, 21 April 2011.

67   Dan Hodges, 'We should all be in the dock on immigration', *Labour Uncut*, 19 August 2010.

68   'Prime Minister's questions: The Full Story', *BBC News*, 9 June 2010.

69 Hélène Mulholland, 'Labour will make cuts to welfare budget if it wins 2015 election, says Liam Byrne', *Guardian*, 2 October 2012.

70 Richard Seymour, 'Authoritarianism and free-market orthodoxy in Liam Byrne's welfare ideas', *Guardian*, 4 January 2012.

71 Tom Newton Dunn, 'Prime Minister's questions: The Full Story', *Sun*, 22 April 2011.

72 Rowena Mason, 'Emily Thornberry resigns from shadow cabinet over Rochester tweet', *Guardian*, 20 November 2014.

73 'Miliband steps up attack on SNP as any post-election deal ruled out', *The Herald*, 10 April 2015

74 Andrew Grice, 'Ed Miliband lost the election because he ditched New Labour, says Tony Blair', *Independent*, 10 May 2015.

75 Rowenna Mason, 'Beckett report: Labour lost election over economy, immigration and benefits', *Guardian*, 14 January 2016.

76 Oliver Wright, 'Miliband shows he's a control freak too', *Independent*, 17 February 2011; Patrick Wintour, 'Ed Miliband signs up top Obama adviser David Axelrod for UK election', *Guardian*, 17 April 2014; Rowenna Davis, 'Arnie Graf: The man Ed Miliband asked to rebuild Labour', *Guardian*, 21 November 2012.

77 Adam Bienkov, 'Ed Balls wouldn't reverse anything from Osborne's Budget', Politics.co.uk, 19 March 2015.

5. Two Years Before the Mast: Corbyn's Subaltern Leadership

1 Jane Merrick and Mark Leftly, 'Jeremy Corbyn: Labour MPs are plotting a coup against the potential leader if he is elected', *Independent*, 18 July 2015; Christopher Hope, 'Jeremy Corbyn could face Labour MPs' coup "within days of being elected leader"', *Telegraph*, 20 August 2015; Adam Bienkov, 'Labour MPs plotting coup against Jeremy Corbyn "on day one"', Politics.co.uk, 12 August 2015.

2 Tim Ross and Emily Gosden, 'Jeremy Corbyn faces coup plot if he wins Labour leadership', *Telegraph*, 27 July 2015.

3 Alison Little, 'Lord Mandelson implores Labour to delay coup against Jeremy Corbyn', *Express*, 25 September 2015.

4 Heather Stewart and Rowena Mason, 'Leaked list of "hostile" Labour MPs lays bare party divisions', *Guardian*, 23 March 2016; Anushka

Asthana, 'Labour MPs back call for Jeremy Corbyn to stand down', *Guardian*, 25 March 2016.

5　Jamie Stern-Weiner, 'Jeremy Corbyn hasn't got an "antisemitism problem". His opponents do', *Open Democracy*, 27 April 2016; Baroness Jan Royall, 'Allegations of anti-Semitism: Oxford University Labour Club', at www.ousu.org.

6　Jonathan Freedland, 'Labour and the left have an antisemitism problem', *Guardian*, 18 March 2016; anonymous, 'Labour's shame', *Jewish Chronicle*, 17 March 2016; Daniella Peled, 'The anti-Semitic clouds gathering over U.K.'s Labour Party', *Ha'aretz*, 17 March 2016; Thomas Jones, 'Labour and antisemitism', *LRB* blog, 4 May 2016; Jamie Stern-Weiner, 'Jeremy Corbyn hasn't got an "antisemitism problem". His opponents do', *Open Democracy*, 27 April 2016.

7　Howard Jacobson, 'Corbyn may say he's not anti-Semitic, but associating with the people he does is its own crime', *Independent*, 4 September 2015; Rowena Mason, 'Jewish Labour MP hits out at Jeremy Corbyn's record on antisemitism', *Guardian*, 14 August 2015.

8　Tom Harris, 'The Labour Party is increasingly anti-Semitic', *Telegraph*, 14 March 2016; Camilla Turner, 'Labour anti-Semitism row threatens to divide the party', *Telegraph*, 6 March 2016; Kate McCann, 'Jeremy Corbyn must tackle anti-semitism within Labour or face "almighty row", warns MP', *Telegraph*, 13 March 2016; 'IJV Statement on allegations of antisemitism in the Labour Party', Independent Jewish Voices, 1 May 2016.

9　The Shami Chakrabarti Report, 30 June 2016, at labour.org.uk; 'Jewish Labour movement reaction to Chakrabarti inquiry report', Jewish Labour Movement, 30 June 2016.

10　Geoffrey Evans and Jonathan Mellon, 'Working class votes and Conservative losses: solving the UKIP puzzle', *LSE* blog, 30 April 2015; Chris Curtis, 'UKIP is a "gateway drug" – but more are going straight for the hard stuff', *YouGov*, 5 May 2017.

11　Matt Dathan, 'EU referendum: 5 ways the launch of the In campaign was a disaster', *Independent*, 12 October 2015; Hugo Dixon, 'Britain stumbles into long EU-referendum campaign', *Financial Times*, 16 October 2015; Britain Stronger in Europe, YouTube, 11 October 2015.

12　Ben Riley-Smith and Peter Foster, 'Rapists and murderers harder to deport if Britain leaves EU, "In" campaign claims', *Telegraph*, 12 October 2015.

13   'Corbyn launches Labour In for Britain campaign battlebus', *Telegraph*, 10 May 2016.

14   Rowena Mason, 'Jeremy Corbyn "not on same side" as David Cameron in EU debate', *Guardian*, 29 February 2016.

15   Andrew Sparrow and Claire Phipps, 'EU referendum live: Gordon Brown compares Leave campaign to Trump's', *Guardian*, 13 June 2016; Angela Phillips, 'The BBC's obsession with balance took Labour off-air during the referendum campaign', *LSE* blog, 10 August 2016.

16   John McDonnell MP, DiEM 25 – Another Europe Is Possible, London, 28 May 2016.

17   'Media coverage of the EU referendum (report 5)', Centre for Research in Communication and Culture, Loughborough University, 27 June 2016; 'The people hoping to persuade UK to vote to stay in the EU', *BBC News*, 13 June 2016; Lucy Fisher, 'Johnson takes to skies for last stand', *The Times*, 22 June 2016; 'Alan Johnson launches Labour's "keep UK in the EU" campaign', BBC, 1 December 2015.

18   Phil Wilson, 'Corbyn sabotaged Labour's remain campaign. He must resign', *Guardian*, 29 June 2016.

19   Editorial, 'The culpability of Jeremy Corbyn', *The Economist*, 24 June 2016.

20   John Curtice, 'Where's the evidence that Jeremy Corbyn is to blame for Brexit?', *New Statesman*, 4 July 2016; John Curtice, 'Don't blame Jeremy Corbyn – polls show only Tory voters could have kept us in the EU', *New Statesman*, 30 June 2016; Anushka Asthana, 'Labour In for Britain chair criticises Jeremy Corbyn's campaign involvement', *Guardian*, 26 June 2016; Andy McSmith, 'Brexit: Jeremy Corbyn undermined and sabotaged Remain campaign, claims Peter Mandelson', *Independent*, 6 August 2016; Lord Ashcroft, 'How the United Kingdom voted on Thursday … and why', Lord Ashcroft Polls, 24 June 2016.

21   Heather Stewart, 'Ed Miliband calls for Jeremy Corbyn to resign as Labour leader over Brexit', *Guardian*, 29 June 2016; 'Former Labour leader Kinnock urges Corbyn to resign', BBC, 22 July 2016; Gloria de Piero, 'If you think the country need new leadership, I am begging you to join our Party and give Labour the champion they need', *Sun*, 3 July 2016; Jamie Reed, 'My letter to @jeremycorbyn tonight', *Twitter.com*, 29 June 2016.

22   Robert Peston, 'Corbyn opponents try to fix vote', *ITV News*, 12 July

2016; Julia Rampen, 'Anti-Corbyn campaigners are recruiting lapsed Labour members – but is it legal?', *New Statesman*, 18 July 2016.

23   Anoosh Chakelian, 'Labour suspends local party meetings to avoid intimidation – will it work?', *New Statesman*, 14 July 2016; Aubrey Allegretti, 'Labour suspends local party meetings to prevent intimidation of MPs and activists', *Huffington Post*, 13 July 2016.

24   John McTernan, 'Why Angela Eagle is exactly what Labour needs', *Telegraph*, 29 June 2016; John McTernan, 'Is change afoot in the British political weather?', *Policy Network*, 1 February 2011.

25   Rachel Cooke, 'Angela and Maria Eagle: "We were brought up to believe that there was nothing we couldn't do"', *Guardian*, 7 February 2016.

26   Mikey Smith, 'Who is Angela Eagle? All about Jeremy Corbyn's first challenger and her policies', *Mirror*, 10 July 2016.

27   Hilary Benn, 'Why I'm backing Angela Eagle for Labour leader', *Sun*, 17 July 2016; Craig Woodhouse, 'The Eagle has crash landed', *Sun*, 11 July 2016.

28   Gabriel Samuels, 'Angela Eagle accuses BBC interviewer of pandering to "Corbynista meme" during Iraq War questioning', *Independent*, 12 July 2016.

29   Amanda Devil, 'Vandals target Eagle', *Sun*, 12 July 2016.

30   Alexandra Sims, 'Angela Eagle's constituency branch issues statement supporting Jeremy Corbyn as Labour leader', *Independent*, 6 July 2016.

31   Anne Perkins, 'Angela Eagle was never going to be Labour leader. You can guess why', *Guardian*, 19 July 2016.

32   Anoosh Chakelian, '"I've got a wife and children": Owen Smith's Andrea Leadsom moment', *New Statesman*, 18 July 2016; Adam Bienkov, 'Owen Smith says sexist Nicola Sturgeon tweet was "just banter"', Politics.co.uk, 5 September 2016; Aubrey Allegretti, '"29 inches – inner leg measurement of course"', *Huffington Post UK*, 30 August 2016.

33   Dan Hodges, 'Spineless, incoherent, incompetent – and how Owen Smith's house of cards is collapsing', *Mail on Sunday*, 21 August 2016.

34   Heather Stewart, 'Isis should get round the table with UK, says Owen Smith', *Guardian*, 17 August 2016; Anushka Asthana, 'Owen Smith: Labour leadership more crucial than my NI peace role', *Guardian*, 19 September 2016.

35   Mark Chandler, 'Keep Corbyn protest: defiant leader addresses huge crowds after "catastrophic" meeting with MPs', *Evening Standard*, 27

June 2016; Adam Boult, 'Rally in support of Jeremy Corbyn cancelled due to "overwhelming public demand"', *Telegraph*, 29 June 2016; Julia Rampen, 'Inside the Momentum rally: meet the Jeremy Corbyn supporters challenging Labour's rebel MPs', *New Statesman*, 28 June 2016; Lizzie Dearden, 'Jeremy Corbyn says he is "proud to carry on" as Labour leader in defiant speech amid calls for resignation', *Independent*, 29 June 2016; Sarah Pine, 'Top Unite official to attend Momentum's "Keep Corbyn" rally tonight', *LabourList*, 27 June 2016; Sarah Pine, 'Momentum set to mobilise thousands to back Corbyn this weekend', *LabourList*, 1 July 2016.

36   Ellesmere Port Unite Community, 'Keep Corbyn rally – Liverpool 2nd July 2016', YouTube, 2 July 2016.

37   Len McCluskey, general secretary, Unite the union; Dave Prentis, general secretary, Unison; Tim Roache, general secretary, GMB; Dave Ward, general secretary, CWU, Brian Rye, acting general secretary, Ucatt; Manuel Cortes, general secretary, TSSA; Mick Whelan, general secretary, Aslef; Matt Wrack, general secretary, FBU; Ronnie Draper, general secretary, BFAWU; Chris Kitchen, general secretary, NUM, 'Joint trade union statement on the Labour party', 29 June 2016, at unitetheunion.org.

38   Robert Fisk, 'Bad luck Jezza: Jeremy Corbyn has 0% chance of winning majority in the next general election, electoral report says', *Sun*, 9 August 2016; Robert Fisk, '"Not in my lifetime": ex-Labour leader Neil Kinnock warns there will not be a Labour government if Jeremy Corbyn is re-elected', *Sun*, 18 September 2016.

39   Jonathan Walker, 'Jess Phillips says she could resign as a Labour MP if Jeremy Corbyn wins', *Birmingham Mail*, 20 July 2016.

40   Caroline Mortimer, 'Rebel Labour MPs "to form new group to force Jeremy Corbyn to resign" if party loses election', *Independent*, 9 May 2017.

41   Jon Stone, 'Labour's right wing draws up new plan to undermine Jeremy Corbyn', *Independent*, 1 June 2017.

42   Kate McCann, 'Why can't Labour MPs get rid of Jeremy Corbyn before the June general election?', *Telegraph*, 19 April 2017.

43   Graeme Demianyk, 'Jeremy Corbyn was NOT "dancing a jig" before Remembrance Sunday service', *Huffington Post*, 13 November 2016.

44   Jon Craig, 'Labour leader Jeremy Corbyn denies supporting or meeting IRA', *Sky News*, 26 May 2017

45   Andrew Gilligan, 'Revealed: Jeremy Corbyn and John McDonnell's close IRA links', *Telegraph*, 10 October 2015; Claire Newell, Hayley Dixon, Luke Heighton, and Harry Yorke, 'Exclusive: MI5 opened file on Jeremy Corbyn amid concerns over his IRA links', *Telegraph*, 19 May 2017; Laura Hughes and Edward Malnick, 'Revealed: Jeremy Corbyn's three decades of blocking terror legislation', *Telegraph*, 26 May 2017; Richard Dearlove, 'Corbyn would not be allowed into security services, so he's not fit for No 10', *Telegraph*, 8 June 2017.

46   Sean O'Callaghan, 'Jeremy Corbyn might not have planted a bomb but he made it easier for those who did, says former IRA man', *Sun*, 22 May 2017; Tom Newton Dunn, 'Jeremy Corbyn boosted morale of IRA killers with his support and prolonged the violence leading to more deaths, IRA killer reveals', *Sun*, 22 May 2017; Sean O'Callaghan, 'Finucane should not have been killed – but he was in the IRA', *Telegraph*, 18 April 2013; Cory Collusion Inquiry Report: Patrick Finucane, House of Commons, April 2004.

47   David Trayner, 'Claims Jeremy Corbyn funded "IRA bomber" turn out to be 30 years old – and inaccurate', *Independent*, 20 September 2015.

48   'Jeremy Corbyn quizzed over IRA comments', *ITV News*, 21 May 2017; Jessica Elgot, 'Johnson accuses Corbyn of siding with UK's enemies in fight on terror', *Guardian*, 6 June 2017; Robert Booth, Martin Belam, and Maeve McClenaghan, 'Tory attack ad misrepresents Corbyn views on IRA, says Labour', *Guardian*, 2 June 2017.

49   Kate Devlin, 'Labour MPs urge Smith to attack Corbyn over IRA', *Evening Times*, 18 August 2016; Kate McCann, 'Labour's Stoke candidate branded Jeremy Corbyn "IRA supporting friend of Hamas" and criticised Brexit', *Telegraph*, 27 January 2017.

50   James Forsythe, 'Jeremy Corbyn always blames Britain first', *Spectator*, 28 May 2017; Simon Heffer, 'Jeremy Corbyn has long hated Britain', *Telegraph*, 28 May 2017; editorial, 'Jeremy Corbyn's intervention on terror is tasteless and wrong', *Telegraph*, 26 May 2017; Steve Hawkes, 'RED FLAG: outrage as it's revealed Jeremy Corbyn will claim Britain's war on terror is to blame for Manchester terror attack', *Sun*, 25 May 2017; editorial, 'An important speech from Jeremy Corbyn – but made at the wrong time', *Independent*, 26 May 2017; Matthew Smith, 'Jeremy Corbyn is on the right side of public opinion on foreign policy: except for the Falklands', *YouGov*, 30 May 2017.

51   Tom Batchelor, 'British voters overwhelmingly back Labour's mani-
      festo policies, poll finds', *Independent*, 11 May 2017.

52   Will Dahlgren, 'Voters choose greater equality over greater wealth',
      YouGov, 30 April 2014; Will Dahlgren, 'Nationalise energy and rail
      companies, say public', *YouGov*, 4 November 2013; Patrick Butler,
      'UK survey finds huge support for ending austerity', *Guardian*, 28 June
      2017.

53   Editorial, 'The Guardian view on the Labour election manifesto: wid-
      ening the bounds of the thinkable', *Guardian*, 16 May 2017; editorial,
      'The Observer's view on the Labour manifesto', *Observer*, 14 May 2017;
      Andrew Grice, 'Labour's manifesto will be popular, but this election is
      about trust, not policies', *Independent*, 16 May 2017; Nick Robinson, 'No
      one should be surprised ...', Twitter.com, 20 May 2017; Jeremy Culley,
      'REVEALED: Labour plans to "TREBLE Council Tax plunging
      people into negative equity"', *Daily Star*, 30 May 2017; Gordon Rayner,
      'Tax on homes "to treble under Labour plans for Land Value Tax"',
      Telegraph, 29 May 2017; Jon Stone, 'Labour looks to replace Council
      Tax with a Land Value Tax', *Independent*, 16 May 2017.

54   Macer Hall, 'May's plan for a Fairer Britain', *Daily Express*, 18 May
      2017; editorial, 'DAILY MAIL COMMENT: as Mrs May unveils her
      manifesto, at last, we have a PM who is not afraid to be honest', *Daily
      Mail*, 19 May 2017; editorial, 'THE SUN SAYS: never in our history has
      a UK election thrown up such a clear-cut and obvious choice for Sun
      readers', *Sun*, 19 May 2017; editorial, 'The Guardian view on Theresa
      May's manifesto: a new Toryism', *Guardian*, 18 May 2017.

55   Dawn Foster, 'Theresa May's manifesto shows that she is more right
      wing than Cameron ever dared to be', *Independent*, 18 May 2017.

56   Robert Booth, 'Conservatives launch online offensive against Corbyn',
      Guardian, 15 May 2017.

57   Nicholas Cecil, 'How Jeremy Corbyn beat Theresa May in the social
      media election war', *Evening Standard*, 14 June 2017.

58   Jim Waterson and Tom Phillips, 'People on Facebook only want to
      share pro-Corbyn, anti-Tory news stories', *Buzzfeed*, 7 May 2017; Ben
      Kentish, 'Tories "spent more than £1m" on negative Facebook adverts
      attacking Jeremy Corbyn', *Independent*, 11 June 2017; Giles Turner and
      Jeremy Kahn, 'U.K. Labour's savvy use of social media helped win
      young voters', *Bloomberg*, 11 June 2017; Richard Fletcher, 'Labour's

social media campaign: more posts, more video, and more interaction', *Election Analysis*, 2017, electionanalysis.uk; Robert Booth and Alex Hern, 'Labour won social media election, digital strategists say', *Guardian*, 9 June 2017.

59 Paul Hilder, 'How people power can beat the big donors – from crowdfunding to tactical voting', *Left Foot Forward*, 6 June 2017.

60 Dan Hodges, 'This isn't a vote, it's a game of Russian roulette', *Daily Mail*, 4 June 2017; Nick Cohen, 'Don't tell me you weren't warned about Corbyn', *Observer*, 19 March 2017; 'Final reckoning: May on track for sweeping win', *Independent*, 8 June 2017; John Rentoul, 'Why I don't believe the YouGov model predicting a hung parliament', *Independent*, 31 May 2017; Sam Coates and Frances Elliott, 'Tory lead grows in election's final poll', *The Times*, 8 June 2017; editorial, 'THE SUN SAYS: don't chuck Britain in the Cor-bin – vote Tory unless you want a friend of terrorists who's ready to open our borders and hike up taxes as your next PM', *Sun*, 7 June 2017.

61 Oscar Rickett, 'Weighing Up Theresa May's Leadership Prospects', *Vice*, 14 June 2017; 'Conservatives' Evans: we've shot ourselves in the head', *BBC News*, 9 June 2017; George Parker, 'Conservatives fear descent into chaotic leadership battle', *Financial Times*, 15 July 2017.

62 Georgina Lee, 'Here are 10 Tory U-turns since the election was called', *Channel 4 News*, 26 July 2017; Anushka Asthana, 'Here are 10 Tory U-turns since the election was called', *Guardian*, 21 July 2017.

6. Prospects: Can Corbyn Win?

1 Charles Eliot Norton, 'The advantages of defeat', *The Atlantic*, September 1861, available at atlantic.com.

2 Liz Davies, *Through the Looking Glass: A Dissenter Inside New Labour*, Verso: London, 2001, p. 174

3 William Green, 'Ronnie Campbell calls for honesty over public sector job cuts', *The Journal*, 15 April 2010.

4 Leo Panitch points out that I got this argument from him. For insightful commentary, see Leo Panitch, *Working Class Politics in Crisis: Essays on Labour and the State*, London and New York: Verso, 1986.

5 Sam Coates, 'Corbyn still first choice for Labour grass roots', *The Times*, 24 November 2015.

6   Serina Sandhu, 'Tony Blair: I'm the face on the placard, I'm that bastard', *iNews*, 26 September 2016.

7   Perry Anderson, 'Origins of the present crisis', *English Questions*, London and New York: Verso, 1992, p. 42.

8   This notwithstanding the extraordinary class-based invective of some on the party's right, like John Mann MP: 'In the Dog and Duck, they could understand his words. Nationalise the railways. Alf and Bert could agree with that – sounds reasonable enough. Stop austerity. Samantha and Craig can smell a pay rise for themselves here.' John Mann, 'More positions than the Kama Sutra – and not up to the job', *Daily Mail*, 13 September 2015.

9   Although, as is always the case, it depends on how you ask the polling question. See Patrick Worrall, 'FactCheck: does Britain want to scrap Trident?', *Channel 4 News Factcheck* blog, 4 November 2015; Will Dahlgreen, 'Nationalise energy and rail companies, say public', *YouGov*, 4 November 2013; Tom Clark, 'Energy giants more disliked than banks, poll finds', *Guardian*, 25 January 2015; Will Dahlgreen, 'Voters choose greater equality over greater wealth', *YouGov*, 30 April 2014; 'Corbyn still first choice for Labour grass roots', Office for National Statistics, 22 January 2015, at ons.gov.uk.

10   Jeremy Corbyn, 'Building a social movement', in Tom Unterrainer, ed., *Corbyn's Campaign*, Nottingham: Spokesman Books, 2016, p. 10.

11   George Eaton, 'How John McDonnell is trying to reframe the economic debate', *New Statesman*, 20 November 2015.

12   Chris Giles, 'Team McDonnell: meet Labour's seven economic advisers', *Financial Times*, 28 September 2015.

13   Gavin Stamp, 'What we learnt about Labour's economic policy from McDonnell's speech', *BBC News*, 28 September 2015; Mariana Mazzucato, *The Entrepreneurial State: Debunking Public vs. Private Myths in Risk and Innovation*, New York: Anthem Press, 2013.

14   See Tony Wood, 'Good riddance to New Labour', *New Left Review* 62, March–April 2010.

15   Andrew Grice, 'It's time that we valued people over profits, poll results show', *Independent*, 24 December 2011.

16   The British Social Attitudes Survey of 2009 found this shift across the board: 'The public now appear less supportive of "big government" than at any time since the late 1970s.' 'British Social Attitudes 27th

Report', NatCen, December 2010, at natcen.ac.uk.

17 James Schneider, 'Jeremy Corbyn can lead the Labour Party back to power', *Prospect*, 12 February 2016.

18 Ipsos Mori, 'Generations', at ipsos-mori-generations.com; Andrew Grice, 'Voters "brainwashed by Tory welfare myths", shows new poll', *Independent*, 4 January 2013; Will Dahlgreen and Will Jordan, 'Osborne's first all-Tory Budget: initial scorecard', *YouGov*, 9 July 2015.

19 Raymond Williams, 'Culture is ordinary', in Williams, *Resources of Hope: Culture, Democracy, Socialism*, London and New York: Verso, 1989.

20 Freddie Sayers, 'Bernie Sanders, Jeremy Corbyn and their new coalitions on the left', *Guardian*, 15 February 2016.

21 Monica Poletti, Tim Bale, and Paul Webb, 'Explaining the pro-Corbyn surge in Labour's membership', *LSE* blog, 16 November 2016; Anushka Asthana, 'Big majority of Labour members "want UK to stay in single market"', *Guardian*, 17 July 2017.

22 Tim Bale, Monica Poletti, and Paul Webb, 'Speed data: who are Labour's members?', *Prospect*, 19 January 2017.

23 Hilary Wainwright, quoted in Tom Gann, 'A Million Member Party, Concluding Thoughts: Democratisation, Delivering Consequences, Disalienation', *New Socialist*, 24 July 2017

24 Nicholas Watt, 'Labour split exposed as Tom Watson describes Momentum as a "rabble"', *Guardian*, 4 December 2015; Heather Stewart, 'Tom Watson sends Corbyn "proof of Trotskyist Labour infiltration"', *Guardian*, 10 August 2016; Adam Bienkov, 'Owen Smith: Momentum members could be banned by Labour party', Politics.co.uk, 16 September 2016.

25 Tom Peck, 'Trotskyists are trying to take over Momentum, says senior member', *Independent*, 6 December 2016.

26 Paul Waugh, 'Momentum activists take control of local Labour parties ahead of Brighton conference', *Huffington Post*, 20 June 2017; Emma Rees, 'Grassroots create momentum to vote Jeremy Corbyn into office', *Financial Times*, 22 July 2017; Emma Bean, 'Corbynista slate pulls ahead in battle for key conference committees', *LabourList*, 18 July 2017; Ashley Cowburn, 'Momentum: what happens to the Jeremy Corbyn-backing organisation after the general election?', *Independent*, 7 June 2017.

27　Luke Akehurst, 'Competing visions', *Progress*, 11 February 2017.

28　Andrew Gilligan, 'Revealed: the radical hard-left Momentum activists mounting a ruthless purge of Labour', *Telegraph*, 13 February 2016; Rachel Shabi, 'Opening Labour', *Jacobin*, 16 July 2017.

29　Glen O'Hara, 'How is Jeremy Corbyn's Labour faring in elections so far?', *New Statesman*, 4 January 2016.

30　Hardeep Matharu, 'Britain could be more left-wing than people assume, study finds', *Independent*, 15 January 2016; Jon Stone, 'Labour seen as "indistinguishable from the Tories" to Scottish voters, leaked internal report warns', *Independent*, 25 January 2016.

31　Ian Johnston, 'Labour was not too left wing for voters at last election, review concludes', *Independent*, 15 January 2016.

32　'Labour opinion poll ratings "worst since World War II"', *Herald*, 19 January 2016.

33　Glen O'Hara, 'How is Jeremy Corbyn's Labour faring in elections so far?', *New Statesman*, 4 January 2016.

34　Leon Watson, Helena Horton, and David Millward, 'Crawling back to Corbyn: the Labour rebels eating their words after benefiting from Jeremy Corbyn's popularity', *Telegraph*, 10 June 2017; Laura Hughes, 'Yvette Cooper would "consider" serving in Jeremy Corbyn's shadow cabinet', *Telegraph*, 10 June 2017.

35　Tony Blair, 'Brexit and the centre', Tony Blair Institute for Global Change, 15 July 2017.

36　Michael Savage, 'Tom Watson: "If we can reassure our traditional voters, we'll be unbeatable" ', *Guardian*, 2 July 2017.

37　Phil Wilson MP, 'Labour's purpose', *Fabian Society*, 4 July 2017.

38　Rajeev Syal, 'Senior Labour figures clash over concerns of working-class voters', *Guardian*, 4 July 2017.

39　Ashish Ghadiali, '"The Labour Party is its members" – Chris Williamson MP interview', *Red Pepper*, 13 July 2017.

40　On the City and Brexit, see the new afterword to Tony Norfield, *The City: London and the Global Power of Finance*, London and New York: Verso, 2017; Carl Emmerson, Paul Johnson, Ian Mitchell, and David Phillips, 'Brexit and the UK's Public Finances', Institute for Fiscal Studies, IFS Report 116, May 2016.

41　Owen Smith, BBC *Question Time*, 9 February 2017; Kiran Stacey, 'India dents UK trade hopes with lapsed deal', *Financial Times*, 5 April 2017;

on the framework of likely deals, Jon Henley and Dan Roberts, 'Reality check: will it take 10 years to do a UK–EU trade deal post Brexit?', *Guardian*, 15 December 2016; and Jonty Bloom, 'Reality check: can there be a quick UK–USA trade deal?', *BBC News*, 16 January 2017.

42   Martin Sandbu, 'Free lunch: sheep in wolf's clothing', *Financial Times*, 27 September 2016.

43   'A national investment bank for Britain: putting dynamism into our industrial strategy', report to the shadow chancellor of the exchequer and shadow secretary for business, energy and industrial strategy on implementation, Labour 2016, at labour.org.uk; John Marlow, 'National investment banks: a radical proposal?', *Open Democracy*, 6 September 2016.